High Profit Candlestick Patterns

Turning Investor Sentiment Into Profits

Stephen W. Bigalow

Profit Publishing
Houston, TX

Published by Profit Publishing, LLC

This publication is designed to provide accurate and authorized information in regard to
the subject matter covered. It is sold with the understanding that the publisher is not
engaged in rendering professional services. If professional advice or other expert of
sustenance is required the services of a complement professional should be sought.

Printed in the United States of America

Library of Congress Cataloging-in-Publication Data

Bigalow, Stephen

High Profit Candlestick Patterns; Turning Investor Sentiment Into Profits

p. pp (Profit Publishing LLC)

Includes index.
ISBN 0-9773757 - 0 - 6 (cloth, alk. Paper)
I.   Stocks—charts, diagrams, etc. 2. Investment analysis. 3. Stocks — prices — Japan -
— charts, diagrams, etc. 1. Title 2. Series.

10 9 8 7 6 5

Preface

As candlestick signals become more indoctrinated into the investment arenas. the information conveyed in the signals is being better understood. Candlestick analysis is becoming a very powerful investment technique. Up until recently, it's under-use was a function of not fully understanding how candlestick signals truly worked. As more investors become acquainted with the benefits that candlestick signals provide, an additional benefit is developing. Candlestick signals, developed over the last few centuries, makes it the oldest investment technique in existence. The information and implications that are revealed, by centuries of observations, is now being enhanced with computer related techniques. Overlaying the information derived from candlestick signals on top of technical analysis that has been dramatically improved with computer generated programs makes for a very powerful trading platform.

There have been a number of books written about candlestick signals. At the time they were written, they conveyed the best possible knowledge attributed to candlestick signals at that time. As computer generated scanning programs and research techniques improve with the development of computer software programming, the utilization of candlestick analysis constantly improves.

This book was written to educate investors on how to use Japanese candlestick analysis profitably. The easy-to-follow procedures detailed in this book provide the reader with profit-making techniques that can be learned quickly. More importantly, learning of the principles detailed in this book will provide the reader with investment techniques they can use immediately. As candlestick signals become better understood, their applications to high profit patterns allows investors to exploit profits from high profit situations.

Candlestick signals produced good returns in their own right. Investment patterns, the reoccurring psychology found in all trading markets goose by investor sentiment, also are capable of producing good returns. Combining the two techniques produces an investment platform that dramatically improves high profit probabilities. This is not a difficult process.

Having the ability to recognize what candlestick signals are conveying creates a tremendous investment advantage. Witnessing those signals appearing as potential trading patterns are forming creates a format for establishing potentially high profit trades as well as common sense stop loss procedures.

Not only does the knowledge of what a signal looks like benefit the candle-stick educated investor, but learning the common sense psychology that formed a signal provides the investor with a whole new perspective into successful investing. Somebody is making huge profits in the markets. It is those that have established successful trading methods for interpreting when to buy and when to sell. Reading this book should and enhance your investment abilities forever. The improved perspective of what dictates low risk, high profit situations creates a very positive investment structure. Utilize the information that hundreds of years of profitable observations have produced. Utilize the capabilities found in computer related sorting techniques. The probabilities of producing significant profits will always be in your favor when visually identifying signals and patterns that have worked a high percentage of the time in the past. Learn candlestick signals and patterns and reap the benefit of that knowledge put into a very simple graphic form.

Stephen W. Bigalow
Houston. Texas

Acknowledgments

Writing a book is not a stand-alone effort. The writing of this book involved the efforts of many people. The constant support of a loving family makes the lengthy endeavor much easier. My mother, June Bigalow, has been a constant source of encouragement.

My brother Andy and my sister Diane, along with their families, have been a constant supply of support through the years.

Pat Johnson, the business manager of the Candlestick Forum LLC, provided invaluable services for making sure the many details for publishing a book was in place. The huge time and effort that she expended will always be greatly appreciated.

David Elliott has been a good friend and has provided many profitable applications of technical analysis in conjunction with candlestick signals. His spirit of sharing profitable uses of modern technical applications and combining them with candlestick signals has produced some very easy to use trading setups.

Ken Melber deserves a special thanks for his patience and friendship through many years of developing candlestick trading programs. Also, Mark Storey needs to be acknowledged for the many hours of business consultation.

Many thanks go to my Cornell University, DU fraternity buddies and families for their constant support. They have been an inspiration in striving to provide quality information.

Many thanks go to Bill Johnson and Tina Logan for their generous contribution of actual trading experience and knowledge. They both unselfishly contributed their knowledge of candlestick analysis with their expertise to help make this book provide information from different insights.

A special thank you goes to Donna Love, Kermit and Karin Prather, and Rick Saddler for the generous contribution of editing the writing of this book. Unfortunately for them, the task was probably much greater than they anticipated. Their time and efforts are greatly appreciated.

Ron Kaye and Connie Schmidt of Schmidt Kaye & Company deserve special acknowledgment for their work in assembling and formatting the book. Their professional literary services made the publication of this book very smooth.

Thanks to the CQG company for providing clear and easy to work with charts. Also, thanks to Worden Brothers for providing an efficient search software program.

Many thanks go to the members of the Candlestick Forum website. The spirit of sharing information and successes has been a great contribution in the continuing learning process of how to use candlestick signals successfully.

To keep from possibly blemishing any reputations associated with those acknowledged as providing something toward the completion of this book, it should be noted that any factual errors or a missions found with in this book are solely the responsibility of the author.

Contents

Chapter 1

Altering Your Investment Perspectives

> *Bring ideas in and entertain them royally, for one of them may be the king.*
>
> *Mark Van Doren*

Japanese candlestick investing has inherent aspects that cannot be ignored. This book was written based on one major assumption. If you are reading this, you are looking for a better investment program than what you have been experiencing. You have come to the right place. Candlestick analysis has some very compelling aspects. *It will completely alter your investment perspectives.* This book was written to educate investors on *how* to use the Japanese Candlestick technique profitably. The easy-to-follow practices described will provide the reader with profit-making techniques that can be quickly learned. **More importantly, learning the principles of market psychology underlying the Candlestick methodology will revolutionize your overall investment psyche** *forever.* This statement can be made because candlestick signals have already proven themselves. Fortunes have been made using the Japanese Candlestick techniques.

Knowing *"how"* to use the candlesticks and *"why"* they work will immediately improve the reader's investment profitability and permanently alter overall investment perceptions. This newly acquired perception will produce consistent profits along with an associated mental re-programming designed to maximize investment returns. Once one becomes convinced of the reliability of the Candlestick methodology, one also acquires a pre-programmed investment discipline. As a result, Candlesticks add a whole new dimension to enhancing the investor's profit-making capabilities.

You will be exposed to an investment philosophy that will immediately jar you out of your current investment viewpoints. The information that you glean from this reading will not be something new or provocative. All the investment concepts incorporated into candlestick signals are derived from commonsense applications. Additionally, the signals are easy to visualize. Do not be surprised to see smatterings of information directly out of "Profitable Candlestick Trading," the previous book and the basis for the writing of this book. There are many aspects of candlestick analysis that bear repeating.

In learning and using Candlestick analysis effectively, a few assumptions need to be made up front. The signals have been developed through hundreds of years of actual usage. Japanese traders started charting the price movement of rice, utilizing the application of the open, close, high and low. Much the same as western bar charting but with the addition of boxing in the open and close. This method of charting created a new analysis tool, a tool that was used as a statistical analysis centuries before the advent of the computer. The details of how candlesticks were developed will not be illustrated in this book. That information is better studied in previously written books. (See suggested reading list.)

Japanese Candlestick signals possess one major attribute that is not present in other technical systems. ***The signals are created by the CHANGE in investor sentiment.*** This point is the crux of the success of Candlestick analysis. Again, to emphasize the importance of what you have just read. ***THE SIGNALS ARE CREATED BY THE CHANGE IN INVESTOR SENTIMENT***. Understanding this truism will make it easy for your investment psychology to become acclimated to this successful trading discipline.

The secrets of the effectiveness of the signals can be learned in a fast and easy process. An investor does not need to be highly knowledgeable about technical charting to take *immediate advantage* of the signals. A signal's graphic formation makes it visibly easy to identify reversals. A Candlestick formation provides a visual graphic of investor psychology during a specific time period. For the purpose of illustration in this book, the standard time frame will be one day. The trading entity will be stock, equity as opposed to commodity. Investment strategies can be structured, of course, for whatever time period is suited for your trading style: minute-to-minute all the way through monthly. Applicable trading instruments include any vehicle that has the key elements of investor ***fear and greed.***

Forming the Candlesticks

Horizontal lines represent the open and the close. Once both lines are added to the chart, they are boxed. This box is called the **BODY.** If the close is higher than the open, the body is white or empty. If the close is lower than the open, the body is black or filled. Keep in mind, this does not necessarily mean that a white body represents that the price was up for the day or that a black body represents that the price was down for the day.

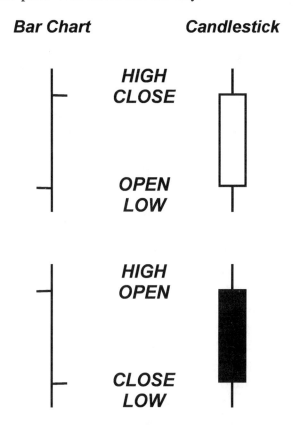

The body color only illustrates where the close was as compared to the open. The contrasting colors of the bodies provides for rapid visual interpretations. A declining column of dark candles is obviously interrupted when a white candle appears. This attracts the attention of the eye immediately. This is something that would not occur when viewing conventional bar charts. The lines extending from the body represent the extremes of the price movement during the day. These are known as the **SHADOWS.** The shadow above the body is known as the upper shadow. In some Japanese analytical circles, the upper shadow is also described as the **HAIR.** The shadow below the body is known as the lower shadow or the **TAIL**. The length of the shadows has important impli-cations to the strength of reversal moves.

The bodies with shadows look very much like candles, thus the name 'Candlesticks.' But don't let the unsophisticated name throw you. The informa-tion provided by the formations puts the Candlestick analyst giant leaps ahead of other technical analysts.

The colors of the boxes are not important. For visual clarity, white and black easily show contrast. Some computer software may have green for up and red for down. The purpose of the chart is to provide a clear indication of what signals are being formed. Once you have become accustomed to the candle-stick charts, the visual aspects to the candlestick charts will make all other charting techniques obsolete.

However, the important facts that should be considered about the history of candlestick signals are first they made Japanese rice traders immensely wealthy. Not just wealthy, but legendarily wealthy. Songs were written about the wealth that the Homma family acquired through their rice trading exploits, using candlestick signals. Second, the signals are still here after hundreds of years of use. It can safely be assumed that if candlestick signals did not work effectively, we would not be looking at them today.

Candlestick signals work! Not because a computer generates back-tested facsimile showed hypothetical positive results, but results produced from ac-tual trading and real live profits. More so, real live fortunes.

Assumption, if the signals are interpreted and used correctly, they can produce inordinate rates of return for the investor. This is already proven by the Homma trading family, making a huge fortune from trading rice.

Taking that point of view, the purpose of this book is to cut to the crux of using Candlesticks to maximize your profit potential! Background information about the history of candlestick investing in this book will be minimal. That information is better found in excellent books that have been written about Candlesticks. "Profitable Candlestick Trading" provides a more general over-view of how to use the signals profitably. Steve Nison is credited with introduc-ing Candlestick investing into the U.S. markets. Greg Morris also has written excellent books describing the candlestick signals. The serious candlestick in-vestor should make obligatory reads of their books during the road to master-ing the signals.

Some of the information found in this book will also been seen in "Profit-able Candlestick Trading" Some duplication will be witnessed, but only for preparing the further development of investment strategies and pattern analy-sis of high profit trading patterns.

In staying with the purpose of this book, analyzing and implementing high profit strategies, the background information about the signals and their history will be sparse. The direction will be towards educating the investor on how and why the signals, along with the psychology behind the signals, can be utilized for increasing investment profits. Fear not, you will not be inundated with investment theory, or new investment concepts. When learning candlestick analysis, the predominant reaction will be "yeah, I knew that." The common sense aspects will be evident constantly. No formulas. No preconceived deep- rooted psychological visions. Just plain commonsense put into a graphic depiction.

Misconceptions about candlesticks will be erased. An often asked question is "If Candlestick signals are so effective, then why isn't everybody using them?" When using the signals correctly, and realizing the ease and simplicity of using the signals, it will become a rhetorical question from all those who correctly use the signals. Please note the term "correctly." For the uneducated user of candlesticks, those not using the proper tools to analyze the signals, there are many reasons that an uneducated investor could perceive that the signals are not accurate. The same analogy of a golfer never improving his game, thinking he/she will always be a 24 handicap, until they get proper lessons, correcting what they may have been doing wrong for many years.

In reading this book, you will be exposed to the proper methods of interpreting the signals. Additional, the pitfalls will be laid out so you need not learn them through experience. More importantly, high profit patterns will be illustrated for the sole purpose of cutting to the chase, maximizing the use of investment funds.

> *Never tell people how to do things. Tell them what to do and they will surprise you with their ingenuity.*
>
> *General George S. Patton*

The purpose of these writings will have a dual intention. Educating the investor in using potential high profit patterns and altering the moderated investment programming espoused by so-called investment professionals! These professionals, of an industry that dictate an extremely low threshold of returns, making the incompetent capable of looking good!

Learning how to use the candlestick signals correctly will elevate the serious investor so they will never have to rely on professionals again. Especially from an investment industry that recently has been exposed for not having the investors' interest anywhere near the top of the list.

Where Do We Learn to Invest?

Consider this question. Where do we learn to invest**?** Where did you learn to invest? Did you take a semester of "The Correct Investment Methods for Making Money in the Market" when you were in high school or college? No way. At best, maybe we got an investment course, which consisted of stocks were equities, bonds were debt, and preferred stock was a combination. Were you taught on how to analyze the movements of stock prices or index directions? Were you taught how to recognize panic selling and the indications that the bottom had been hit? Very doubtful. Who was going to teach you?

Most investors learn how to invest solely through unguided experience. The process of investing usually consists of asking friends, family, or investment broker what should be bought with your initial investment funds. Little thought is put into learning investment programs or techniques. We hear about a good story stock. We buy it. No buying plan, no selling plan.

The two most important areas of our lives where we should all have mentors are sex and investing. But we have to muddle through both, learning as we go, hoping that we eventually become good at it.

Until recently, candlestick investing fit into that category, trying to learn it on our own. Wanting to learn how to use the signals correctly was a lonely road. There have been books written on what candlesticks are. This book will show you how to use candlestick signals profitably. There were very few people that could talk intelligently about how to use candlestick signals. Because of the proficiency of candlestick charting, many professional investors have taken to using candlestick graphics. The difference between bar charts and candlestick charts is that the candlestick charts are dramatically more revealing as far as conveying information. They visually tell a complete story.

Today the learning process is not a solo endeavor. That problem has been eliminated in the past few years. Websites, such as www.candlestickforum.com have been established exclusively for the education of those who want to learn about candlestick analysis. Having somebody to provide clarification on various interpretations of the signal formations greatly enhance the learning curve.

Learning an investment method should be the responsibility of every person. This should be the third leg of the three-legged stool. The first leg, we spend becoming educated so we can go out and have an occupation. The second leg, we spend the majority of our lives earning income to support our families and ourselves. Consider that, we work most of our lives to earn money, not a frivolous endeavor. Yet, after all that time and effort, we take those hard earned bucks and hand them over to a "professional" that wants to earn us a moderate return, mostly concerned about protecting capital. Not a program that maximizes the use of the funds to be invested. That is like kissing your sister. Those assets should be put to work with just as much energy and dedication as what it took to earn them.

Learning candlestick analysis is the third leg of that stool. It is an investment technique, imbedded with common sense investment conception, for the sole purpose of maximizing investment returns with the control of investment risk. Where do you learn to invest? You learn to invest by making it your responsibility to educate yourself in the techniques of extracting the best returns from your investments.

Learning High Profit Patterns

High profit patterns, patterns that put the probability of extracting gains from the markets, dramatically in your favor. Investor psychology, how do most investors think? Those that do not have a trading program! Those that do not have the correct mental investment training! That is the basis for the success produced by candlestick analysis. It visually depicts the flaws in the human emotions of the average investor. It will be no surprise when FEAR and GREED are mentioned.

An immense advantage is created when one understands those emotions. Most of us have experienced them ourselves. Panic at the bottom! After a stock continues its downtrend to the point that investors can not stand the pain of owning that stock any longer, because all indications show that stock is going to zero. They panic and want to get rid of the stock at any price, "Just get me out." Conversely, after a stock has steadily gone up for weeks on end, everybody finally realizes that stock is going to go up forever. They can't wait to get in, at any price, exuberance. Completely opposite from rationale decision making - emotional decision making! Candlestick analysis easily interprets those investor emotions. It allows an investor to exploit the "wrong-way" thinking of the majority of investors.

Recognizing the signals, that reveal the 'thinking' process of the masses, creates huge profit potential. Realizing that those weaknesses can be graphically illustrated allows investors to understand their own weaknesses and converts them to being able to identify buying opportunities. *Opportunities develop from what normally would have been our own loss-contributing investment behavior.*

Turning Your Weaknesses into Profits

Candlestick signals and Candlestick analysis benefit the investor in a twofold manner. First, the graphic signals are the representation of what most investors are doing wrong. Learning what the signals represent, the fear and exuberance of the majority of investors, prepares the candlestick investor for a profitable trade situation. Secondly, knowing that the signals depict what the masses are doing wrong, allows the investor to alter their own emotional habits by being ready to profit from the situation versus being part of the situation. This becomes the first step in reforming your investment perceptions. You are now in the position, knowing what to look for when the panic selling sets in, to be a buyer, not one of the panic sellers. Conversely, when a position is showing great exuberance, the media is proclaiming how great the company/industry is doing and the future is more than rosy, you will recognize the signs for the pending 'sell' signals.

This book will expose you to those signs. Becoming educated in what occurs at the bottom of a trend and what occurs at the top of a trend becomes a valuable tool for not jumping in or out of a position at the wrong times. More so, it produces an easy-to-see format for getting investors in and out of positions at the right times. The most revealing question, at the time everybody is capitulating, selling out at any price, because the future prospects appear to be so bad, should be "Who is buying this stock at these levels?" Also, when a stock being promoted as having such a bright future and everybody can't buy fast enough, who is selling the stock?

Understanding what makes people buy and sell investment positions creates advantageous insights for extracting consistent profits from the market. The Candlestick signals entail hundreds of years of actual experience. Witnessing the reaction of the majority of investors at the turns of trends has revealed insightful results that can be utilized in any trading entity. Use this book to become familiar with those signs of human investing weaknesses. More than likely you will see the obvious weaknesses that you yourself exhibit. Having those weaknesses illustrated as a profit opportunity blatantly suggests that we should recognize them as our own weakness and revert from continuing them. The candlestick signals provide that self-induced discipline.

How do you make money in the market? Buy at the bottom and sell at the tops. Easy! But do you remember the last time any of the so-called "Professionals of Wall Street" recommended a stock at the bottom? Or shorting at the top?

Do Wall Street Professionals Make You Money?

Consider the investment advice we are given from the Wall Street experts. If you analyze all their advisory statements, you begin to understand why you seem not able to make more than a moderate rate of return at best.

As witnessed in the recent past, Wall Street may not have your best interests as their main objective. A daunting revelation, isn't it? To understand why altering your investment psychology should be important to you, we should first illustrate why and how you have the investment perceptions that you have already. Where did you learn the basic information about investing? Mostly from the "professionals" of Wall Street is the logical answer. What are those basic assumptions that Wall Street teaches the populous?

The market historically provides 10% return annually. That is the usual guideline. The guideline repeated from Wall Street. **The question should not be what will the market give us, but what can we make from the market**. Year after year, it is drummed into our heads that the only way to make money in the market is find good, well run companies and hold them through the ups and downs. You will make out best that way. Great, but ask those who saw their portfolio's drop 50%, 70%, 90% over the past four years. Cisco Corporation is a well run company. Three years ago, it could be bought for $65.00 a share, today it is near $18.00. Not a buy-and-hold that is working.

You Can Not Time the Market

How many so-called investment experts have you heard on the T.V. financial stations, all professing that you can not time the market? If that is so, why do the names Warren Buffet and George Soros stand out from the crowd? When somebody says that you can not time the market, that is the person that you should stay as far away from as possible. *You cannot time the market?* That is usually the statement made by somebody that does not have the ability to understand that prices do not move based upon the fundamentals of a company, but prices move based upon the PERCEIVED results of the fundamentals of a company. This is the most important aspect for making money in the markets. The best run company in the world will not make you a cent if it is not perceived by investors to have potential. Conversely, the worst run company in the world can make huge profits for you if it is perceived that they have a positive future. Case in point, it was clearly demonstrated in the last of the bull market of the 90's where fortunes were made in stocks that had not made a single penny while the stalwarts of industry hardly moved.

Hold for Long Term

Another tried and true axiom from investment counseling. The question should be "why." Only two reasons for being told to hold long term. First, it sure gives the investment advisor more time to handle your investment funds before you recognize that their recommendation was not working. Second, it probably stems back to the original problem. They do not know how to time the markets.

Of course, there is rationale that tax rates are better for the long term hold. This mindset now takes an investor completely away from the purpose of buying the position in the first place. To maximize profits! How does one relate to the other? Buying a position in a stock should be based upon maximizing profits. Placing the arbitrary criteria of holding long term has nothing to do with maximizing profits. If a stock goes up 40% in the next three months, followed by dismal prospects of staying up at those levels, why would the position continue to be held? To save on the tax bill? The markets do not give a hoot what your investment criteria is.

CONSULT THE MARKET ABOUT THE MARKET

When analyzing the market, attention should be paid to the market movement itself. One has to follow the market movement like the cat that wishes to catch the mouse. Charts reflect the past. Theoretically, it is not possible to predict the market's future. Yet, analyzing identifiable patterns, as a prelude to a "high probability" result, is as close as an investor can get. Repeating patterns are not 100% accurate, but visually proven probabilities can adjust the odds immensely in your favor. Identification of certain events provides a basis for an occurrence happening. Otherwise, truisms such as "Red skies at night, sailor's delight" would not be in existence. Hundreds of years of weather observations have produced a reliable result the next day. The same observations have made Candlestick signals highly accurate.

Bottom line, the name Sokyu Homma, in Japan, through Candlestick recognition, is associated with successful investing, as Bill Gates' name is associated with successful computer program marketing in the United States. Learning to "consult" the market, as Homma did hundred of years ago, will greatly enhance your investing probabilities in the markets today.

The market is going to move in whatever manner it needs to. The process for maximizing profits is to exploit the profits that the market is producing. The Japanese traders say, *"Let the market tell you what the market is doing."* Candlestick analysis is oriented towards reacting to the signals that the prices are revealing. This makes available much higher profits versus trying to fit a pre-structured investment philosophy to a trading program. The market does not care what you are doing. You have to develop the best strategy for what the market is doing.

That is one of the immense advantages of candlestick signals. It is the *"cumulative knowledge all the investors that participated in the buying and selling of that trading entity during that time frame."* This statement is the ultimate focal point for successful investing. Consider this statement very carefully and use it as the underlying guide for the Candlestick technique. Prices move based upon this knowledge. Candlestick signals clearly illustrate what is happening to investor sentiment during the course of that time frame. The combination of one, two, three, and four day candlestick formations have been thoroughly analyzed through hundreds of years of observations. Use that information to put your investment probabilities in your favor.

How does that benefit you in reversing some of the years of indoctrination to the theories put forth buy Wall Street professionals? The signals tell you exactly what investors are thinking now. It allows the Candlestick investor to create strategies using that knowledge. It brings the concept of making the best use of your money in to sharp focus, moving away from the "sage???" counsel of most investment professionals.

Diversify

Diversify, the conservative advice that most investors should heed. So we are led to believe. What is the definition of 'diversify?' In investment language, it is the process of having your funds in different forms of investments. This is to protect the assets, if something is not working well, it does not affect the whole asset base dramatically. In simple terms, it usually means if something is going down, the rest of the assets, placed in other investments will help offset the losing position. Aren't we advised to separate investment funds in this manner? However, doesn't this also imply that not everything is going to go up? We need to protect ourselves by being in different investments?

Isn't that a vanilla way to use your investment funds? Shouldn't the purpose of having investments is too maximize returns? Wouldn't it make more sense to monitor positions so that the ones that do not look promising can be liquidated and those funds moved to better probabilities?

Again, this is the sage counsel of those that lack the knowledge to time investments. They do not have the skill to search for the investments that indicate that investors are moving money to those stocks/sectors. Candlestick analysis concentrates investment funds to the areas that are working, intensifying that criteria for investing in the first place. Maximization of profits!

One T.V. investment 'guru' advocates having no more than 4% of your investment funds in any one position. Yet, there are many highly paid Wall Street research analysts, being paid seven figure incomes, to follow eight or ten companies. And they can't do that all that well. But the average Joe is supposed to have 25 positions. They are expected to produce successful results following that many positions while having careers and other activities in their life.

Diversify if you can not analyze the direction of the trends. But if you are serious about enhancing your returns, then the process of creating high profit strategies using candlestick signals will change the mundane investment return syndrome.

> *He who cannot change the very fabric of his thought will never be able to change reality.*
>
> *Anwar el-Sadat*

How about this for an investment strategy. Your broker recommends selling a profitable position and at the same time recommends selling a position with a big loss to offset the tax gains. What a progressive investment strategy that is! Not a bit of concern for what is the potential for the losing position, such as, is it time to be buying at these lower prices. What name should be given to that type of investing? Running is quicksand sounds good.

Hopefully, to this point, this has been preaching to the choir. If you are reading this book, it is assumed that the standard Wall Street investment practices are not satisfying you. The third leg of the life cycle, learn to put your assets to the best return applications. Learning the candlestick method fine tunes the use of your investment strategies. It should be clear to most everyone that the business of Wall Street brokerage firms is to make money. Not necessarily to make **you** money, but for them to make money. The average investor, being happy to make moderate returns, is the fodder for the brokerage business.

The following chapters will be oriented towards developing your investment arsenal. You will be given in-depth description of the major signals. The major signals will produce more high profit trades than most investors will ever be able to employ. The advantage will be clearly evident. Not too many years ago, most investors had to rely on their brokers to be able to do any research. The availability of investment data was very limited. Now the Internet provides loads of investment services. Investors have the capability to do any amount of research and testing that they can imagine. With easy to use stock screening software, investors are able to find the best candlestick trades everyday in the matter of minutes. The supply and demand ratio is now where an investor can fine tune the investment search, cultivating an overabundance of high profit potentials, right down to the cream of the crop.

The remaining signals do not have to be aggressively learned. Knowing what they look like is helpful. They will show up occasionally, but not enough to spend any great amounts of time studying.

Option strategies will be described, best utilizing the aspect of having a high probability for detecting the direction of price. Knowing the direction with reasonable certainty, at least a beneficial probability, easy to learn option strategies can be incorporated. Bill Johnson, one of the nations leading writers in option strategies, has written a chapter for identifying undervalued options.

David Elliott, of www.Wallstreetteachers.com, is one of the leading technical experts for identifying patterns and waves in price movements. The application of his research techniques dramatically enhances the probabilities of being in a correct trade. His chapter will illustrate how to use current computer techniques to improve candlestick analysis.

Protecting assets can be enhanced using common sense stop loss procedures. This peace of mind program allows the nervous to sleep comfortably at night. As introduced in "Profitable Candlestick Trading" the explanation of an emotion free money management strategy will be discussed. It will be further enhanced with some very simple variations for completely eliminating emotions in the investment decisions. Techniques, using the basic characteristic of candlestick analysis, will consistently revert back to one factor, common sense.

Tina Logan, well respected for her analytical capabilities, has written a chapter demonstrating stop loss techniques. Her input brings to light simple stop loss techniques.

Candlestick signals are excellent reversal indicators on their own. However, utilizing expertise in other forms of technical analysis and trading programs can only enhance the potential trading results.

Utilize This Information

Information is pretty thin stuff unless it is mixed with experience.
Clarence Day

The major signal explanations will be more descriptive into the psychology that formed the signals. Understanding what the mindset of investors in the formation of the signals will furnish revealing perspectives on how prices move. This knowledge becomes invaluable for the rest of your investment career. That is why you are here!

Illustrations of high profit candlestick patterns will be described. Having the foreknowledge of what can occur during a specific pattern allows investors to maximize the profit potential. Additionally, knowing immediately when to liquidate the trade, if it is not working, becomes a practiced procedure. Expanding your experience to profitable situations prepares investors for acting when the time is right. When the masses are panic selling, who is buying? As evidenced time and again, the smart money is buying. You can be trading with the professionals, be with the smart money.

Chapter 2

The Major Signals

> *They teach in academies far too many things, and far too much that is useless.*
>
> *Goethe*

Candlestick signals have gained popularity in the recent years. Why, if the signals demonstrate such a high degree of accuracy, have they not been actively used until recently? The common answer has been that there were too many of them to learn expeditiously and they did not always seem to work. It was a common assumption that becoming proficient at candlestick analysis required a long and steep learning curve.

Fortunately, the productive utilization of candlestick signals has revealed an important factor. Of the 50 or 60 candlestick signals, only a dozen signals need to be learned. These are considered the 12 major signals. What constitutes these signals being considered the major signals? Most importantly, the frequency in which they occur during trend analysis!

Although the other signals are effective for analyzing reversals or continuations of trends, the frequency in which they occur is very small. The mental effort, to learn and remember the majority of candlestick signals, is not worthwhile. Do not disregard them! It is suggested that the remaining signals be recognized. This means visually reviewing the secondary signals and the continuation patterns. If the eye can be trained to recognize what appears to be a signal, it becomes more time-effective to go to a reference to verify that a candlestick signal is occurring. References would include other candlestick books that have a full description of those signals. The Candlestick Forum site provides a set of flash cards that have all the signals graphically illustrated. A description of the signal is on the reverse side. Keep these near your computer screen for quick reference.

The reason for downplaying the secondary signals is simple. For every 100 occurrences of a major signal, a secondary signal or continuations signal may occur once. The occurrence of a secondary signal does not carry as much predictability as a major signal. There are better trading opportunities available containing the major signals. Simply stated, the major signals will provide more trade opportunities and trend analysis situations than most investors require. The major signals incorporate an extensive amount of information relating to investor psychology. Your time is best spent concentrating on learning the major signals. It will develop an immense amount of insight into why and where reversals occur.

Because of the frequent appearance of the major signals, investors are provided with more opportunities to make profits once the significance of these signals is understood. For example, a Doji represents indecision. It is a significant signal when viewed in overbought or oversold conditions. However, Doji appear quite often during a trend or during a flat trading period. Understanding the relationship between the Doji signal and its meaning, depending upon where it appears in a trend, produces a great advantage for an investor.

The purpose of evaluating each of the major signals in depth is for the preparation of exploiting profitable situations. When the eye recognizes a potential pattern, the mind can be prepared to implement the correct trading strategy. The following illustrations of the major signals should help investors spot high probability situations.

Western charting has patterns that indicate reversals of major trends. Head and shoulders, double tops or double bottoms, island reversals, are a few formations that have exhibited high degrees of accuracy for identifying change in the current trends.

Candlestick analysis enhances an investor's ability to prepare for trend changes. Being familiar with the psychology behind specific candle formations provides immense advantages. Candle signals can identify a trend reversal in one day. More often, the Candlestick signals can *forewarn* when a trend is preparing to change.

A major trend will probably not have a one-day reversal. It may take a few days or weeks for the force (psychology of investors) to expend itself and reverse direction. The appearance of a reversal signal alerts the investor that a change of investor sentiment has or is about to occur.

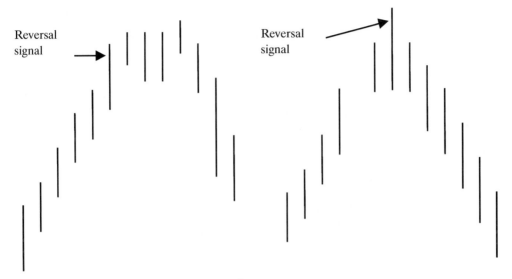

Fig. 2-1

Viewing a 'sell' signal at the top of a long up-trend should inform an investor that the trend might now be losing stream. Will the trend continue up from here? Maybe, but not with the same potential as putting your investment funds elsewhere! The trend is starting to lose steam. Quite often, a reversal of a trend can be clearly illustrated with a candlestick signal at the ultimate reversal point. Other instances may see a trend reversing slowly with the appearance of major signals occurring during the reversal pattern. In either case, being able to identify a major signal in overbought or oversold conditions provides an alert system for the candlestick investor.

With these principles in mind, review the rest of this chapter. Learn to visually recognize these major signals as they will provide more trading opportunities than most investors can use in a single day. Keep in mind; these signals are the results of hundreds of years of cultivation. The most important aspect of this cultivation being PROFITS! Additionally, utilizing other indicators along with candlestick signals provides a format for identifying not only profitable trades, but also the <u>high</u> profit trades.

The signal would have indicated that sellers were stepping in at these levels.

The force of the trend may still take prices higher. However, with the indications that the sellers may be stepping in, the strength of the up-trend should be greatly diminished. The investor can now prepare for the appearance of the next sell signal. Not all trends reverse immediately. Candlestick signals can illustrate when a trend is starting to lose strength.

Before going into the descriptions of the major signals, let us do a quick review of the basic candlestick formations. Japanese candlestick charting dramatically increases the information conveyed by visual analysis. Each formation, or series of formations, clearly illustrates the change of investor sentiment. This interpretation process is not apparent in standard bar charts. Each candle formation has a unique name. Some have Japanese names, others have English names. When possible in this book, the English name and Japanese name are given. The Japanese names are illustrated in Romanji, writing so that English-speaking people can say the names.

Single candles are often referred to as YIN and YANG lines. These terms are actually Chinese, but are used by Western analysts to account for opposites; in/out, up/down, and over/under. *INN* and *YOH* are the Japanese equivalents. YIN is bearish. YANG is bullish. There are nine basic YIN and YANG lines in Candlestick analysis. These are expanded to fifteen to cover all possibilities. The combination of most patterns can be reduced to one of these.

Long days

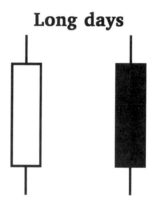

Fig. 2-2

A long day represents a large price move from open to close. 'Long' represents the length of the candle body. What qualifies a candle body to be considered long? That question has to be answered relative to the chart being analyzed. The recent price action of a stock will determine whether a "long" candle has been formed. Analysis of the previous two or three weeks of trading should be a current representative sample of the price action.

Short Days

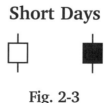

Fig. 2-3

The same analytical process of the long candles can interpret short days. There are a large percentage of the trading days that do not fall into either of these two categories.

Maruboza

In Japanese, Marubozu means close cropped or close-cut. Bald or Shaven Head are more commonly used in candlestick analysis. Its meaning reflects the fact that there are no shadows extending from either end of the body.

Black Marubozu

Fig. 2-4

A long black body with no shadows at either end is known as a Black Marubozu. It is considered a weak indicator. It is often identified in a bearish continuation or bullish reversal pattern, especially if it occurs during a downtrend. A long black candle could represent the final sell off, making it an alert to a bullish reversal setting up. The Japanese often call it the Major Yin or Marubozu of Yin.

White Marubozu

Fig. 2-5

The White Marubozu is a long white body with no shadows on either end. This is an extremely strong pattern. Consider how it is formed. It opens on the low and immediately heads up. It continues upward until it closes, on its high. Counter to the Black Marubozu, it is often the first part of a bullish continuation pattern or bearish reversal pattern. It is called a Major Yang or Marubozu of Yang.

Closing Marubozu

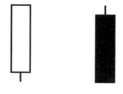

Fig. 2-6

A Closing Marubozu has no shadow at its closing end. A white body will not have a shadow at the top. A black body will not have a shadow at the bottom. In both cases, these are strong signals corresponding to the direction that they each represent.

Opening Marubozu

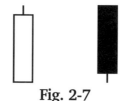

Fig. 2-7

The Opening Marubozu has no shadows extending from the open price end of the body. A white body would not have a shadow at the bottom end; the black candle would not have a shadow at its top end. Though these are strong signals, they are not as strong as the Closing Marubozu.

Spinning Top

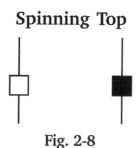

Fig. 2-8

Spinning Tops are depicted with small bodies relative to the shadows. This demonstrates some indecision on the part of the bulls and the bears. They are considered neutral when trading in a sideways market. However, in a trending or oscillating market, a relatively good rule of thumb is that the next day's trading will probably move in the direction of the opening price. The size of the shadow is not as important as the size of the body for forming a Spinning Top.

Doji

Fig. 2-9

The Doji is one of the most important signals in candlestick analysis. It is formed when the open and the close are the same or very near the same. The lengths of the shadows can vary. The longer the shadows, the more significant the Doji becomes. More will be explained about the Doji in the next few pages. ALWAYS pay attention to the Doji.

Being able to recognize the basic formations creates a visual awareness of potential changes in a trend. For example, the formation of a long candle demonstrates more buying or selling sentiment than a normal candle. It may be simplistic but being able to recognize what the formations represent provides valuable information. A long black candle or a series of long black candles after an extended downtrend reveals important information regarding investor sentiment.

A long black candle at the bottom of an extended downtrend should be a forewarning that the panic selling is coming into the price. It becomes time to watch for a candlestick buy signal. The same is true when long white candles start forming at the top of a trend. That reveals exuberant buying at the top. Watching for a candlestick sell signal becomes prudent.

The mainstay of candlestick analysis comes from centuries of observing what occurs when specific candlestick formations appear. The process of boxing in the open and the close provides an immense amount of information not found in other charting techniques.

The following illustrations demonstrate where the major signals work most effectively. It will incorporate the analysis of candlestick formations leading up to a potential reversal. This is depicted by purely visual observations. The candlestick investor has the huge advantage of visually identifying the weaknesses of human nature.

The utilization of the 12 major signals is greatly enhanced when the surrounding investor sentiment can be visually identified prior to a major reversal.

The remainder of this book will concentrate on how and when the major signals work most effectively. That will include identifying trend formations that warn a reversal signal is potentially forming. Also, high profit patterns will be demonstrated when utilizing candlestick signals. There will not be formulas; there will not be heavy interpretations. Candlestick analysis is purely a visual evaluation. The following major signals will be explained in depth. Being able to recognize chart patterns that have high a profit potential prepares an investor to take advantage of profitable trades from their inception. Learning these major signals will greatly simplify the formation of a consistently profitable trading program.

Scanning for candlestick signals makes for finding the potential of a reversal. However, the final analysis reverts back the visual analysis.

The following illustrations will be of the major signals. The description of these signals will be done in much greater depth than the descriptions found in *Profitable Candlestick Trading*. You may find some of the explanations repetitive. The important features of the will be repeated to insure that their relevance is fully understood.

THE MAJOR SIGNALS

THE DOJI
BULLISH ENGULFING
BEARISH ENGULFING
HAMMER
HANGING MAN
PIERCING PATTERN
DARK CLOUD
HARAMI – BULLISH
HARAMI – BEARISH
SHOOTING STAR
INVERTED HAMMER
MORNING STAR
EVENING STAR
KICKER SIGNAL

THE DYNAMIC DOJI

(Doji Bike)

DOJI STAR

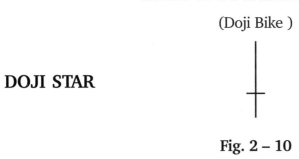

Fig. 2 – 10

Description

The Doji it is the most recognized candlestick signal. Its formation, essentially looking like a cross, has relevant implications. It illustrates indecision during a specific time period between the Bulls and the Bears. The Doji is also comprised of one candle. The Japanese say when a Doji occurs, one should always take notice. It is one of the most important Candlestick signals. The formation is created when the opening price and closing price are the same or nearly the same. This forms a horizontal line. It is an important alert at both the top and bottom of trends. At the top of a trend, the Doji signals a reversal without needing confirmation. The rule of thumb is that you should close a long or go short immediately.

However, the Doji occurring during the downtrend requires a bullish day to confirm the trend reversal. The Japanese explanation is that the weight of the market can still force the trend downward. The Doji is an excellent example of the Candlestick method having superior attributes compared to the Western bar charting method. The deterioration of a trend is not going to be as apparent when viewing standard bar charts.

Criteria

1. The open and the close are the same or very near the same.
2. The length of the shadow should not be excessively long, especially when viewed at the end of a bullish trend.

Signal Enhancements

1. A gap, away from the previous days close, sets up for a stronger reversal move.
2. Large volume on the signal day increases the chances that a blow-off day has occurred although it is not a necessity.
3. It is more effective after a long candle body, usually an exaggerated daily move compared to the normal daily trading range seen in the majority of the trend.

A Doji at the Top

*** *Illustrations in the following chapters will not have explanations of every indicator. The stochastic settings for all the charts are 12,3,3. The moving averages are the 50 day and 200 day simple moving averages. If a question of which is which, the 50 day MA will be the more volatile of the two.*

The Doji becomes an extremely significant reversal signal when viewed at the top of a trend. The definition of a top of a trend is a function of the stochastic's in an overbought condition. The Japanese rice trader's scenario is easy-to-understand. After an extensive uptrend, the appearance of a Doji is an illustration the Bulls and the Bears have reached a point of equilibrium. The price has finally reached a level where the bullish buying pressure is being equalized by the Bears selling into them. A Doji at the top becomes an immediate sell signal. The Japanese Rice traders say to start taking your profits. A Doji in the overbought condition becomes more relevant following a large white candle or a gap-up. A large white candle or a gap-up signifies the exuberant buying coming in at the top of a trend. That exuberance, followed by a Doji, becomes a very strong signal that a reversal is about to occur.

In early 2004, Fig.2-11, TASER International Inc. was the stock that just would not quit. It moved from the low single-digit price range up to the mid 30s in just a few months. Of course it was well-publicized on the financial news stations. The higher it moved, the more it became debated as to whether it still had huge upside potential or was way over-priced.

If you were long, where did you take profits? If you are looking to short the stock, where did you want to get in? The Doji at the top in mid-April provided a very clear answer. Notice how the price of TASER stock started moving exuberantly in the first part of April, 2004. The long bullish candle, after a small gap-up, with stochastics in the overbought condition, should have been an alert to start watching for a candlestick 'sell' signal. That signal became clearly apparent the following day with a large Doji signal.

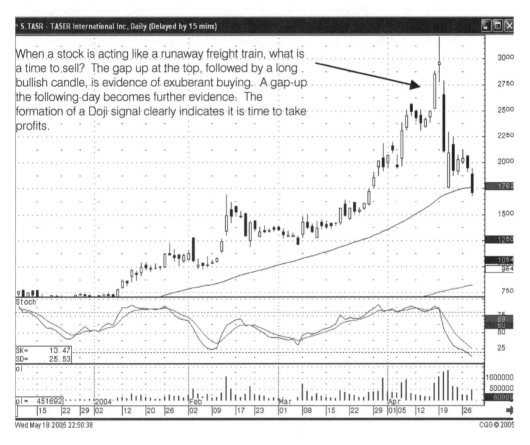

Fig. 2-11 *TASER International Inc. - early 2004*

The Doji became the sell signal. The evidence of exuberant buying, followed by a Doji formation, would have allowed an investor to take profits near the very top of the trend. Could the price have continued higher? Certainly! However, remember that the Japanese Rice traders have analyzed these circumstances for hundreds of years. The probabilities of a top reversal signal occurring is a function of witnessing exuberant buying followed by a gap up Doji signal. The Japanese Rice traders have recognized that this is time to sell. The gap-down open, the following day, clearly illustrates that the sellers have stepped into this trade.

If it is assumed that the signals have significance, then we would not be looking at them today if they did not work. Selling upon the appearance of a Doji is a high-probability profitable result. Exuberant buying followed by a Doji equals 'sell'!

> *Learning is a treasure that will follow its owner everywhere.*
> **Chinese proverb**

When the greed sets in, and the exuberant buying becomes visually apparent, be prepared to take profits. Viewing big price moves at the top of a trend, followed by a Doji, especially when that Doji gaps up at the top, take the profits. What is occurring when these formations occur? Investor sentiment deciding that everything is apparently so rosy for the future, they want to get in at any price. The question always needs to be raised "If everything is so great, who is selling?" The answer is usually the smart money.

The price of TASER International Inc. Fig.2-12, illustrated again the Doji at the top creating the reversal at the end of 2004. A long bullish candle, in the overbought condition, followed by a gap up Doji illustrates that the uptrend should be over. How do you exit the trade? Investors that have access to computer screens during the final 30 minutes of trading will be able to witness a Doji forming near the end of the day. They can close out their position on the close

Fig.2-12 *Taser International Inc. - late 2004*

For the investor that does not have access to the markets during the day, the 'sell stop' can be placed for the next days trading. A logical stop loss point would be at the low of the trading of the previous days Doji signal. If the selling came back down through that point, that would be a clear indication that the sellers had now started coming into the trade.

The gap-up at the top of a trend can have many conclusions. A gap-up followed by a long bullish candle has different implications than a gap-up that forms a Doji. As illustrated in the Photonics Inc. chart, Fig. 2-13, a gap-up Doji indicated the top of the trading. Profits should have been taken at the close of the Doji day or on the lower open the following day. Could a higher price been achieved?

Fig. 2-13 *Photonics Inc.*

As seen in this chart, a better price could have been obtained approximately a week later. However, what is the main point of investing? To maximize your returns and to do so with the least amount of risk! Holding onto this position for another week would not have produced the percentage returns to make the risk of holding that position worth while. As can be seen, the majority of the profits were made when the price gapped up and formed a Doji.

The point of investing is not to maximize your profits on each individual trade. It is to maximize your profits for your account. The majority of the profits were extracted from this trade at the gap up Doji. Those funds now should be moved to a lower risk trade, one that would have the upside potential as was seen at the beginning of this trade in mid to late January.

The appearance of a Doji at an important resistance level such as a trend line also has significance. Notice in Fig.2-14, the Cadence Design Systems Inc. chart, how a Doji, in the overbought, condition forms right at a trend line. The major advantage of candlestick signals is that they indicate immediately what the investor sentiment is doing at important levels.

Fig. 2-14 *Cadence Design Systems Inc.*

Witnessing a Doji, at what everybody else might be anticipating as a resistance level, provides an immediate confirmation that the buyers and sellers have participated in indecisive trading. The Doji illustrates that the trend-line has become resistance once again. It is further confirmed by seeing the selling the next day when prices gap to the downside.

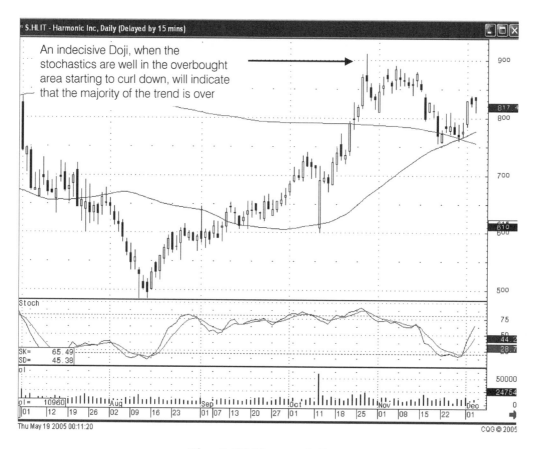

Fig. 2-15 *Harmonic Inc.*

A Series of Doji

If one Doji represents indecision, a series of Doji represents a lot of indecision. Finding a series of Doji is the set up for some powerful trades. Observing a series of Doji should alert investors that the Bulls and the Bears are having a hard time deciding which direction the trend should be moving. The more extensive the series, (the longer the indecision time frame) the more convincing the trend will be once it breaks out.

A series of Doji is an excellent warning device. It illustrates that something is about to happen. Logically, if a series of Doji occur in oversold condition, what should occur is a move to the upside. Conversely, a string of Doji, seen in the overbought condition, usually indicates the trend is about to turn down. The caveat to witnessing a large number of Doji forming is analyzing the previous chart formations. A trading entity that has Doji forming a high percentage of the time will not be as significantly influenced by more Doji. A series of Doji becomes more significant when found in a normal trading chart.

As illustrated in Fig. 2-16, the Frontier Oil chart, after a mild sell-off the investors became very indecisive. This indecision occurred as the stochastics came into the oversold condition. One Doji, in an oversold condition, calls to the attention of an investor to watch for a reversal. Watching a series of Doji develop allows an investor to take advantage of a strong trend developing right from the very start.

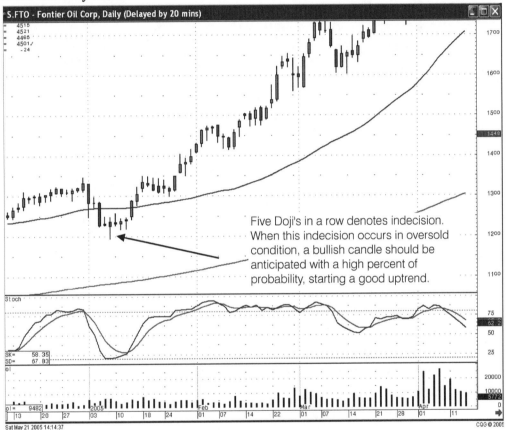

Fig.2-16 *Frontier Oil Corp.*

What does a series of Doji represent? Indecision! What does the bullish candle illustrate after the series of Doji? The investors have now made up their mind which direction to take the trend. With that knowledge, it becomes an easy process to watch which direction the trading will move from that indecisive period. The candlestick investor can start putting on the trade as soon as the price movement has indicated that the indecision is over. A strong move, from an indecisive trading range, is an extremely high probability indicator. It can be acted upon immediately. An indecisive trading range can have many configurations. As witnessed in Fig. 2-17, the SIRF Technology Holdings Inc. chart, the indecision after the slight pullback could be viewed. The Doji illustrated that the downward trajectory was running into indecisive trading.

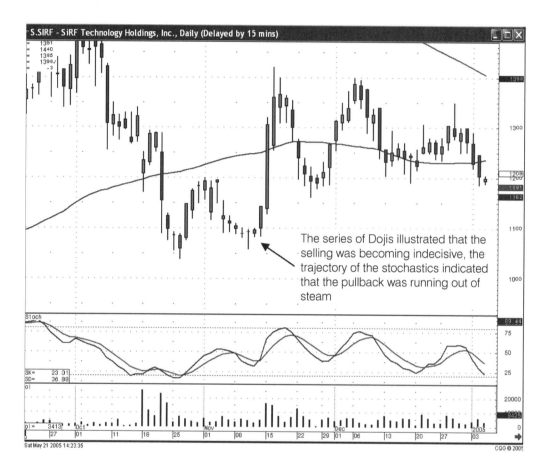

The series of Dojis illustrated that the selling was becoming indecisive, the trajectory of the stochastics indicated that the pullback was running out of steam

Fig.2-17 *SIRF Technology Holdings Inc.*

Although the stochastics were in mid-range, the series of Doji illustrated that the selling was waning, giving time for the stochastics to start curling to the upside. When the trading becomes indecisive at important moving averages, the investor should become aware of a potential trend change.

That scenario becomes relatively clear in Fig.2-18, the Champion Enterprises Inc. chart. Doji/Spinning Tops occurring at a major moving average while stochastics are starting to move up should be watched. The appearance of a Long-legged Doji at the end of the series creates additional relevance. The indecisiveness is growing.

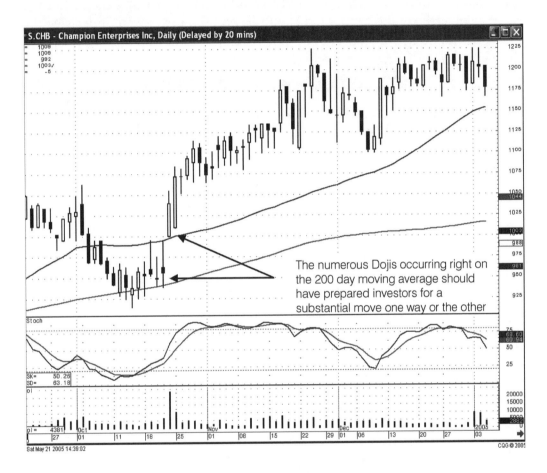

Fig.2-18 *Champion Enterprises Inc.*

Being prepared for a major consequence to occur allows an investor to make a purchase decision quickly. What is expected after a series of Doji? A significant move! If that is the case, a gap-up or a gap-down immediately illustrates what has been decided.

In the case of the Champion Enterprises Inc.chart, Fig. 2-18, a gap up above the 50 day moving average, followed by the immediate buying, should have activated a purchase immediately.

Allow your eyes to evaluate what the major signals are doing. Keep it simple. As seen in Fig. 2-19, the Alamosa Holdings Inc. chart, a series of Doji indicated a bottom in early September. Another series of Doji occurred at the same level at the end of a month. The Bulls and the Bears were indecisive the first time the trend pulled back. The Bulls and the Bears were just as indecisive the second time the trend pulled back to that level.

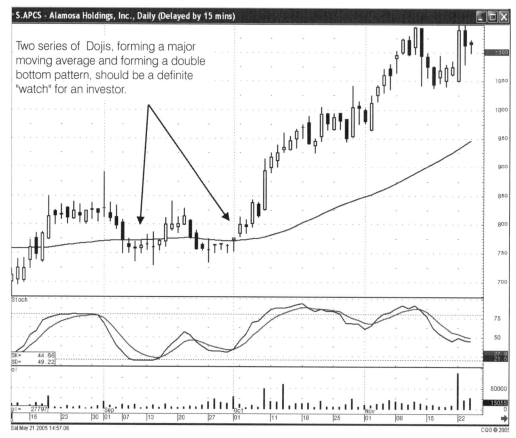

Fig.2-19 *Alamosa Holdings Inc.*

Both times the series of Doji were revealing valuable information. Something should happen from these levels. The first rally failed. Is this not contrary to the implication that a series of Doji, followed by a strong move out of that trading range, should produce a strong rally? The key word is "probabilities". Not all series of Doji are going to be followed by high profit trend. However, an extremely high percentage of the trends will be strong.

The fact that the first trend failed does not negate the probabilities that the second series of Doji will have any less likelihood of being followed by a strong trend. Realistically, the second time the series of Doji indicated that there was great indecision at approximately the $7.50 level. A new buying indicator appeared. The gap up from the 50 day Ma and the stochastics curling back up. The sellers recognize the persistency of the Bulls.

A series of Doji occurring near a major moving average has significant implications. Two series of Doji at the same level, creating a double bottom formation, creates stronger implications. Will a series of Doji in the oversold condition always preclude a bullish trend? Will any series of Doji in the overbought condition always preclude a bearish trend? No! The Doji indicate a major move is about to occur. The "probabilities" point to a bullish trend after Doji have formed in the oversold condition. The "probabilities" point to a bearish trend when Doji are viewed in an overbought condition. The important factor that the Doji portray is that a major move is likely to occur. As illustrated in Fig. 2-20, the Dick's Sporting Goods Inc. chart, the series of Doji was just an indecisive congestion area in a strong up trend.

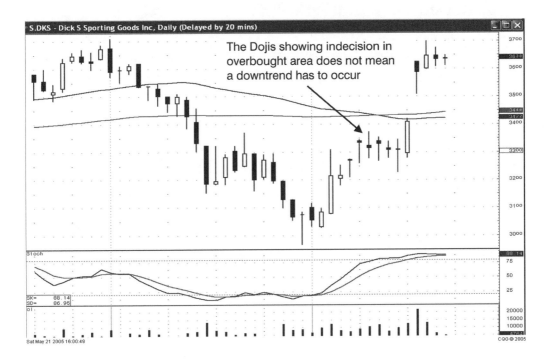

Fig. 2-20 *Dicks Sporting Goods Inc.*

One Doji, be prepared. Two Doji, be more prepared. Three Doji, definitely start looking for something major to happen one way or the other. This can be applied to any trading entity. Whether you are analyzing the long-term trends in the indexes or trading minute-by-minute in E-mini S&P trades, the appearance of a large number of Doji becomes an excellent trade entry warning.

Series of Doji Observations

1. **The bigger the series of Doji, the more powerful the resulting move from that level will be.**

2. **A series of Doji, forming in an oversold condition, represents an extremely high probability that a major uptrend is about to start.**

3. **A series of Doji forming in an overbought condition represents an extremely high probability that a major downtrend is about to start.**

4. **The initiation of the trend will be illustrated by a strong candle moving away from the indecision area.**

ENGULFING PATTERNS

(Tsutsumi)

BULLISH ENGULFING

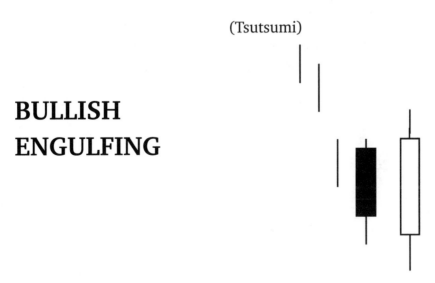

Fig. 2 – 21

Description

The Bullish Engulfing pattern is a very easy signal to identify. At the end of a down trend, it becomes evident that the Bulls are now involved. The Bullish Engulfing pattern is a major reversal pattern comprised of two opposite colored bodies. It opens lower than the previous day's close and closes higher than the previous day's open. Thus, the white candle completely engulfs the previous day's black candle body. This produces a clear visual graphic that in the early part of the trading, the Bears were still in control. As the time frame moves on, the Bulls started stepping in and continue to buy all the way past the open of the previous day. The graphic itself illustrates that there is now strong bullish sentiment in the price at these levels. The Engulfing Signal can be formed with the open and the close of one end of the pattern being equal but not open and close of both days being equal.

Engulfing patterns are considered major signals for two reasons. First, they occur often and second, they produce a high probability that the trend has reversed. Not only has the trend reversed, but the buyers have come in with enthusiasm. The most obvious element of the engulfing signal is a candle body color that is completely opposite of the previous trend.

Criteria

The body of the second day completely engulfs the body of the first day. Shadows are not a consideration. Prices have been in a definable down trend, even if only for a short term. The body of the second candle is the opposite color of the first candle, and the first candle is the color of the previous trend. The exception to this rule is when the engulfed body is a Doji or an extremely small body.

Signal Enhancements

1. A large body engulfing a small body. The small body shows the trend is running out of steam. The large body indicates the new direction has started with good force.
2. When the engulfing pattern occurs after a fast move down, there is less supply of stock to slow down the reversal move. A fast move makes a stock price over-extended and increases the potential for profit taking. Large volume on the engulfing day increases the chances that a blow-off day has occurred.
3. An engulfing body which engulfs more than one previous body demonstrates power in the reversal. If the engulfing body engulfs the body and the shadows of the previous day, the reversal has a greater probability of working.
4. The greater the open price gaps down from the previous close, the greater the probability of a strong reversal.

The appearance of a Bullish Engulfing signal when stochastics are in an oversold condition produces an extremely high probability that the trend will move to the upside. Some features of the engulfing body can make it more convincing. The bigger the engulfing body is compared to the last down trending body, the more likely the uptrend will move with significant force.

The Alliance Gaming Corp. chart Fig. 2-22 (following page), is a prime example of a reversal signal. A large bullish engulfing signal occurring with oversold stochastics and an inordinate amount of volume. This clearly represents that the existing negative sentiment of the trend has been completely altered.

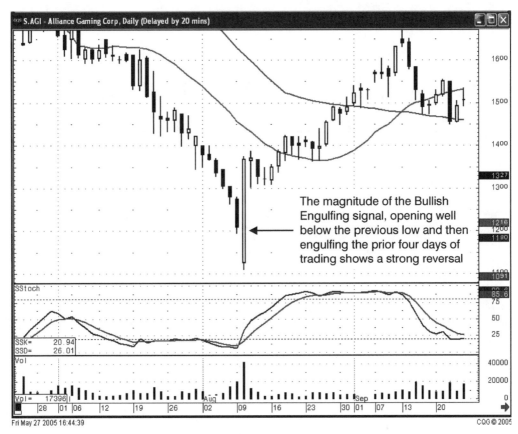

The magnitude of the Bullish Engulfing signal, opening well below the previous low and then engulfing the prior four days of trading shows a strong reversal

Fig.2-22 *Alliance Gaming Corp.*

The further the engulfing body opens below the close and/or the trading range of the previous day, and then closes above the previous days open, the higher the probability and the more forceful the uptrend will be. This incorporates the common sense aspects that candlestick analysis conveys. Where do most investors sell? Panic selling at the bottom! That is where the Bullish Engulfing signal starts its formation. The deeper the selling, starting the Bullish Engulfing formation, the more convincing that all the weak stock has finally been sold into the strong hands. The further a Bullish Engulfing signal closes above the previous day's candle, engulfing one, two, three or more previous candles, the more compelling the reversal signal.

Stochastics are Excellent Indicators for Overbought and Oversold Conditions

When are you near a bottom? When you're indicators, such as stochastics, tell you the trend is in an oversold condition. Also, when you can identify selling at the bottom. Keep in mind, the oversold condition can last for a long period of time as shown in the Alliance Gaming Corp. chart. A gap down at the bottom, then the formation of a strong bullish engulfing signal bringing the stochastics of the oversold condition becomes a very relevant reversal signal.

> *If you have an apple and I have an apple, and we exchange these apples, then you and I will still each have an apple. But if you have an idea and I have an idea and we exchange ideas, each of us will have two ideas.*
> *George Bernard Shaw*

Fig. 2-23, the Digene Corp. chart illustrates the classic reversal signal. The last day of the downtrend shows aggressive selling. This should be the first alert for watching for a candlestick "buy" signal. The following day forms a Bullish Engulfing signal. A Bullish Engulfing signal has more significant ramifications when both candles have "long days".

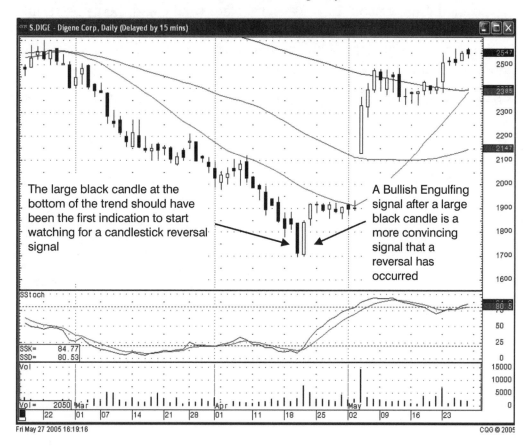

The large black candle at the bottom of the trend should have been the first indication to start watching for a candlestick reversal signal

A Bullish Engulfing signal after a large black candle is a more convincing signal that a reversal has occurred

Fig. 2-23 *Digene Corp.*

(Long days are identified when the size of the candle is larger compared to the majority of the other candles within the immediate preceding area on the chart. Generally, two or three weeks of previous candle formations are sufficient to judge the average candle size.) Simply stated, the sellers were in a hurry to get out of the trade. The next day, the Bulls clearly demonstrated that they were getting into the trade

The Taro Pharmaceutical Industries Ltd. chart Fig. 2-24, is an example of investors wanting to get out, no matter what. After nearly a month of selling, the final gap-down demonstrates the extensive desire for investors to get out of the position. The fact that once the price opened, started moving up, and finished above the previous day's trading, clearly signifies the Bulls had stepped into this position. The previous day was not a black candle and therefore, technically not a Bullish Engulfing signal, nonetheless the fact that you had a huge Bullish Engulfing signal that actually engulfed the previous four days of trading provides a significant message. The buyers had stepped in at the bottom.

Fig 2-24 *Taro Pharmaceutical Industries Ltd.*

Does identifying a candlestick reversal signal always foretell that a new trend is starting? Not all the time! But the "probabilities" are extremely high a reversal will occur. Will that new trend start up immediately? Not necessarily, but the signal occurring in the correct conditions increases the likelihood a new trend should be starting. If not immediately, very soon.

Witnessing a bullish signal in oversold condition conveys the information an investor should be looking for. The buyers have started moving into the position. The uptrend may not start immediately. As witnessed in Fig. 2-25, the IXYS Corp. chart, the first Bullish Engulfing signal occurred with stochastics in the oversold condition. The uptrend fizzled. However, that did not negate the fact that a bullish signal formed in an oversold condition. Even though that uptrend did not get started, the oversold condition was still in existence.

One Bullish Engulfing signal conveys information. Two Bullish Engulfing signals confirms that information.

Fig. 2-25 *IXYS Corp.*

If the first Bullish Engulfing signal failed, the second Bullish Engulfing signal will be more significant. The Bears see the buying from the first bullish signal. They are relieved when there is no follow-through buying. However, when they see the second Bullish Engulfing signal, the Bears realize that the Bulls are back again. They finally step out of the way. If one Bullish Engulfing signal indicates the buyers are stepping in, then two Bullish Engulfing signals indicate the buyers are serious.

It makes good sense that when a Bullish Engulfing signal is witnessed in an oversold condition, a trend reversal is likely to occur. But what happens if you see a bullish engulfing signal occurring in an overbought condition? As a Bull, that would be a comforting event. However, the Japanese Rice traders used a Bullish Engulfing signal in overbought condition as an 'alert' to start watching for candlestick "sell" signals. The rationale is that the Bullish Engulfing signal, at the top of a trend, is usually the last gasp buying.

> *Learning is like rowing upstream: not to advance is to drop back.*
> *Japanese proverb*

How can this information be used to the candlestick investor's advantage? First, if long a position and you observe some toppiness with a Bullish Engulfing signal, be prepared to close out the position. If short a position, based upon a candlestick sell signal, such as a Bearish Harami, followed by a Bullish Engulfing signal, you should be less inclined to cover the short position. The trend would require further buying after the Bullish Engulfing signal to indicate the uptrend is still in force. Otherwise, be prepared for the price to start heading down.

Fig. 2-26, The Wyeth chart illustrates the Bullish Engulfing signal occurring in the overbought condition acting as the last gasp buying. The logical stop loss in this trade, if long, would have been at the low of the Bullish Engulfing signal day. The logic being; that if this stock was still in an uptrend, it should not be coming back down through the low of the last bullish candle.

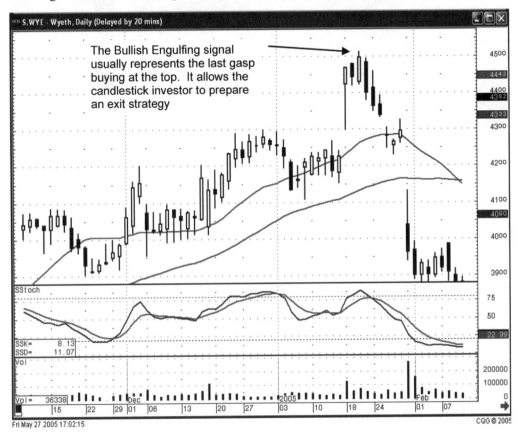

Fig. 2-26 *Wyeth*

The Bullish Engulfing signal has graphic characteristics that make it easily identified. As a major signal, a Bullish Engulfing signal will be viewed often during scans. They will appear every single day somewhere. They work very effectively when stochastics are in oversold conditions. They also work effectively at important support levels such as a trend lines or major moving averages.

The information conveyed in a Bullish Engulfing signal is very simple. The Bulls have come into a position with reasonable force. That buying force more than negated the previous days trading. Use that knowledge to your advantage.

ENGULFING PATTERNS

(tsutsumi)

BEARISH

ENGULFING

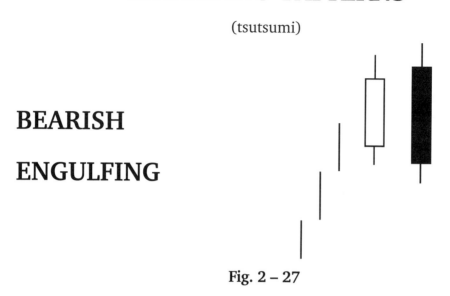

Fig. 2 – 27

Description

The Bearish Engulfing signal is exactly opposite the Bullish Engulfing signal. The Bearish Engulfing pattern is a major reversal pattern comprised of two opposite colored bodies.. The Bearish Engulfing Pattern (Figure 2-23) is formed after an up trend. It opens higher that the previous day's close and closes lower than the previous day's open. Thus, the black candle completely engulfs the previous day's white candle. Engulfing can include either the open or the close being equal to the open or close of the previous day but not both.

Criteria

1. The body of the second day completely engulfs the body of the first day. Shadows are not a consideration.
2. Prices have been in a definable uptrend, even if it has been short term.
3. The body of the second candle is opposite color of the first candle, the first candle being the color of the previous trend. The exception to this rule is when the engulfed body is a Doji or an extremely small body.

Signal Enhancements

1. A large body engulfing a small body. The previous day was showing the trend was running out of steam. The large body shows that the new direction has started with good force.
2. When the engulfing pattern occurs after a fast spike up, there will less supply of stock to slow down the reversal move. A fast move makes a stock price over-extended and increases the potential for profit taking and a meaningful pullback.
3. Large volume on the engulfing day increases the chances that a blow-off day has occurred.
4. The engulfing body engulfing more than one previous body demonstrates power in the reversal.
5. If the engulfing body engulfs the body and the shadows of the previous day, the reversal has a greater probability of working.
6. The greater the open price gaps up from the previous close, the greater the probability of a strong reversal.

The Bearish Engulfing signal is created with the same investor psychology as the Bullish Engulfing signal. After an uptrend, the open of the Bearish Engulfing signal is above the close of the previous day's bullish body. Once again, the investor psychology that illustrates exuberance, began the formation. A Bearish Engulfing signal requires only to have an open above the previous days close. The demonstration of exuberant buying, an open price much higher than the previous day's close and/or above the previous day's trading range is more significant. Where do most investors buy? Exuberantly at the top!

The further to the upside that the Bearish Engulfing signal opens, the more convincing the Bearish Engulfing signal becomes. It clearly illustrates that the Bears have now taken over control of the trend. As with the Bullish

Engulfing signal, the Bearish Engulfing signal is visually clear to identify. It is a dark candle after an uptrend of bullish candles.

A Bearish Engulfing signal following another candlestick sell signal adds more conviction to a downside move. As illustrated in Fig. 2-28 the Novatel Wireless Inc. chart, the Bearish Engulfing signal is initially created with a gap-up in overbought conditions..

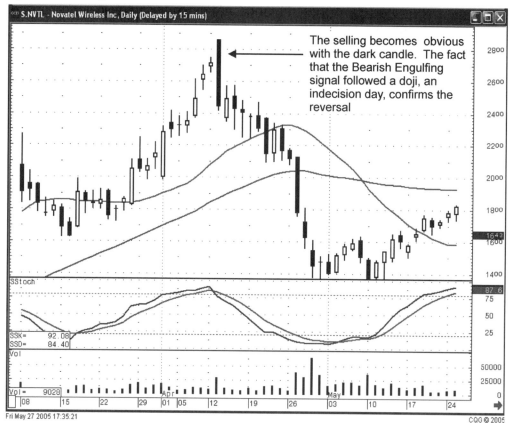

Fig.2-28 *Novatel Wireless Inc.*

A gap-up in price, followed the Doji/Spinning Top formation of the previous day. The bearish trading of that day confirms the indecision that was developing in the previous day's signal. As with all the major signals, the signal itself is the most important factor. Confirming indicators, such as stochastics, are just that, confirming indicators.

The Bearish Engulfing signal witnessed in Fig. 2-29 (following page), the Abgenix chart, occurred at a significant level. Although the stochastics were not near an overbought condition, a Bearish Engulfing signal occurring exactly at the 200 day moving average is meaningful.

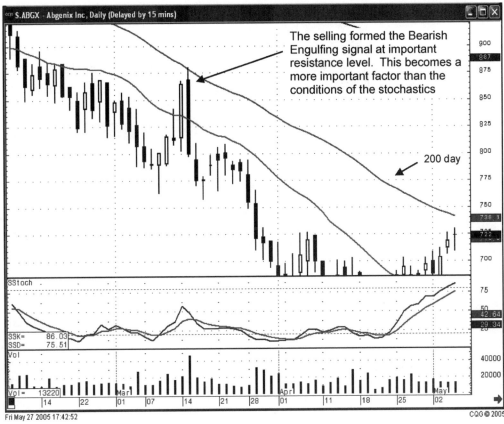

Fig. 2-29 *Abgenix Inc.*

It clearly illustrated that the sellers made their presence known once an important resistance level had been touched

A Bearish Engulfing signal gains more credibility after witnessing the obvious topping signals of a trend. Notice in fig. 2-30, the Sonic Solutions chart (following page), the uptrend shows topping signals with a gap up in the overbought condition. This would be the area to start looking for a candlestick sell signal. The formation of the Bearish Engulfing signal, the following day, is more relevant after the gap-up. The second Bearish Engulfing signal four days later reaffirms that the sellers have come into this price. Both long dark candles provide more evidence that the sellers are now in control.

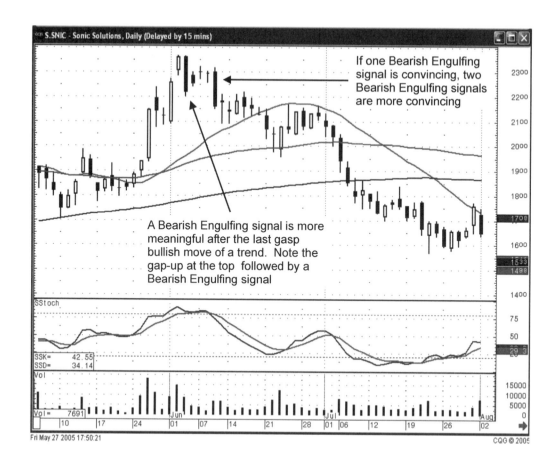

Fig. 2-30 *Sonic Solutions, Inc.*

The Bearish Engulfing signal can be created by opening higher than the previous day's close. If the open is higher than the previous days trading range, stop-loss procedures can easily be implemented. Stop-loss procedures will be further discussed in the Entry and Exit Strategy chapter. The completion of a Bearish Engulfing signal, in an overbought condition, allows investors to prepare for short trade potentials.

Notice in Fig. 2-31, the Millicom International Cellular chart, the gap up in the overbought condition was the first indication of a bearish signal being formed. A 'close' below the previous days open, as well as the open on the candle two days prior, made for a strong Bearish Engulfing signal. Not only should this have closed out any long positions, it should have set the stage for shorting the stock.

Fig. 2-31 *Millicom International Cellular*

The Bearish Engulfing signal portrays the same characteristics as found in the Bullish Engulfing signal. A Bearish Engulfing signal viewed in an overbought condition projects an extremely high probability of the trend turning down. What happens when a Bearish Engulfing signal is seen in an oversold condition? As with the Bullish Engulfing signal viewed in the overbought condition, representing last gasp buying, a Bearish Engulfing signal provides the same alert. A Bearish Engulfing signal in an oversold condition demonstrates the final selling.

When viewing a Bearish Engulfing signal in oversold condition, an investor should be prepared for a bullish signal to occur very soon. As an alert for the bull to start watching for a buy signal, it should also forewarn the investor with a short position to be prepared to cover as seen in Fig. 2-32, the Google chart

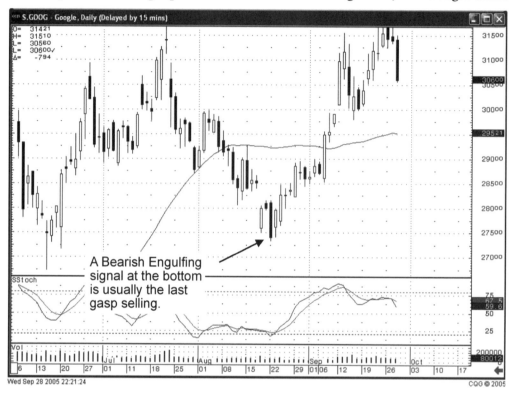

Fig. 2-32 *Google*

The Bullish and the Bearish Engulfing signals are both highly effective candle-stick signals.

They can easily be recognized visually on a chart. Incorporating investor psychology that is built into those signals allows the candlestick investor to take advantage of tread reversals at the most opportune times. The signals, occurring in overbought or oversold conditions, make their effectiveness that much greater. The engulfing patterns reveal a significant change in investor sentiment. They should always be addressed. The Bullish and the Bearish En-gulfing signal, occurring at other major technical levels, provide a significant meaning. Do not ignore these signals.

HAMMER
(TAKURI)

HAMMER

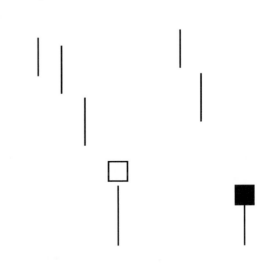

Figure 2-33

Description

The Hammer signal is aptly named. It looks like a hammer. The Hammer is comprised of one candle. It has one defining feature. The extensive shadow or tail to the downside!

Found at the bottom of a downtrend, this signal shows evidence the Bulls started to step in. The signal is usually formed after an extensive downtrend has been in effect. The price opens and continues to head down. However, before the end of the day, the Bulls start moving in.

One of the few formulas that an investor has to learn when analyzing candlestick signals is the length of the "shadow" or "tail." In the case of a Hammer signal, the lower shadow or tail should be at least <u>two</u> times greater than the body. The body can be either black or white. When viewed in the oversold condition, one should watch for a bullish confirmation the following day.

The important aspect of a Hammer signal illustrates that the Bears were pushing the prices down. Then the Bulls started entering the trade. The Japanese say, "The Bears were hammering out the bottom." The term "takuri" in Japanese is defined as "searching or probing for the depths," testing for the bottom.

The strength in which the Bulls started coming into the position is depicted by the color of the body. The buyers stepping in at the bottom of a trend, bringing the price back up into the top third of the trading range for the day is illustrated as a hammer signal with a black body. The significance of this signal is that the Bulls have moved in.

Criteria

1. The lower shadow should be at least two times the length of the body.

2. The real body is at the upper end of the trading range. The color of the body is not important although a white body should have slightly more bullish implications.

3. There should be no upper shadow or a very small upper shadow.

4. The following day needs to confirm the Hammer signal with a strong bullish day.

Signal Enhancements

1. The longer the lower shadow, the higher the potential of a reversal occurring.

2. A gap down from the previous day's close sets up for a stronger reversal move, provided the day after the Hammer signal opens higher.

3. Large volume on the Hammer day increases the chances that a blow-off day has occurred. (Blow-off day – see glossary)

The signal gains more strength if the Bulls bring the price back up through the open and close at or above that price, creating a white body. This illustrates more strength coming from the buyers than a black body.

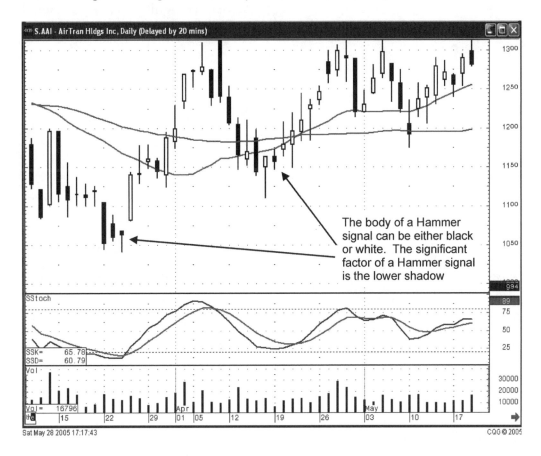

The body of a Hammer signal can be either black or white. The significant factor of a Hammer signal is the lower shadow

Fig. 2-34 *Airtran Holdings Inc.*

What do investors want to see after a Hammer signal? Continued buying! Does that continued buying need to come in the next day? Not necessarily. As will be experienced with many candlestick reversal signals appearing at the end of a downtrend, residual selling may occur for another day or two before a trend starts its move. The reversal signal indicates a change of investor sentiment. The trend, from that point, has a high probability of moving in an upward direction. However, it may take another few days to soak up the remainder of the sellers. As illustrated in Fig. 2-35 (following page), the AMB Properties chart, the large shadow to the downside is the clear reversal of the trend.

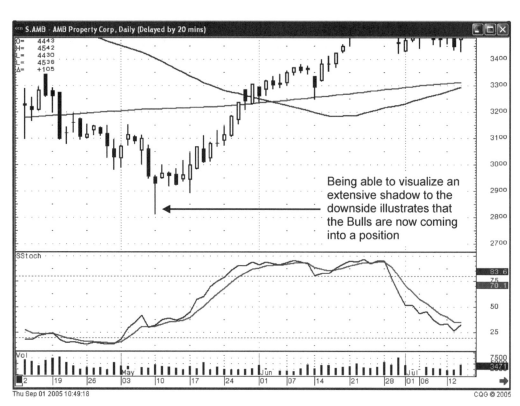

Fig. 2-35 *AMB Property Corp.*

Being able to visualize an extensive shadow to the downside illustrates that the Bulls are now coming into a position

A man with little learning is like the frog who thinks its pond is an ocean.
Japanese proverb

Fig. 2-36, the Celgene Corp. chart shows how one signal might have multiple names. The hammer signal could also be considered a Bullish Harami. The length of the shadow is an important indicator in itself. The further the prices were knocked down and then bought back, the more convincing the reversal.

The name of the signal is less important than being able to identify that a reversal signal has formed. The long lower-shadow, forming a Hammer signal, at a major moving average, while the stochastics are in an oversold condition, are the parameters aligning for a high probability trade.

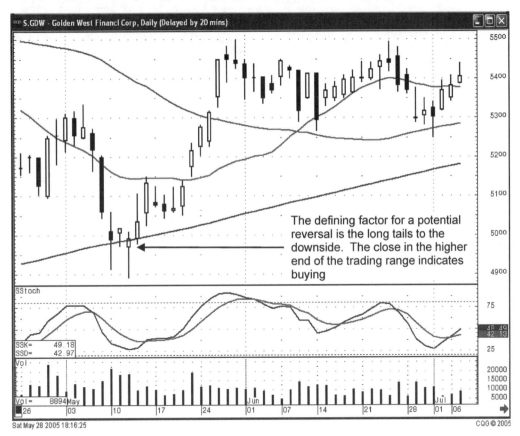

The defining factor for a potential reversal is the long tails to the downside. The close in the higher end of the trading range indicates buying

Fig. 2-36 *Celgene Corp.*

The true Hammer signal is depicted with no upper shadow or a very small upper shadow above the body. The evaluation of whether a Hammer signal is a true Hammer signal, a Spinning Top, or a Dragonfly Doji is not highly relevant.

The importance of evaluating the signal is to discern whether the signal demonstrates a reversal possibility.

As witnessed in Fig. 2-37, the Golden West Financial Corp. chart, a long shadow to the downside provides the indication that a reversal possibility is in the making.

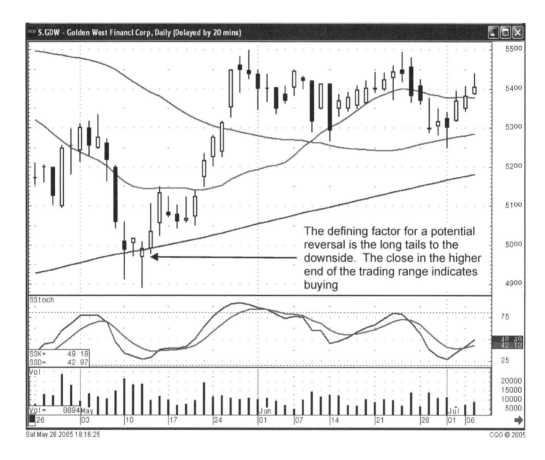

Fig. 2-37 *Golden West Financial Corp.*

The actual description of the signal is much less important than evaluating what the formation is conveying. In addition, the analysis should include the condition of the stochastics and the presence of a major moving average. However, the most foretelling attribute, the long lower shadow, should be the main consideration.

The defining element of a Hammer signal is the shadow to the downside. It illustrates that when the Bears knocked the price down, the Bulls stepped in. That same analysis can be better defined when witnessing a series of Hammer signals. Those signals produce a visual scenario that demonstrates the Bears are running out of steam. As illustrated in Fig. 2-38 the Black & Decker Corp. chart, a number of Hammers occurring as stochastics start rising illustrates that the Bulls are buying each time the Bears are trying to sell. The shadows to the downside make it clear for the candlestick investor to visualize buying support. An uptrend should be anticipated. A bullish candle, coming out of this type of trading area, should reveal immediately that the Bears have given up.

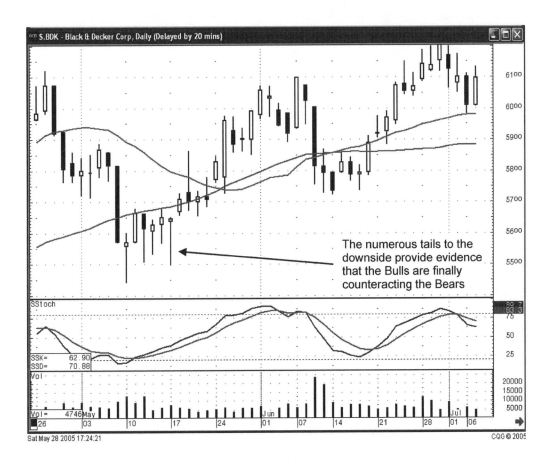

Fig. 2-38 *Black & Decker Corp.*

HANGING MAN
Paper Umbrella (Karakasa)

HANGING MAN

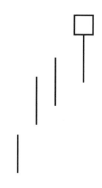

Fig. 2 –39

Description

The Hanging Man is comprised of one candle. It requires a lower tail two times greater than the body. Its name is derived by the Japanese; explaining it looks like a hanging man. The body is the head and the tail is the dangling feet. The Hanging-Man and the Hammer signal have the same characteristics but the Hanging Man is found at the top of a trend while the Hammer is found at the bottom of a trend.

After a strong up-trend has been in effect, the atmosphere is bullish. The price opens higher but starts to move lower. The Bears take control. Before the end of the day, the Bulls step in and take the price back up to the higher end of the trading range, creating a small body for the day. This could indicate the bulls still have control when analyzing a Western bar chart. However, the long lower shadow represents that the sellers started stepping in at these levels. Even though the Bulls may have been able to keep the price positive by the end of the day, the evidence of the selling was apparent. A lower open or a black candle the next day reinforces the fact that selling is starting.

The Hanging Man signal has a deeper analysis applied to its message. An investor, being in a bullish frame of mind, will be a little bit nervous upon seeing the selling during the day. However, by the end of the day the price has moved back up toward the top of the trading range. Although a little bit nervous during the day, the Bulls are relieved that the buying still seems to be around.

What the Japanese have witnessed is the nervousness that the Hanging Man signal creates. If prices opened lower the following day, the nervous Bulls from the previous day start saying " shoot, the Bears are back again, get me out of this trade." Essentially, the Hanging Man signal is the first sign that the sellers might be coming in. A lower open, or more selling the following day convinces the Bulls that is time to get out of the position.

Criteria

1. The upper shadow should be at least two times the length of the body.
2. The real body is at the upper end of the trading range. The color of the body is not important although a black body should have slightly more bearish implications.
3. There should be no upper shadow or a very small upper shadow.
4. The following day needs to confirm the Hanging Man signal with a black candle or better yet, a gap down followed by a lower close.

Signal Enhancements

1. The longer the lower shadow, the higher the potential of a reversal occurring.
2. A gap-up from the previous day's close sets up for a stronger reversal move provided the day after the Hanging Man signal trades lower.
3. Change Large volume on the signal day increases the chances that a blow-off day has occurred although it is not a necessity.

The Hanging Man, followed by continued selling the next day, is a relatively high probability 'sell' signal. When a trend is in the overbought condition, the hanging man signal definitely needs to be addressed. As with the Hammer signal, the longer the lower shadow in a Hanging Man signal, the more likely the Bulls will be nervous upon seeing a lower open the next day.

A gap-up at the top, followed by selling also signifies the sellers were showing up immediately after the opening price. This is in keeping with the candlestick analysis of where to start looking for candlestick sell signals, the exuberant buying indications at the top. As viewed in Fig. 2-40, the PMC Sierra chart, the gaps up in the overbought condition provided a forewarning that a top was near.

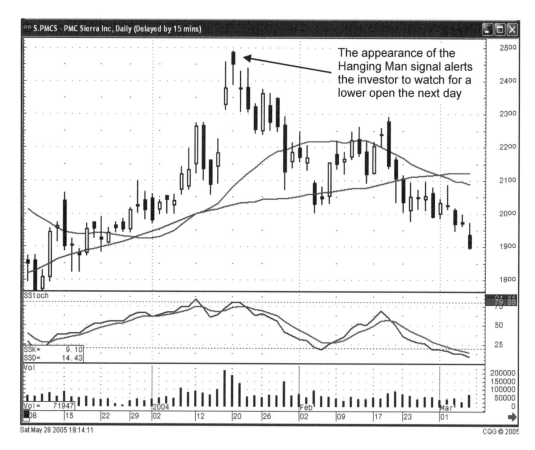

The appearance of the Hanging Man signal alerts the investor to watch for a lower open the next day

Fig. 2-40 *PMC Sierra Inc.*

The immediate sell-off indicated there was no new buying after the open. Although some buying occurs before the close, the Hanging Man signal now becomes an alert. This is a signal that would definitely not show up in Western charts. The gap down in price the following day would have been an immediate indication that the sellers were now controlling the trend.

Identifying a Hanging Man signal, along with other candlestick signals at major potential resistance levels, adds more credence to a reversal signal occurring. Illustrated in Fig. 2-41, the Micrel Inc. chart, the Hanging Man signal occurred right on a major moving average. This allows the candlestick investor to immediately evaluate what might be happening at an important technical level that other investors are watching.

Fig. 2-41 *Micrel Inc.*

Understanding what should occur after a Hanging Man signal, with a high probability that a downtrend is in the making, allows an investor to close out a position more quickly and confidently than other investors waiting for better confirmation.

The ultimate Hanging Man is the "Dragonfly Doji", which has an open and close near or at the very top of the trading range. As illustrated in Fig. 2-42, the Brightpoint Inc. chart, a Hanging Man/Doji formation creates a visual alert. Witnessing a much lower open the next day provides confirmation that the uptrend is over.

Fig. 2-42 *Brightpoint Inc.*

The Hanging Man signal, in an overbought condition, requires immediate attention. The lower trading during the day made the Bulls nervous. More selling the following day convinces the Bulls to be out of a trade. Remember, centuries of observations have revealed this to be a major signal.

PIERCING PATTERN
(Kirikomi)

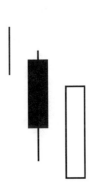

PIERCING

PATTERN

Fig. 2–43

Description

The Piercing Pattern, a bullish signal, is composed of a two-candle formation in a down-trending market. The first candle is black, a continuation of the existing trend. The second candle is formed by opening below the low of the previous day. It closes more than midway up the black candle, near or at the high for the day. The Piercing pattern has almost the same elements as the Bullish Engulfing signal. The differences are that the open, unlike the Bullish Engulfing signal, opens well below the previous day's trading range. The Bullish Engulfing signal only requires the open below the previous day's close. This lower open is now a gap down in an oversold condition. Again, this incorporates the aspect that most sellers "panic sell" at the bottom. The remainder of the day shows buying. That buying continues into the close, closing more than half way into the previous day's black candle. Closing above the halfway point of the previous black candle is the most important factor. A close below the halfway point produces other candlestick evaluations.

As with other candlestick 'buy' signals, the magnitude in which the lower open occurs is important. The lower the Piercing signal opens, the further down the gap down open occurs, the stronger the probabilities of a reversal occurring as well as the implied strength of the new uptrend. Additionally, the higher the close occurs in the previous day's black candle, the better the probabilities of a strong reversal. It is not unusual to see a large volume day occurring in a severe Piercing signal pattern. The increase in volume implies that the weak have sold their shares to the smart money.

Criteria

1. The body of the first candle is black; the body of the second candle is white.
2. The downtrend has been evident for a good period. A long black candle occurs at the end of the trend.
3. The second day opens lower than the trading of the prior day.
4. The white candle closes more than half-way up the black candle.

Signal Enhancements

1. The longer the black candle and the white candle, the more forceful the reversal.
2. The greater the gap-down from the previous day's close, the more pronounced the reversal.
3. The higher the white candle closes into the black candle, the stronger the reversal potential.
4. Large volume during these two trading days is a significant confirmation.

The gap-down in an oversold condition becomes the first indication that a candlestick reversal signal might occur. The open price, occurring below the previous day's low, followed by a close more than halfway up the previous black candle, makes this a viable buy signal. Additional parameters such as the stochastics being in the oversold condition lend more credibility to the signal. Although not as strong a candlestick signal as the Bullish Engulfing signal, the Piercing signal conveys the same information. Once the sellers capitulated at the bottom, the buyers came back into the price trend. As can be seen in Fig. 2-44, the Marathon Oil Corp. chart, the downtrend was reversed with the appearance of the Piercing pattern.

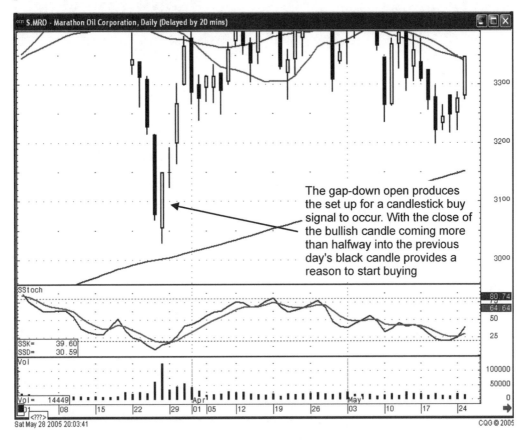

The gap-down open produces the set up for a candlestick buy signal to occur. With the close of the bullish candle coming more than halfway into the previous day's black candle provides a reason to start buying

Fig.2-44 *Marathon Oil Corp.*

A gap-down at the bottom of the trend, followed by obvious buying, reveals that there has been a change of investor sentiment. What confirmation is needed after a Piercing signal? A positive open the following day demonstrating the buying revealed in the signal is still present. This provides evidence that the buyers are still involved.

Fig. 2-45, The Petroleum Development Corp. chart illustrates the characteristics found in a Piercing signal. After observing a lengthy downtrend, prices gap down below the previous day's trading range. The previous day illustrated a somewhat indecisive day, a Spinning Top.

Fig. 2-45 *Petroleum Development Corp.*

The evidence of buyers stepping in after the open reveals that the selling was the last gasp sales of the weak investors. The large bullish candle clearly demonstrates that once the last of the selling occurred, the buyers started coming in with force. The additional buying strength of the following day added further confirmation that the uptrend was now in progress.

Fig. 2-46, The Home Depot chart illustrates a Piercing signal after the apparent exuberant selling at the bottom. The previous day gapped down on hefty volume. The gap down on the day of the formation of the Piercing signal, with stochastics in the oversold condition, would have alerted the candlestick investor to get ready for a candlestick buy signal to form soon.

Watching the buyers move the price well above the halfway point of the gap-down black candle would have informed the candlestick investor that the buyers were now back in the trade. The visibility of this large white candle against the black candle downtrend makes it obvious that something has changed in investor sentiment.

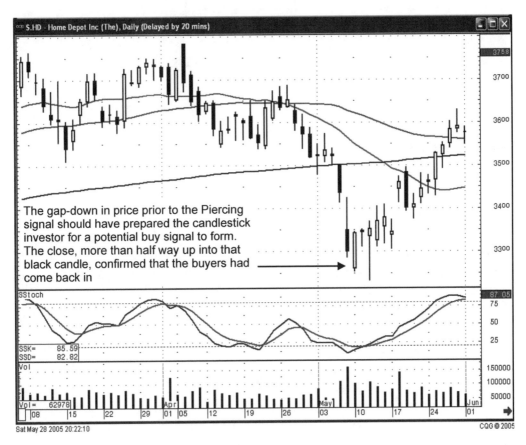

Fig. 2-46 *Home Depot Inc.*

DARK CLOUD COVER
(Kabuse)

DARK CLOUD

COVER

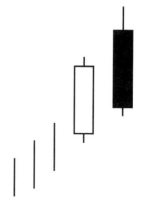

Fig. 2–47

Description

The Dark Cloud Cover is the bearish counterpart to the Piercing pattern. It gets its name from the ominous dark candle that is formed after a nice bright uptrend. The first day of the pattern is a long white candle at the top end of a trend. The second day's open price is higher than the high of the previous day. It closes at least one-half the way down the previous day's candle. The further down the white candle, the more convincing the reversal. 'Kabuse' means to get covered or to hang over.

The Piercing Pattern has almost the same characteristics as a bullish engulfing signal. Likewise, the Dark Cloud signal has almost the same characteristics as the Bearish Engulfing signal. The difference is that a Dark Cloud is formed as it opens higher than not only the previous day's close of the white candle, but it gaps up above any of the previous days trading range.

The gap up becomes the first alert indicating that a candlestick sell signal is in the making. The exuberant buying at the top should be viewed with suspicion. Once the selling has occurred, it continues into the close. As the Piercing Signal requires a close more than halfway up into the previous day's black candle, a Dark Cloud signal requires a close below the halfway point of the last white candle. The same parameters enhance the credibility of a Dark Cloud as seen in the Piercing signal. The higher the gap-up open, the higher the probability a downtrend is in progress and the greater the potential force of the downtrend. The further the close comes below the midway point of the previous day's candle, the stronger the downward trend should be. Once again, like the Piercing Signal parameter, a Dark Cloud signal requires a close below more than the midway point of the previous bullish candle.

Criteria

1. The body of the first candle is white; the body of the second candle is black.
2. The up-trend has been evident for a good period. A long white candle occurs at the top of the trend.
3. The second day opens higher than the trading of the prior day.
4. The black candle closes more than half-way down the white candle.

Signal Enhancements

1. The longer the white candle and the black candle, the more forceful the reversal.
2. The higher the gap up from the previous day's close, the more pronounced the reversal.
3. The lower the black candle closes into the white candle, the stronger the reversal.
4. Increased volume during these two trading days is a significant confirmation

A Dark Cloud signal is not difficult to spot. Keep in mind the very simple rules that established a Dark Cloud signal. A gap up above the previous days trading and closing well into the last bullish candle forms a signal that clearly indicates an up trend is over.

Fig. 2-47, The American Tower Corp. chart has a nice uptrend in progress for a month and a half. It started at a major moving average with a Morning Star signal. The top was clearly illustrated with a dark candle that showed a change of investor sentiment.

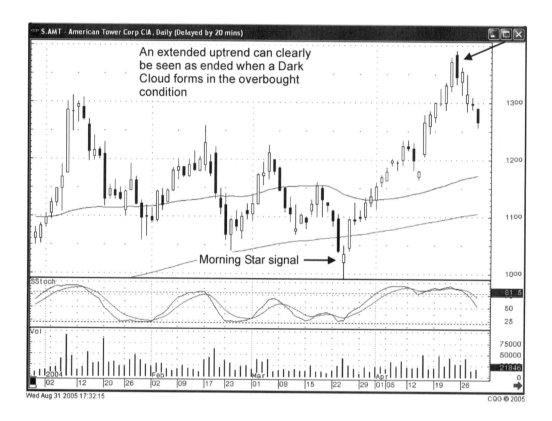

Fig. 2-47 *American Tower Corp.*

Opportunity doesn't travel on any schedule - you just have to watch for it.

Japanese proverb

The trend in Fig. 2-48, the Brightpoint Inc. chart showed signs of weakness in mid June with a bearish candle. However, that bearish candle was not a reversal signal. When the Dark Cloud signal was formed a couple days later, the fact that some weakness had occurred a few days prior made the Dark Cloud signal that much more significant. Although all candle formations are not signals, the interpretation of surrounding candles in overbought or oversold conditions can add credibility to the actual candlestick signal when it is formed.

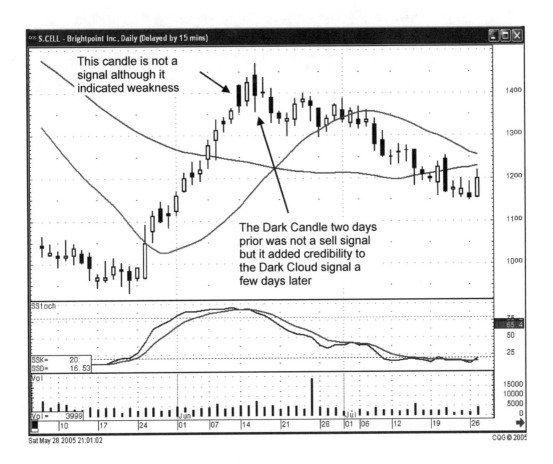

Fig. 2-48 *Brightpoint Inc.*

Notice how the Dark Cloud formed twice in Fig. 2-49, the AirT Inc. chart. The first Dark Cloud signal produced a very good indication that the breakout in price was now over. A few days later the second attempt to take the price of the stock back up was also stifled by the appearance of a second Dark Cloud. Simple visual observation, observing two Dark Cloud signals, in close proximity of each other, should have made it apparent that the sellers had stopped the uptrend.

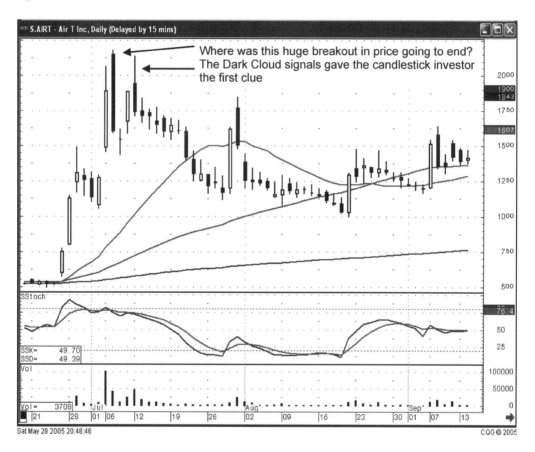

Fig. 2-49 *Air T Inc.*

Use the dark candle signal to prepare to take profits or be ready to establish short positions. The Dark Cloud signal lives up to its name. It does cast a dark cloud over nice up-trends. What other investors are 'hoping' for, a continued upward move in prices, the candlestick investor can visually evaluate. The probabilities an uptrend is over when a Dark Cloud signal forms, takes the emotion out of an investment decision.

HARAMI
(Harami)

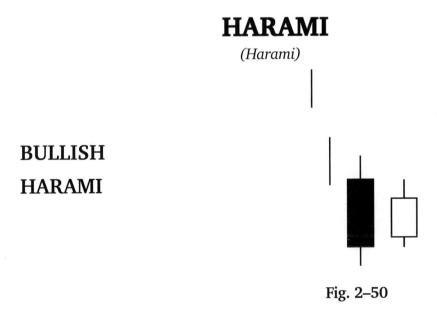

BULLISH

HARAMI

Fig. 2–50

Description

The Japanese definition for Harami is "pregnant woman" or "body within". Western terminology would call the Harami an inside trading day. It is comprised of two candles. The first candle is black, a continuation of the existing trend. The second candle, the little belly sticking out, is usually white, but that is not always the case (See Homing Pigeon, *Profitable Candlestick Trading*, p. 96). The location and size of the second candle will influence the magnitude of the reversal.

The Harami signal conveys some important information. It says that the previous trend is over. The appearance of a Harami signal will convey the same information after an extended downtrend or one or two days of a pullback.

After a strong down trend has been in effect and after a 'long candle' selling day, the bulls open the price higher than the previous close. The short's become concerned and start covering. The price finishes higher for the day.

This is enough support to have the short sellers take notice that the trend has been violated. A bullish day after that would convince everybody that the trend was reversing. Usually the volume is above the recent norm due to the unwinding of short positions. One of the visual benefits provided by the Harami signal is the indication of how strong the potential of the new trend will be. It acts as a barometer. The signal works most effectively after an extended downtrend concluded with the large black candle at the bottom of the trend or a gap down black candle. The appearance of a Harami signal the following day reveals that the selling has stopped. The size of the Harami or where it is formed in the previous days black candle is significant.

Criteria

1. The body of the first candle is black; the body of the second candle is white.
2. The downtrend has been evident for a good period. A long black candle occurs at the end of the trend.
3. The second day opens higher than the close of the previous day and closes lower than the open of the prior day.
4. Unlike the Western "Inside Day", just the body needs to remain in the previous day's body, where as the "Inside Day" requires both the body and the shadows to remain inside the previous day's body.
5. For a reversal signal, further confirmation is required to indicate that the trend is now moving up.

Signal Enhancements

1. The longer the black candle and the white candle, the more forceful the reversal.
2. The higher the white candle closes up on the black candle, the more convincing that a reversal has occurred despite the size of the white candle.

A Harami forming at the very lower end of the last bearish candle of a downtrend provides some insights. Although it illustrates that the selling has stopped, it also illustrates that there is not much buying impetus. The potential uptrend may not be immediate or very strong.

As seen in Fig. 2-51, the EchoStar Communication Corp. chart, the Bullish Harami was very small and stayed near the bottom of the previous black candle's trading range. The subsequent buying took a while to get started, not showing any great immediate strength.

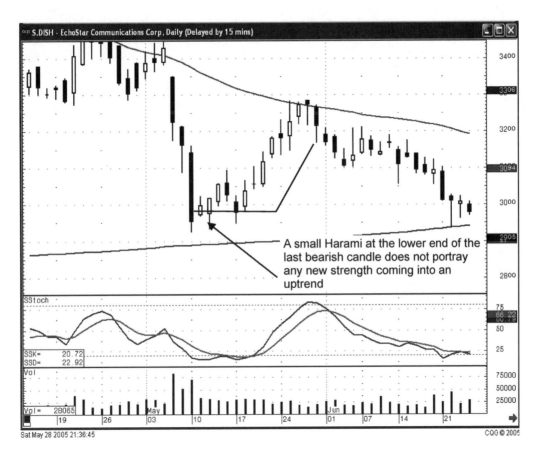

Fig. 2-51 *EchoStar Communication Corp.*

The higher the close of Harami into the previous days black candle, the stronger the trajectory of the new uptrend. The Harami requires bullish confirmation the following day. The Harami signal itself indicates the downtrend has stopped. Continued buying the next day reveals the uptrend is now in progress.

As viewed in Fig.2-51A, the Television Azteca chart, the Harami closing just above the bottom third of the previous black candle, followed by a bullish open the following day, started a decent up trend. The stochastics are an additional confirming parameter.

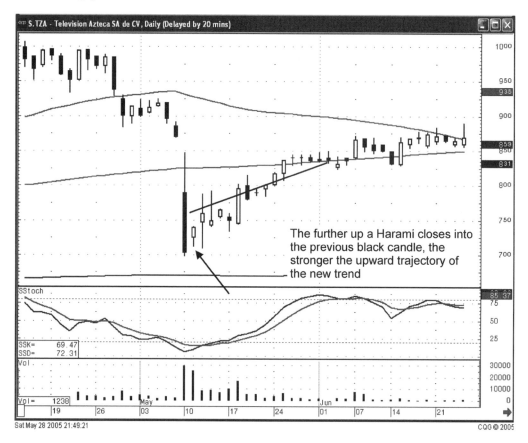

Fig.2-51A *Television Azteca*

The Harami works very well for indicating whether important support levels are going to hold. As seen in Fig. 2-52 (following page), the Standard Pacific Corp. chart, a bullish Harami revealed that the uptrend was going to continue after the pullback. A pullback moving very near to the 50-day moving average. Although the stochastics were not in the oversold condition, it could be deduced that the pullback was over, the price stayed above the moving average, in the process of continuing the uptrend. Remembering that the Harami indicates selling has stopped, it becomes an effective visual indicator when trying to analyze existing trends.

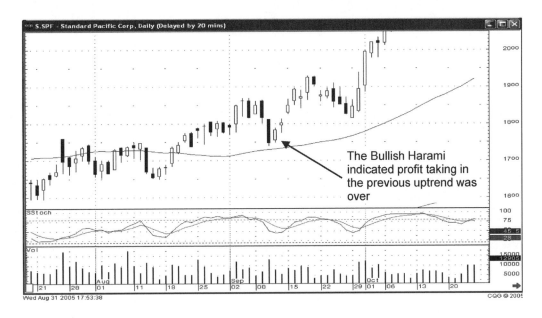

The Bullish Harami indicated profit taking in the previous uptrend was over

Fig. 2-52 *Standard Pacific Corp*

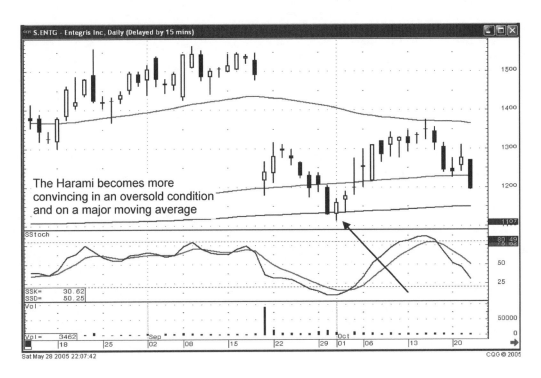

The Harami becomes more convincing in an oversold condition and on a major moving average

Fig. 2-53 *Intergroup Corp*

HARAMI
(Harami)

BEARISH

HARAMI

Fig. 2–54

Description

The Bearish Harami is the exact opposite of the Bullish Harami. The pattern is composed of a two candle formation. The body of the first candle is the same color as the current trend. The first body of the pattern is a long body, the second body is smaller. The open and the close of the second body occurs inside the open and the close of the previous day. The appearance of a Bearish Harami indicates that the uptrend has stopped. The up trend can be extensive or a one- or two-day trend. The Bearish Harami becomes more significant if it occurs at important resistance levels. After a strong up trend has been in effect and after a long white candle day, the appearance of a Harami is more significant. Bears open the price lower than the previous close. The longs get concerned and start profit taking. The price finishes lower for the day. The Bulls are now concerned as the price closes lower. It is becoming evident that the trend has been violated. A weak day after that would convince everybody that the trend was reversing. Volume increases due to the profit taking and the addition of short sales.

Criteria

1. The body of the first candle is white, the body of the second candle is black.
2. The up trend has been apparent. A long white candle occurs at the end of the trend.
3. The second day opens lower than the close of the previous day and closes higher than the open of the prior day.
4. For a reversal signal, confirmation is needed. The next day should show weakness.

Signal Enhancements

1. The longer the white candle and the black candle, the more forceful the reversal.
2. The lower the black candle closes down on the white candle, the more convincing that a reversal has occurred, despite the size of the black candle.

If you break down the aspects of the Bearish Harami, it makes understanding why the signal works much easier. Consider what occurs in the formation of a Bearish Harami. After an uptrend has been in progress, the formation of a Harami is inconsistent with the expectations of the uptrend. The first day of the two-day Harami signal is a bullish candle. The bullish candle coincides with the expectations of the price move in an upward trend. The price opens and continues to move higher. The following day, the price opens lower than the previous day's close. That in itself does not stifle an uptrend.

The factor, not congruent with an up-trending price, is that no further strength is seen in the price move. The lower open may or may not see additional buying during the day. The prices moving lower by the end of the day become the relevant indicator. It becomes obvious that the buying has started waning, especially when stochastics are in an overbought condition. This should be an indication that investor sentiment has taken an obvious turn. Prices opening lower than the previous days close and then continuing to close below the opening price reveals selling pressure.

Fig.2-55, The Cross Country Healthcare chart illustrates a Harami signal. The probabilities become extremely high that the uptrend is over. Will the Harami signal identify the absolute top in all trends? Definitely not! However the signal will suggest that the majority of the move is over.

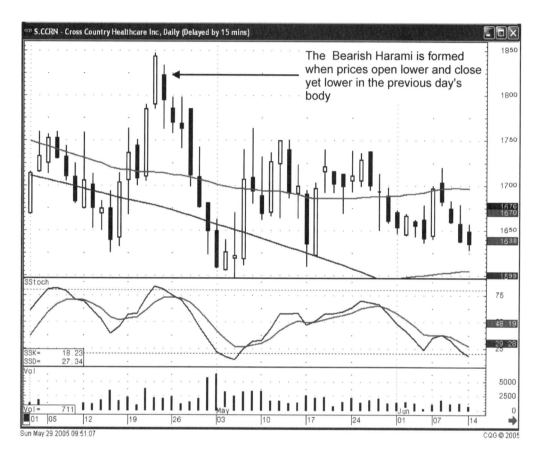

Fig. 2-55 *Cross Country Healthcare Inc.*

A common Bearish Harami signal involves a Doji. An upward price move followed by a Doji/Harami signal is easy to interpret, especially when the trading has moved into the overbought condition. A Doji represents indecision. A Harami indicates the buying has stopped.

What is expected after a Doji/Harami? A high likelihood that the sellers may be coming in, as indicated in Fig. 2-56, the Aspen Corporation chart. A lower open following a Doji/Harami confirms the signal. The probabilities are now extremely high that the uptrend has stopped and a downtrend may be starting. The Bearish Harami followed by additional candlestick 'sell' signals, such as a Shooting Star and/or Doji should be analyzed as a group scenario. The Bearish Harami provides the initial information. The buying has stopped. The following candlestick signals produce additional confirmation to what the Harami is revealing.

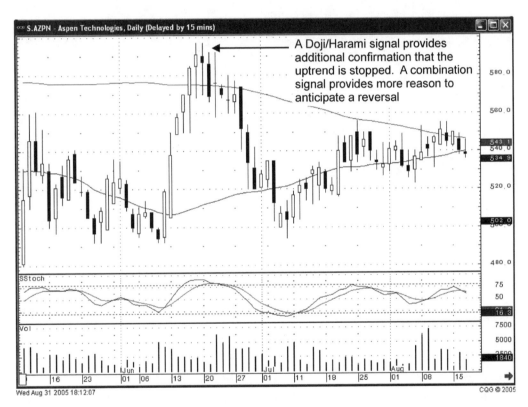

Fig. 2-56 *Aspen Corp.*

Fig. 2-57, The FuelCell Energy Corporation chart provides a clear Harami indicator. The uptrend, now shown to be stopped, is experiencing more indications of indecision at these levels. When the stochastics start turning down, it further confirms the buying forces have disappeared.

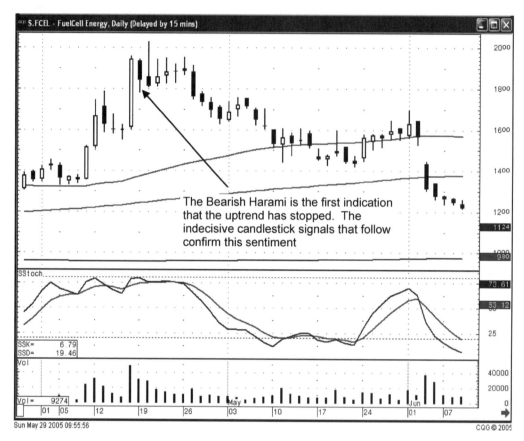

Fig. 2-57 *FuelCell Energy*

If one Bearish Harami signal reveals a potential reversal of a trend, then witnessing two Bearish Harami's in close proximity should be more clear confirmation. The M-Systems Flash Disk Pioneers Ltd. chart reveals simple logic in viewing two Bearish Harami's at the top.

The first signal illustrates that the buying stopped. After pulling back, the Bulls make another attempt to move the price up, followed by another Bearish Harami. This should become obvious that the Bears knock the prices back down when the bulls try to advance.

Bearish signals were occurring right near a major moving average. The stochastics were starting to roll over, making for an easy analysis. The sellers are starting to take control. This is illustrated in Fig. 2-58, the M-Systems Flash Disk Pioneers Ltd. Chart.

Fig. 2-58 *M-Systems Flash Disk Pioneers Ltd.*

As illustrated in Fig. 2-59, the Landrys Seafood Rest. chart, like the Doji acting as a combination signal with the Bearish Harami, the same can be seen with the Hanging Man signal. The analysis should be the same. The Harami indicates that the selling has stopped. The bearish implication the Hanging Man signal conveys, added to the implication a Bearish Harami conveys, produces a strong argument that any further weakness should start a downtrend.

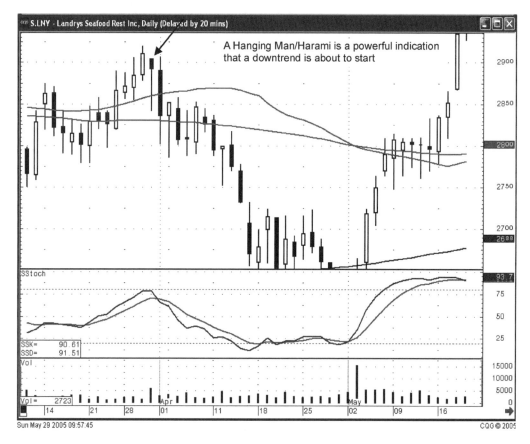

Fig. 2-59 *Landrys Seafood Rest. Inc*

The Bearish Harami has one basic informative fact. The uptrend has ended. Observing the Bearish Harami signal at major technical levels, and appearing when the stochastics indicate an overbought situation, produces a high probability factor. The uptrend has stopped. Now start watching for further selling to confirm that a downtrend is starting.

SHOOTING STAR

SHOOTING STAR
(Nagare Boshi)

Fig. 2–60

Description

The Japanese named this pattern because it looks like a shooting star falling from the sky with the tail trailing it. As with the shooting star, the trend should now be falling to the ground. The Shooting Star is comprised of one candle. It is formed completely opposite the Hammer signal at the bottom. It is easily identified by the presence of a small body with an upper shadow at least two times greater than the body. The Shooting Star is found at the top of an up trend.

The predominant identifying aspect to the Shooting Star signal is the "tail" sticking into the air. The longer the tail, the stronger the evidence that after the Bulls pushed prices up, the Bears knocked it back down. The body of a Shooting Star can be either black or white. The main feature of the signal is that the tail is at least two times greater than the body. After a strong up-trend has been in effect, the atmosphere is Bullish. The price opens and trades higher. The Bulls are in control. But before the end of the day, the Bears step in and take the price back down to the lower end of the trading range, creating a small body for the day. The smaller the body, the more convincing the signal becomes. The fact that the Bears push the price back down to the lower end of the trading range, although forming a white body, still reveals the presence of the sellers. If the sellers pushed the price down through the opening price and closes lower, creating a black body, that is more evidence the sellers have taken control.

The facets built into candlestick signals provide an immense amount of information that would not be found in conventional bar charts. Even though the Bulls may have been able to keep the price positive by the end of the day, the evidence of the selling was apparent. A lower open or a black candle the next day reinforces the fact that selling is going on.

Criteria

1. The upper shadow should be at least two times the length of the body.
2. The real body is at the lower end of the trading range. The color of the body is not important although a black body has implications that are slightly more Bearish.
3. There should be no lower shadow or a very small lower shadow.
4. The following day needs to confirm the Shooting Star signal with a black candle or better yet, a gap down with a lower close.

Signal Enhancements

1. The longer the upper shadow, the higher the potential of a reversal occurring.
2. A gap up from the previous days close sets up for a stronger reversal move, provided the day after the Shooting Star signal opens lower.
3. Large volume on the Shooting Star day increases the chances that a blow-off day has occurred, although it is not a necessity.

The Shooting Star signal indicates failure, the failure of the Bulls to continue the trend. When witnessing an upper shadow that appears to be stretching up to nowhere, start anticipating the change of investor sentiment. The Hammer signal illustrates the failure of the Bears to continue the downtrend. The shooting star signal reveals the same failure of the Bulls at the top. It is not uncommon to see other candlestick sell signals in conjunction with the shooting star signal. Note in Fig. 2-61, the Immtech International chart how a Hanging Man formed prior to the Shooting Star. The stochastics are in the over bought area. The Hanging Man signal indicated the starting weakness of the trend.

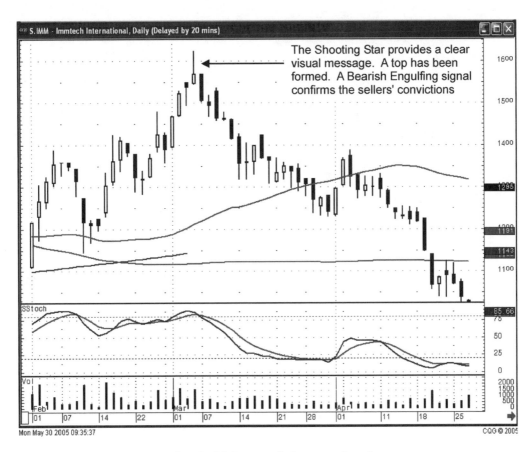

Fig. 2-61 *Immtech International*

The Shooting Star signal illustrates the Bears started taking action. The Bearish Engulfing signal following the Shooting Star confirms that the sellers have entered the trade. Visually the Shooting Star illustrates that the new heights in price were pushed back down. The Shooting Star signal can also indicate the failure of the trend at important resistance levels. A combination of signals creates that much greater evidence that a reversal is occurring.

As illustrated a in Fig. 2-62, the PMC Sierra Inc. chart, the uptrend became indecisive at a major moving average. The scenario of this trend may have been completely different had the Bulls been able to maintain the price up through an important resistance level.

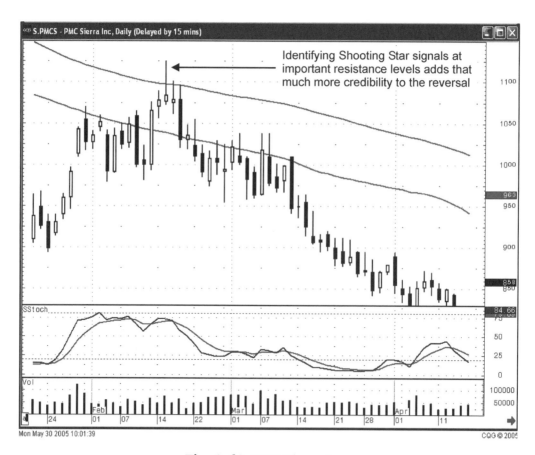

Fig. 2-62 *PMC Sierra Inc.*

INVERTED HAMMER

INVERTED

HAMMER

(Tohba)

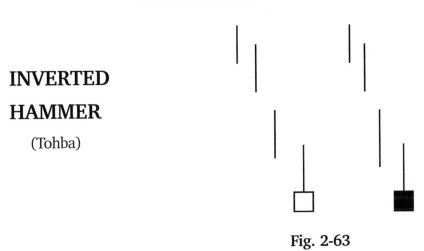

Fig. 2-63

Description

The Inverted Hammer incorporates the reverse interpretation of the Hanging Man signal. Found at the bottom of a downtrend, this shows evidence the Bulls started to step in, but that selling was still going on. After a downtrend has been in effect, the atmosphere is very bearish. The price opens and starts to trade higher. The Bulls have stepped in. But they can't maintain the strength. The existing sellers knock the price back down to the lower end of the trading range. The Bears appear to still be in control. It has the aspects of being a bearish signal.

The mental effect of the Inverted Hammer creates cause for concern for the bears. Although the price closes back down near the low of the day, the buying that day had the Bears worried. The next day, if prices open higher, the Bears are thinking, "darn, the Bulls are still at it." If the Bears see that the Bulls are being persistent, they start getting out of the way. The higher the price moves up before being pushed back down, the more consternation it will have caused for the Bears.

The Inverted Hammer is comprised of one candle. It is easily identified by the presence of a small body with a shadow at least two times greater than the body. The color of the small body is not important but a white candle has slightly more bullish implications than the black body. A bullish candle is required the following day to confirm this signal.

The signal is also a very high probability signal. It does not occur as often as most of the other major signals, but when it does, it will usually produce positive trade results. It also provides an excellent stop loss format. Purchasing a position on a positive open on the following day is the correct entry process. However, if the price would then close below the low point of the Inverted Hammer, a simple deduction can be made. The Bulls were not in control. Close it out immediately.

Criteria

1. The upper shadow should be at least two times the length of the body.
2. The real body is at the lower end of the trading range. The color of the body is not important although a white body should have slightly more bullish implications
3. There should be no lower shadow or a very small lower shadow.
4. The following day needs to confirm the Inverted Hammer signal with a strong Bullish day.

Signal Enhancements

1. The longer the upper shadow, the higher the potential of a reversal occurring.
2. A gap down from the previous day's close sets up for a stronger reversal move provided the day after, the Hammer signal opens lower.
3. Large volume on the Inverted Hammer day increases the chances that a blow off day has occurred.

The most informative factor conveyed in an Inverted Hammer signal is the fact that the buying started. Although the sellers appeared to have maintained control by the end of the day, the Bears had noticed that some buyers had gained confidence in this price area. This may have caused a tinge of doubt to come into the Bear's thinking. The bearish sentiment that may have been stronger in the earlier parts of the downtrend should now create some questions.

A gap up in price clearly indicates that the bullish sentiment is definitely in control. The probabilities become extremely high that an uptrend is in process when the prices gap up following the signal. The definition of a gap up in the case of the Inverted Hammer would be a price opening above the body of the signal. That could mean the price opening up in the upper shadow area or above the high of the Inverted Hammer trading range. Of course, the higher the next days open, the greater the probability that the uptrend will show strength. Fig. 2-64, the Nextel Communications chart reveals a positive open, although a doji day, it still revealed the buyers coming into the price again.

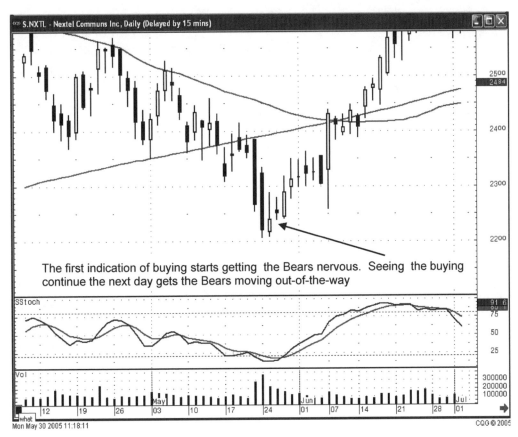

Fig. 2-64 *Nextel Communications Inc.*

The candlestick investor, understanding what this signal is doing to the psychology of the Bears, can now be prepared. If the bearish sentiment is waning, as indicated by an Inverted Hammer signal, then the bearish sentiment should become less pronounced upon seeing more buying. A position entry strategy becomes simple. If the price appears to be opening positive following the Inverted Hammer, the candlestick investor can start buying immediately.

If the eye becomes trained to recognize the signals, then it produces a format for entering trades at the optimal entry areas. The key word in this statement is *areas*. Most investors allow ego to dictate an entry strategy. The sense of pride for entering a trade at the absolute lowest point becomes an overriding factor. What most investors forget is that investing is for the purpose of maximizing profits. The challenge of getting into a trade at the lowest possible entry level diminishes the effectiveness of a good investing program

Fig. 2-65 the Arvinmeritor Inc. chart demonstrates an Inverted Hammer acting as a Harami signal also.

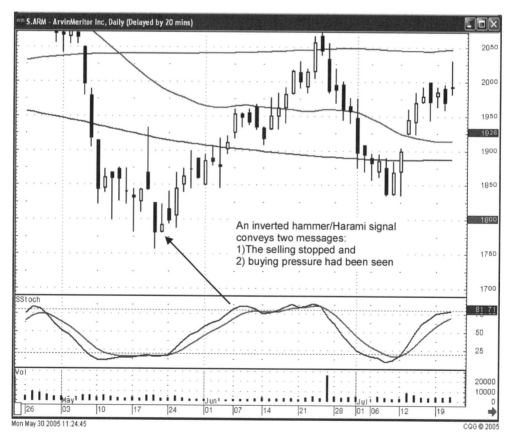

Fig. 2-65 *Arvinmeritor Inc.*

The candlestick signals are a function of a change in investor sentiment. Not a function of anticipating where the absolute bottom will be. The Health Net Inc. chart illustrates what an Inverted Hammer foretells. The appearance of the signal implies that the buyers have stepped in at what could be perceived as the bottom. Will that necessarily mean the uptrend will start immediately? Sometimes it does, sometimes it doesn't. But what it does demonstrate is that buying started, probably putting an end to the downtrend.

The candlestick investor is anticipating strong buying indications. Even though the buying may not appear immediately, the fact that the Inverted Hammer appeared indicates a change in investor sentiment should be experienced soon. Fig. 2-66 the Health Net chat illustrates that the Inverted Hammer signal was the first signs of the buyers stepping in. It took a few days for the remaining selling to be finished.

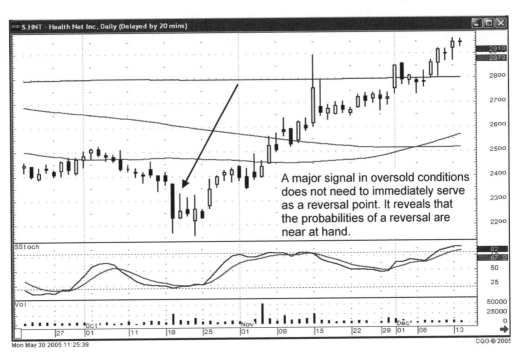

Fig. 2-66 *Health Net Inc.*

The same illustration can be seen in Fig. 2-67, the Broadcom Corp. chart. Although the trading following the Inverted Hammer signal did not reveal dramatic strength immediately, it eventually acted as the bottom. The shadows to the upside indicate buying, which needs to be included into the visual analysis. Something in investor sentiment is changing. That knowledge gives the candlestick investor an advantage. The Japanese Rice traders viewed this signal for centuries. Understanding the psychology that creates a signal aids an investor to understanding what is expected in the trend results.

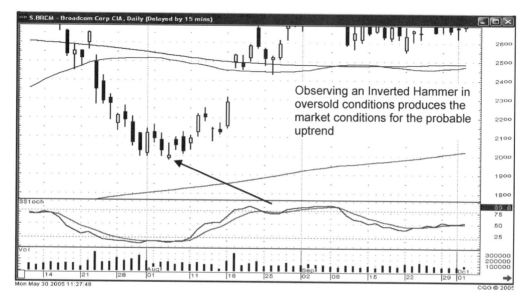

Fig.2-67 *BroadcomCorp.*

MORNING STAR
(Sankawa Ake No Myojyo)

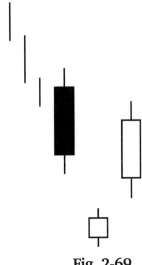

Fig. 2-69

Description

The Morning Star signal is easy to recognize due to its symmetrical elements. It is visually apparent to the eye. The description of the signal in layman's terms makes it easy to understand. It forms after an obvious downtrend. It is made by a long black body, usually fear induced at the bottom of a long decline. The following day gaps down. However, the magnitude of the trading range remains small for the day. This is the star of the formation. The third day is a white candle day representing the fact that the Bulls have now stepped in and seized control. If there is big volume during these days, it shows that the ownership has dramatically changed hands The optimal Morning Star signal would have a gap before and after the star day.

Essentially, the Morning Star signal consists of the sellers wanting to get out at the bottom of a downtrend. The following day, the Bulls and the Bears get into an indecisive trading mode. The third day, the reversal of the previous bearish sentiment becomes obvious. A bullish candle, closing more than half-way up into the previous long black candle, reveals that the Bulls are now dominating.

The Morning Star pattern is named appropriately. Like the planet Mercury, the morning star, the Japanese say it foretells that brighter things, sunrise, is about to occur. Or, prices are going to go higher. The make up of the star, an indecision formation, can consist of a number of candle formations. The important factor is to witness the confirmation of the Bulls taking over the next day. That candle should consist of a closing that is at least halfway up the black candle of two days prior.

Criteria

1. The down-trend has been apparent.
2. The body of the first candle is black, continuing the current trend. The second candle is an indecision formation.
3. The third day shows evidence that the bulls have stepped in. That candle should close at least halfway up the black candle.

Signal Enhancements

1. The longer the black candle and the white candle, the more forceful the reversal.
2. The more indecision that the star day illustrates, the higher the probabilities of a reversal.
3. A gap between the first day and the second day adds to the probability a reversal is occurring.
4. A gap before and after the star day is even more desirable.
5. The magnitude, that the third day comes up into the black candle of the first day, indicates the strength of the reversal.

MORNING STAR DERIVATIVES

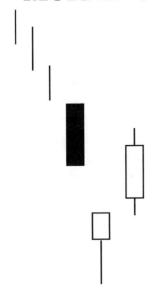

HAMMER

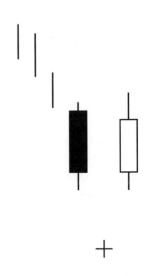

ABANDONED BABY

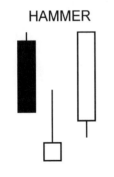

REVERSE HAMMER

DOJI STAR

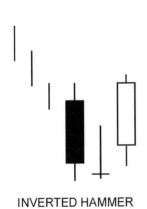

INVERTED HAMMER

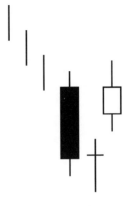

STAR AND GAP

A Morning Star signal makes trend analysis easy. It clearly denotes a change in investor sentiment. Illustrated in the Dow Jones chart are a number of Morning Star signals. Occurring when stochastics, indicating oversold conditions, produces a high probability result. An uptrend is about to occur. As with most candlestick "buy" signals, confirmation is usually required after the signal. What do we want to see after a candlestick buy signal? We want to see that the buyers are still participating. Notice the Morning Star signal that occurred in early August. The analysis of the signal is simplified when understanding what all the parameters are doing. Notice the first Morning Star signal that occurred in early August had stochastics not yet into the oversold condition. As mentioned before, the signal is the most important factor. The stochastics are just a confirming indicator.

The fact that the following day, after the Morning Star signal was formed, did not reveal any follow-through buying will be analyzed different than if there had been another bullish trading day after the signal. The lower trading during the day would have revealed that the Bulls were not participating. This should have immediately suggested that the uptrend was not going to start immediately. The stochastics may have to get to a lower level.

However, the Morning Star signal should have implied that the buyers were coming in at these levels. The bottom should be relatively near. The fact that another Morning Star signal formed over the next three days set the scenario for the same potential. There was a high probability that an uptrend may start. The continued buying the following day confirmed that the bullish sentiment was now in the mix.

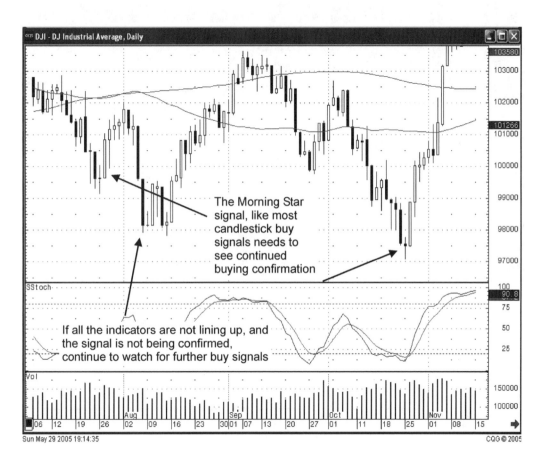

Fig. 2-70 *The Dow*

The Morning Star formation merely requires the evidence of selling at the bottom, followed by an indecisive day, followed by strong buying that closes the trading more than halfway up the previous black candle.

As illustrated in Fig. 2-71, the AirTran Holdings Inc. chart, the third day was not a large body. The fact that it gapped up and then closed well above the black candle's midway point provided the same information. The buyers had come back into this position with force. The fact that the reversal was occurring at a major moving average at the same time that the stochastics were in the oversold condition also provided credibility for this trade.

Fig. 2-71 *AirTran holdings Inc.*

The more confirming indicators that can be added to the analysis, the higher the probabilities that a reversal has occurred and the greater the upside potential becomes. As viewed in fig. 2-72 (following page), the Renaissance RE holdings Ltd. chart, the Morning Star signal has a number of significant indicators. The large black candle, followed by a Bearish Engulfing signal, tells the candlestick investor to start watching for a buy signal. The gap-down of the indecision day is another indicator. Forming indecisive trading, right on a major moving average, is an additional reason to watch this trade. The gap-up and continued buying above the midway point of the large black candle has more credibility. And finally, all this occurring when the stochastics are in the oversold condition makes this a very high probability trade.

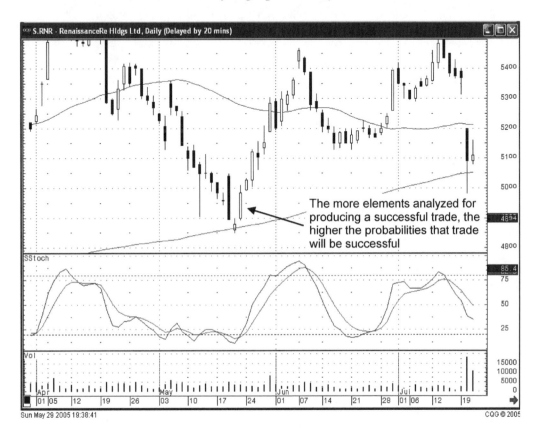

Fig. 2-72 *Renaissance RE Holdings*

Recognizing the Morning Star signal will produce substantial positive results for investors. Visually it incorporates commonsense analysis. Investor sentiment has completely reversed. The implications reveal a Morning Star signal should always be heeded. The selling has exhausted. The Bulls and the Bears are in conflict. The buyers begin to control. Do not make it any more difficult than that.

EVENING STAR

(Sankawa Yoi No Myojyo)

EVENING

STAR

Fig. 2-73

Description

The Evening Star pattern reveals a change of investor sentiment at the top of a trend. It is exactly opposite the Morning Star signal. Like the planet Venus, the Evening Star foretells that darkness is about to set or prices are going to go lower. It is formed after an obvious up trend. It is made by a long white body occurring at the end of an up trend, usually when the confidence has finally built up. The following day shows indecision. Of course, the Doji is the most apparent indecisive day. The same criteria involved for forming the Morning Star can be applied to the Evening Star signal. The indecision day could be a small star trading day, a Shooting Star signal, a Hanging Man signal, or any other candlestick reversal 'sell' signal.

The third day is a black candle day, illustrating the fact that the Bears have now seized control. That candle should close at least halfway down the white candle of two days prior. As experienced in the Morning Star signal, the Bears closing the price, more than halfway down the previous long bullish candle, would indicate they are now in control of the trend. The optimal Evening Star signal would have a gap before and after the star day. The change of direction is seen immediately in the color of the bodies. The symmetry in the reversal is an obvious visual feature. When it occurs in overbought condition, the probabilities of seeing continued selling is very high. The Evening Star signal should have investors closing out long positions and consider establishing short positions.

Criteria

1. The up trend has been apparent.
2. The body of the first candle is white, continuing the current trend. The second candle is an indecision formation.
3. The third day shows evidence that the Bears have stepped in. That candle should close at least halfway down the white candle.

Signal Enhancements

1. The longer the white candle and the black candle, the more forceful the trend reversal.
2. The more indecision that the star day illustrates, the better probabilities a reversal will occur.
3. A gap between the first day or the second day adds to the probability a reversal is occurring.
4. A gap before and after the star day is even more desirable. The magnitude, that the third day comes down into the white candle of the first day, indicates the strength of the reversal.

The Evening Star signal utilizes the normal investment psychology. Where do people usually buy? That can be visually analyzed with the appearance of a large bullish candle in overbought condition. As viewed in Fig. 2-74 (following page), the Biomet Inc. chart, after an extended uptrend a large bullish candle forewarned of the potential of a reversal signal. The Doji at the top becomes a clear indication that a change of investor sentiment could be in the making. The third day, a large black candle closing more than halfway down into the bullish candle confirms the change of investor sentiment. Visually, the reversal is very easy to see.

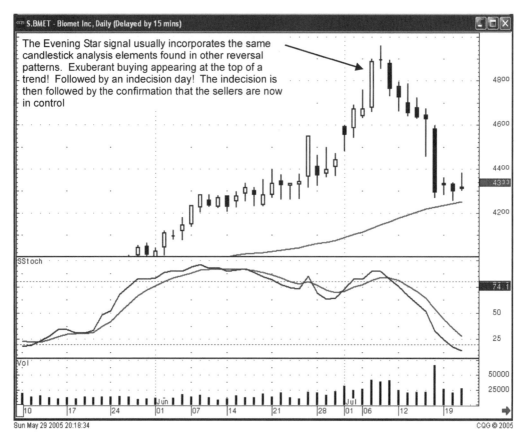

Fig. 2-74 *Biomet Inc.*

The symmetry of the Evening Star signal should be the important element in the analysis. The indecision day, such as the Hanging Man signal or the Shooting Star signal are added benefits. However, the fact that the final day of the signal closes well into the previous white candle's body is the confirmation. Will the downtrend occur immediately? Not necessarily! Nevertheless, important information has already been conveyed. The sellers started taking control.

As illustrated in Fig. 2-75, the Red Hat Inc. chart the Evening Star signal formed and then was followed by two indecisive trading days, two Doji days. The downtrend really got underway after the gap-down on the third Doji day, below the black candle of the Evening Star signal.

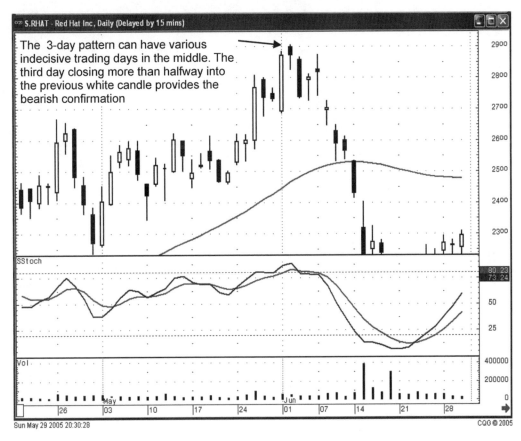

Fig. 2-75 *Red Hat Inc.*

A gap-up Doji after the bullish candle followed by a gap down in price after the Doji indicates more power in the downward reversal. Fig. 2-76, The Protein Design Labs chart reveals the beginning of a strong downtrend coming off an Evening Star signal.

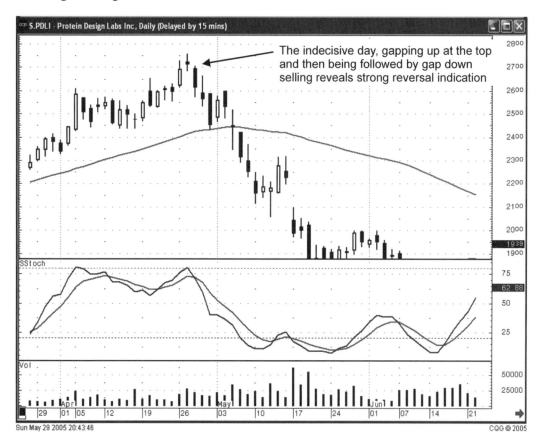

Fig. 2-76 *Protein Design Labs Inc.*

KICKER SIGNAL
(Keri Ashi)

KICKER

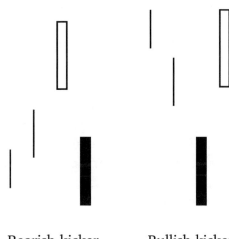

Bearish kicker
Fig. 2-77

Bullish kicker
Fig. 2-78

Description

The Kicker signal is the strongest signal of all the major signals. It demonstrates a dramatic change in investor sentiment. Some occurrence caused a violent change in the direction of price. Usually a surprise news item or a major world/ sector event is the cause of this type of move. The signal illustrates such a dramatic change in the current direction that the new direction will persist with strength for a good while. On a daily chart, that time frame is usually two to three weeks.

While the entry strategy, after most bullish or bearish signals requires confirmed buying or selling, the Kicker signal does not require confirmation. The magnitude of the reversal resulting from a Kicker signal does not preclude some immediate profit taking. Even on a pullback, after a Kicker signal has altered the trend, it is usually safe to buy after a Bull Kicker or to sell into buying strength after a Bear Kicker. The Kicker Signal works equally well in both directions. The occurrence of a Kicker Signal in an overbought or oversold condition magnifies its relevance. It is formed by two candles. The first candle opens and moves in the direction of the current trend. The second candle opens at the same open of the previous day, a gap open, and continues in the opposite direction of the previous day's candle. The bodies of the candles are opposite colors. This formation is indicative of a dramatic change in investor sentiment. The candlesticks visually depict the magnitude of the change.

There is one caveat to this signal. If the next day prices gap back the other way, liquidate the trade immediately. This does not happen very often, but when it does, get out immediately. This usually means the event, which caused the Kicker signal, has been corrected.

A Kicker signal can also be created by a change of recommendation by a major brokerage firm. Although the announcement has created the signal, usually the strength in that scenario may not be as relevant. Be more diligent in watching for selling indicators to occur. The up trend may not possess as much strength as a signal created by announcements or events that would change the fundamental outlook.

Criteria

1. The first day's open and the second day's open are the same or gaps beyond the previous open. . The price movement is in opposite directions from the opening price.
2. The trend has no relevance in a kicker situation.
3. The signal is usually formed by surprise news before or after market hours.
4. The price never retraces into the previous days trading range.

Signal Enhancements

1. The longer the candles, the more dramatic the price reversal.
2. Opening from yesterdays close to yesterday's open already is a gap. Additionally, gapping away from the previous day's open further enhances the reversal.

Witnessing a Kicker signal in an index provides valuable information. Something has happened in an industry/sector that is going to affect a number of stocks participating in that index. Whatever news or event causing the Kicker signal will make bullish signals in individual stocks in that sector that much more effective. As viewed in Fig. 2-79, the Merrill Lynch Internet Holdings index (HHH), a Kicker signal in oversold condition indicated the entire sector had information that will affect a number of stocks.

The true Kicker signal does not have shadows on the body. The gap in price, going in the opposite direction, should open and immediately move away from the previous candle. However, the presence of a shadow should not negate the overall analysis of the signal.

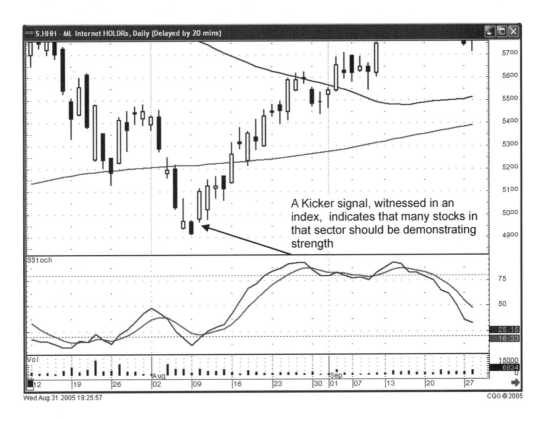

Fig. 2-79 *HHH*

Even when a shadow appears on the new candle, such as in Fig. 2-80, the Alamosa Holdings Inc. chart, the result should still be obvious. The investor sentiment has changed dramatically. The shadow at the bottom of the bullish candle should not deter from the analysis that an uptrend should be starting with force.

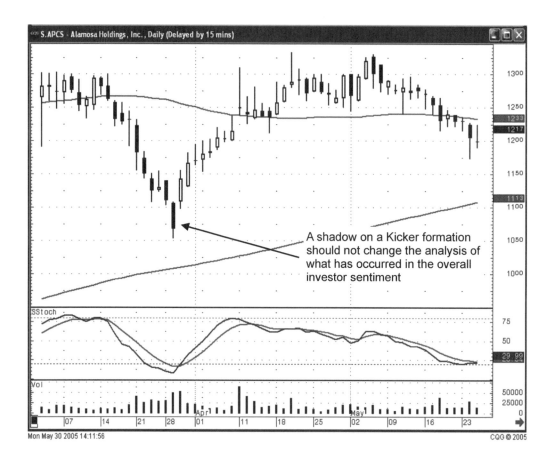

Fig. 2-80 *Alamosa Holding, Inc.*

The signal is considered more effective when the bodies are both long bodies. A long body formation to the downside illustrates strong investor sentiment in the bearish direction. A long body bullish candle now has double connotation. First, the price had to gap up the full length of the black body candle. Secondly, once that gap up occurred, the buying force was shown to have continued with strength.

The affect of a Kicker signal should not be disregarded if one of the two bodies forming a signal is smaller than the other. The result remains the same.

The investor sentiment made the price gap in the other direction and proceeded in that opposite direction.

Technically, a Spinning Top or a Doji with black bodies, followed by a gap-up long bullish body could be considered a Kicker signal. While that pattern is just as effective for identifying a strong reversal it would not necessarily fit into the description of a Kicker signal. The long bodies better define the Kicker signal.

Fig. 2-81, The Alkermes Inc. chart shows the downtrend was progressing with reasonable strength. Whatever news announcement or event that occurred made the new sentiment very bullish.

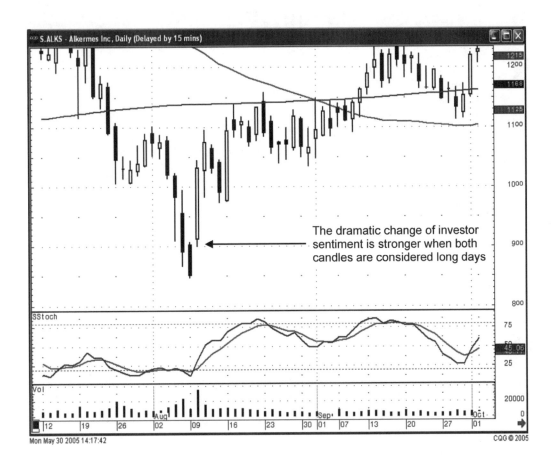

Fig. 2-81 *Alkermes Inc.*

Fig. 2-82, the Zales Corp. chart demonstrates that both candles do not have to be large candles, the kicker signal still reveals a definite change of the trend.

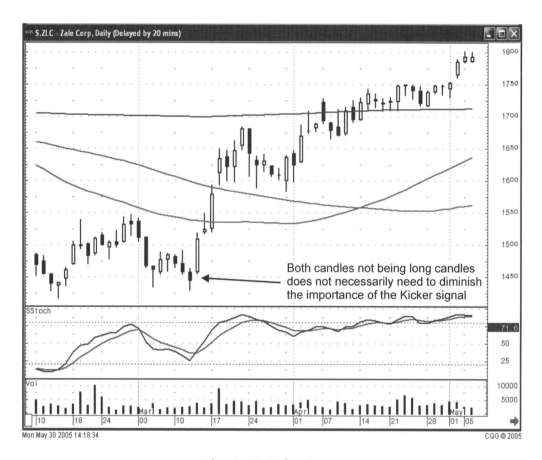

Fig. 2-82 *Zales Corp.*

The magnitude of the gap, above the previous days open, in a bullish candle has great relevance. The gap up in price, followed immediately by added buying, clearly reveals the strength in which buyers wanted to get into a position.

Illustrated in Fig. 2-83, the Macromedia Inc. chart, is a price trend that clearly had no upward bias until the gap up Kicker signal occurred. As mentioned previously, buying at any price during the next few days should be profitable. Some profit taking is likely to occur after a big move to the upside. However, the signal itself illustrates a dramatic change in investor sentiment. That change will not disappear very soon. It can be anticipated that there will be a few weeks to the uptrend.

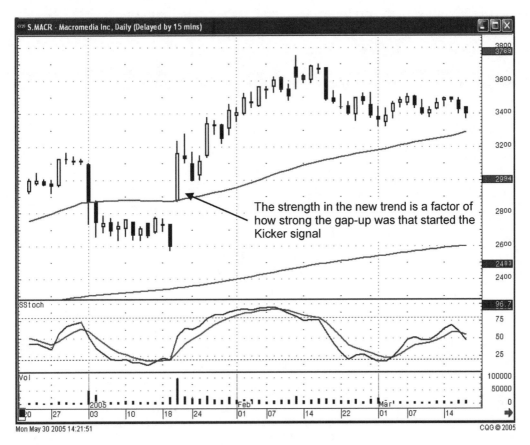

Fig. 2-83 *Macromedia Inc.*

The Kicker signal works equally as well to the downside as it does to the upside. As illustrated in Fig. 2-84, the Motorola Inc. chart, the uptrend was immediately terminated with a gap down in price below the previous days open. The continuation of the selling revealed that the downtrend was going to persist. Understanding the elements forming a Kicker signal allows the candlestick investor to make immediate decisions. An investor that may have been long Motorola Inc., seeing the gap-down open well below the previous days open should have the insight to close the long position immediately. Rarely will a news announcement produce a dramatic gap down open, then see the resuming of the current trend. The results of that dramatic gap-down will usually be a continuation of selling.

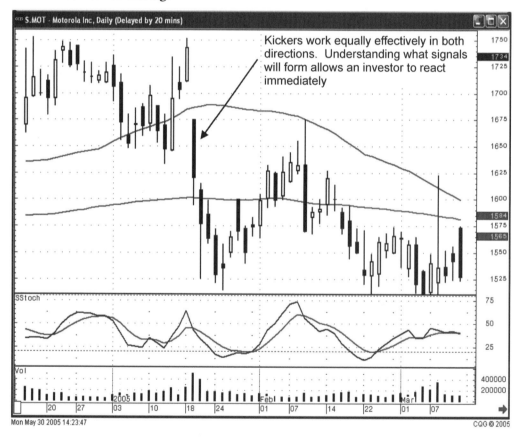

Fig. 2-84 *Motorola Inc.*

Kicker signals produce powerful moves as well as high probability moves. They do not occur very often. When they do occur, they should be analyzed immediately and exploited. They will produce a high percentage of not only correct trades but also very profitable trades.

Concentrate Your Knowledge

Why learn the 12 major signals? Because they incorporate centuries of investment knowledge! Understanding the psychology that forms each signal is an integral part of understanding why prices move. When this knowledge is expanded to the analysis of trend movements, it provides a format for developing profitable investment strategies. How? Because the statistical results of the observations, when viewing a major candlestick signal, is already a high probability outcome. That alone produces the basis for a positive trading program.

Applying candlestick signals to other technical trading factors, that appear to have favorable probabilities, is a vital component for producing confidence. The basic elements of an investment program should produce profitable results. Improving upon the results, utilizing additional technical analysis, becomes much more achievable.

Are the remaining candlestick signals worth while? Definitely, however the frequency in which secondary signals and continuation signals occur does not warrant extensive time spent for learning them. Additionally, the comprehensive investor-psychology revelations are not found in the other signals. Quite often, the other signals are comprised of some derivative of the major signals.

The following chapters will involve the aspects of major signals. High-profit patterns will be better and faster identified utilizing the major signals. The information conveyed in these signals heighten the awareness that a high profit pattern is forming. Stop-loss procedures are better understood when comprehending the information conveyed in a candlestick signal. Use this knowledge to your advantage.

Chapter 3

Moving Averages

Emotions are your worst enemy in the stock market.
Don Hays

Moving averages provide important information regarding the direction of a market. They were created to provide directional information, smoothing out the zigs and zags of a trend. Their use has become much more predominant with the advance of computer software. The automatic calculations for MAs (moving averages) have greatly simplified their applications. They can now be calculated and utilized up to the very second/minute in a trading chart. Their applications, along with candlestick signals, provide a very strong profitable trading format. As with all other technical indicators, MAs have a relevance when correlated to price movement. How the moving averages are utilized can make a big difference between moderate returns and highly profitable returns.

Trading techniques, using moving averages, provide improved entry and exit strategies. The most common use is when the relevant moving averages cross. The feasibility of using MAs "crossing" apparently has some relevance or it would not be widely known as one of their useful aspects. However, the benefits of moving averages become greatly diminished if "crossings" are the only application used. The accuracy of the crossing analysis is moderately successful. However, there are many technical evaluations that are moderately successful. Applying Candlestick analysis in relation to the MAs provides a higher function.

Candlestick signals, along with the moving averages, create a trading program that produces highly profitable trades. Using the important moving averages as support and resistance areas, in conjunction with candlestick analysis, advances the probabilities of participating in a correct trade. Trades are produced with a much greater frequency. The point of investing is to find additional processes for using technical indicators that provide a very high ratio of successful trades. Fortunately, the use of moving averages is very simple. Once applied to candlestick charts, it makes the trend analysis, of probable support or resistance, a very simple, visual process.

The question always arises whether to use the simple moving average (SMA), the exponential moving average (EMA), or the weighted moving average (WMA). The simple moving average is the easiest to calculate; therefore, the reason it was well used before the presence of computers. The exponential moving average has become more popular in recent years due to the quicker calculations computer software provides. It incorporates the latest data in its calculations, allows the older data to fade out, making the current data more pertinent. Weighted moving averages put more importance on current data versus older data. Simple moving averages work very well, providing the information required to successfully trading candlestick signals. Money managers, as well as a majority of technical investors, use the simple moving average.

The moving averages provide a simple visual indicator that shows the direction of a trend's slope. When the moving averages are rising, it indicates an uptrend. When the moving averages are falling, it indicates a downtrend. If the moving averages are trading sideways, it reveals a sideways market.

Traders that use the moving average method for indicating trends follow some very basic rules.

1. **If the SMA is trending up, trade the market on the long side. Buy when prices pullback to, or slightly below, the moving average. After a long position is established, use the recent low as your stop.**
2. **If the SMA is trending down, trade the market to the short side. Short (sell) when prices rally to or slightly above, the SMA. Once a short position is established use the recent high as your stop.**
3. **When the SMA is trading flat or oscillating sideways, it illustrates a sideways market. Most traders, utilizing the moving average to determine trends, will not trade in this market**

Simply stated, traders that use the SMA as a trend go long (buy) when prices are trending above the moving average. They will go short (sell) when prices are trending below the moving average. The candlestick trader has an immense advantage of being able to see what the candlestick signals are telling them at these important moving average levels.

There are numerous timeframes that appear to have relevance when using the moving averages. The 3, 5, 10, 15, 20, 30, 50, 80, 100, 200, 400, 500, 1000 moving averages are all used. Through extensive studies, by David Elliott of www.WallStreetteachers.com, it has been revealed that the 50-day moving average and the 200-day moving average are the most important moving averages. There seems to be a great tendency for prices to support or resist at those averages. Therefore, the 50-day and 200-day moving averages are considered <u>major</u> moving averages. The 20-day and the 80-day moving average are also important but should be considered <u>secondary</u> moving averages. Are there other moving averages that work effectively? Probably, but the major and secondary MAs discussed here seem to have a statistical relevance.

Technical indicators provide important information. An indicator gains importance because of the reoccurring significance of major investment considerations happening at those points. This explanation is put forth so that each investor can become convinced, in their own minds, that moving averages, especially the ones being recommended in this chapter, have some relevance. The major moving averages act like magnets. They attract the price from one moving average to the next moving average.

Give me six hours to chop down a tree and I will spend the first four sharpening the axe.

Abraham Lincoln

Through the following chart evaluations and one's own chart studying, the relevance of these moving averages should become apparent. This does not limit an investor from constantly being aware that other moving averages may start gaining importance in the eyes of other technical investors. The point of using these moving averages, along with candlestick signals, is that historically many investors are watching to see what price movements do at these levels. The advantage of the candlestick signals is that the signals tell you **exactly** what investors are doing at those levels.

Moving Averages as Support

When witnessing a downtrend, how do we tell when a bottom is getting near? As described in other chapters of this book, it could be witnessing the panic selling coming into a price trend, as the stochastics are getting toward the oversold area. That is a helpful alert but does not give us a roadmap to where panic selling might end. Utilizing the 50-day moving average and the 200-day moving average as important support/resistance areas, a target can be established. Being able to evaluate the potential target makes analysis preparation easier. It prepares the investor to anticipate candlestick formations. For example, if a sustained downtrend is now showing large dark candles and is approaching one of the major moving averages, it is evidently indicating the panic bottom may be near. Panic selling with stochastics approaching the oversold area, at or near a major moving average, has a probability of a candlestick reversal signal. This pattern alerts the trader to prepare for a candlestick "buy" signal.

Do all charts work well with moving averages? Definitely not! However, a large majority appear to. The purpose of candlestick analysis is to provide an advantage for the investor to see what is happening at important technical levels. The candlestick signals provide that clarity. If a chart is not providing clear patterns for indicating price movement, then move onto another chart. There are many from which to choose, especially with the availability of easy-to-use computer scanning programs.

Combining technical methods with candlestick signals puts the probabilities in favor of the investor. How do you discover whether the major moving averages are a positive correlation when anticipating price moves? Easy! Investigate what has happened at those moving averages previously in the price trend. This can be done very quickly. Expand the chart. Take a quick visual analysis of what happened in the past.

Fig. 3-1, The United Defense Industries Inc. chart illustrates an example of using past trading patterns to anticipate what might happen. As seen in the chart illustration, the 50-day moving average seems to have importance during May and June.

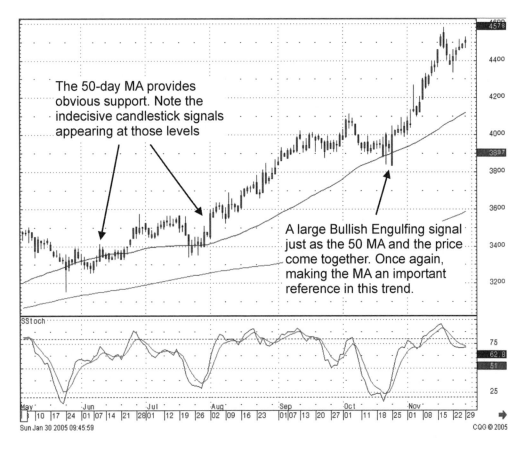

The 50-day MA provides
obvious support. Note the
indecisive candlestick signals
appearing at those levels

A large Bullish Engulfing signal
just as the 50 MA and the price
come together. Once again,
making the MA an important
reference in this trend.

Fig. 3-1 *United Defense Industries Inc.*

In addition, the pullback in late July stopped right on the 50-day moving average with a Meeting Line signal (a secondary candlestick signal), a couple of Doji, then a Bullish Engulfing Signal that came up off the 50-day moving average. That started the next strong run up. As it consolidated through September and October, the 50-day moving average came up to meet the price. Stochastics are back in the oversold area when a very strong bullish engulfing signal forms again right on the 50-day moving average.

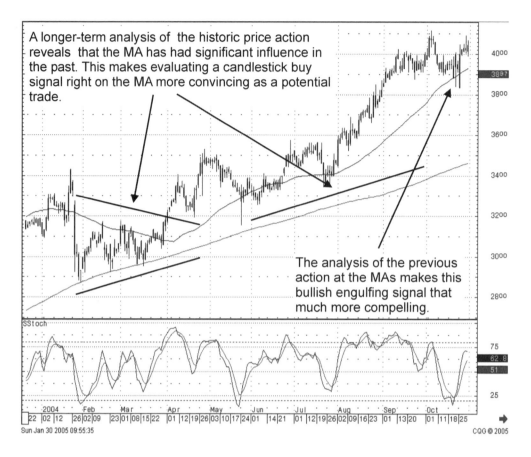

Fig. 3-2 *United Defense Industries Inc. LT*

To further analyze whether the moving averages are important in this stock price move, the charts can be taken back further. It can be clearly seen that back in February and March, the 50-day moving average acted as resistance while the 200-day moving average acted as support. Once the price broke out of the pennant formation from that timeframe, it moved out away from the 50-day moving average before coming back and finding support on it. Bottom line, even without all the verbal description of what happened, it only takes an instant to visually analyze that the price of this stock is greatly influenced by the major moving averages.

The decision to buy, upon seeing the Bullish Engulfing pattern, is that much easier when the signal occurs at the 50-day moving average. This analysis is putting as many factors as possible into making a trade decision. A Bullish Engulfing Signal occurring when the stochastics are in the oversold area, starting to curl up, and doing so right on the 50-day moving average, make a compelling reason to be buying on strength.

When a Resistance Level is Breached, It Becomes a Support Level

In technical analysis, there are some simple basic rules. One is that when a resistance level has been breached during an uptrend; it will now act as support upon any pullbacks. Armed with that little tidbit of knowledge, analyzing price movements becomes a little clearer. Fig. 3-3, The NetGear, Inc. chart illustrates the support concept as well as a few other simple rules when using moving averages.

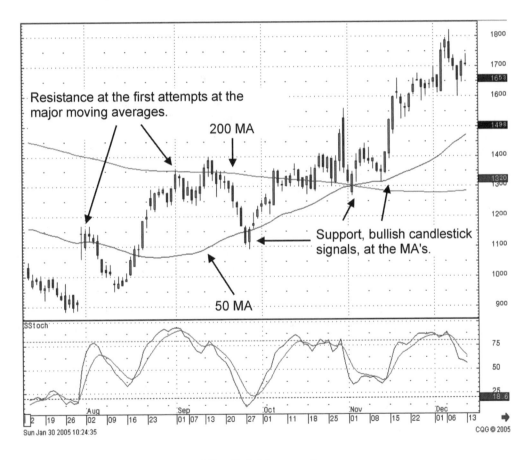

Fig. 3-3 *Netgear Inc.*

Another rule can be applied a majority of the time. When a price tests an important technical level the first time, it will usually fail. However, if it comes back up to test that level again, it will often go through. Notice in the NetGear Inc. chart the last day of July showed a gap up. It formed a Doji just above the 50-day moving average. The uptrend had a hard time continuing the first time it tested the 50-day moving average. As can be seen with the pullback into mid-August. It was then followed by a second test of the 50-day moving average. The advantage of the candlestick signals is that they reveal what the investor sentiment is doing right at those important levels. The second test of the 50-day moving average occurred when the strong bullish candle went through. That revealed the moving average was not going to be a resistance point. If the 50-day moving average is no longer a resistance point, what becomes the next target? The 200-day moving average!

Notice how the 200-day moving average was first tested on September 1. The failure at that level was indicated by a Doji/Harami showing the buying had stopped. This occurring, with the stochastics in the overbought area starting to turn back down, becomes a clear indication the sentiment failed to take prices up through the 200-day moving average. That would be an excellent time to take profits. The next push went through but failed just above the 200-day moving average with the appearance of a Bearish Engulfing signal.

When a moving average fails, what is the next target? The other major moving average! The 50-day moving average now becomes a likely target. This either provides a good short situation or allows an investor to take profits and wait to see what signals will form once the 50-day moving average is touched. As illustrated in this case, when prices got back to the 50-day moving average, a Bullish Harami formed as the stochastics reach the oversold area and started to curl back up. Now what becomes the next target? The 200-day moving average again.

The congestion area from that point remains fairly close to the 200-day moving average. The Piercing Pattern occurring when the 50-day MA crossed the 200-day MA produces important information. As can be seen, that signal, occurring at the intersection of the two major moving averages, was a significant factor in the next strong move upwards. After the initial buying, note how the pullback, with the Doji signal just touching the 50-day moving average, was followed by a Bullish Engulfing pattern that started the strong buying. The analysis of this chart provides a format for when to be looking for significant candlestick signals.

Fig. 3-3a, Cabot Microelectronics Corp. also reveals a failure of the 50-day moving average on July 1, only to come back up through the 50-day moving average with force in the latter part of July. After the initial run up, coming up through the 50-day moving average it pulled back. Notice how it supported exactly on the moving average line before the Bullish Engulfing signal revealed that buying was not going to take the price any lower.

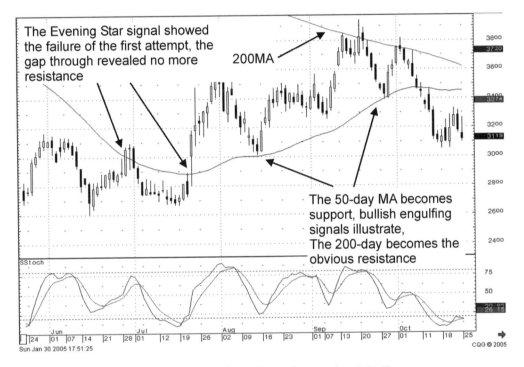

The Evening Star signal showed the failure of the first attempt, the gap through revealed no more resistance

200MA

The 50-day MA becomes support, bullish engulfing signals illustrate, The 200-day becomes the obvious resistance

Fig 3-3a *Cabot Microelectronics CCMP*

Where did the first major resistance come into play? At the 200-day moving average in mid-September! When it fails the 200-day moving average, where is the potential pullback target? The 50-day moving average! The Bullish Engulfing signal at that level indicates the next target is the 200-day moving average again. Once there, the evening star signal reveals another failure of the 200-day moving average.

Notice there is a definite candlestick signal right at the major averages. Once again, it does not take too long to realize that the moving averages are important targets. It was also easy to evaluate what was happening at those targets with the identification of candlestick signals.

Fig. 3-4, the Alamosa Holding Inc. chart also reveals the importance of a major moving average acting as a substantial indicator affecting prices. September revealed two time-periods of great indecision. The series of Doji and Hammer formations were signals that investor sentiment was not able to push the price away from the moving average.

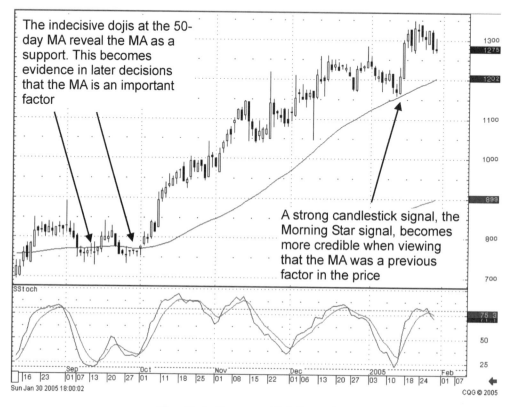

Fig. 3-4 *Alamosa Holdings APCS*

The gap up at the 50-day moving average becomes a signal that strong buying is coming into the trend, as discussed in the chapter on GAPS. As seen in the early part of January, the moving average once again acts as a support level, as indicated by the Doji followed by the Bullish Engulfing signal. Price moves occurring at these major moving averages is not happenstance. Many technical traders watch for these indicators. They are waiting to see what happens at these levels. The advantage provided to the candlestick investor is being able to visually witness what is happening at these levels **immediately**. Other technical investors may require a few trading days of confirmation before they commit funds.

Prices Migrate to the Moving Averages

We cannot hold a torch to light another's path without brightening our own.

Ben Sweetland

An observation made when doing candlestick analysis is that prices tend to stay near a major moving average. If prices move too far away too fast, they have a tendency to come back toward the moving average. It is advisable to start looking for candlestick signals near the moving averages, in conjunction with stochastics. It also becomes obvious to start watching for candlestick signals as the distance of the price becomes extended in moving away from a moving average. The stochastics are also confirming!

As can be seen in Fig. 3-5, the TRM Corp. chart, the signals are the important factor. The moving average is an important secondary target consideration. The Doji at the bottom in late August, followed by bullish candles, indicated where the potential resistance areas were going to be. The bullish candle, moving up through the 200-day moving average, all the way to the 50-day moving average, produces the first resistance level. Selling anywhere in that area produced a reasonably good profit. What will the trend do from there? As seen, just after mid-September, prices came back and just touched the 200-day moving average. The evaluation becomes easy at that point. Continued selling, bringing prices down through the 200-day moving average, would have been a good indication to start shorting the stock. This would have been the time to be observing what was going to happen at these important levels.

The buy signal should have targeted the potential profit taking area at the MAs. It should have also provided an alert for getting in the Kicker signal immediately

Fig.3-5 *TRM Corp.*

The "probabilities" indicate a downtrend was likely to start if the 200 MA was breached to the downside.. Being alert, to watch for something major to happen at the moving average, creates an advantage. A watchful candlestick analyst can take advantage of a powerful signal as it is forming. Upon seeing the gap up from the moving averages and the potential of a kicker signal forming, and knowing that this is the scenario for dramatic moves, the candlestick investor has a map for getting into this trade set up immediately. Would the big price move of the Kicker signal been anticipated? Definitely not! However, having the knowledge that moving averages have a significant influence on price trend is valuable. Seeing a Kicker signal forming produces the opportunity to be in a big move as it happens.

As noted, the indecisive signals over the next few days, the Doji, Hanging Man and Shooting Star formations indicated that the buying pressure had disappeared. The next major opportunity for a good price move occurred on an Inverted Hammer signal occurring right at the 50-day moving average at the end of November. This move would have been exploited by having the knowledge that a candlestick signal, occurring at the 50-day moving average, should have more substantial potential than when occurring without a major average involved. This is not rocket science. This is the accumulation of observations, having positive results an inordinate percentage of the time in the past. Major moves seem to coincide with candlestick signals at the major moving averages. Use this knowledge to your advantage.

> *The aim of education should be to teach us rather how to think, than what to think - rather to improve our minds, so as to enable us to think for ourselves, than to load the memory with thoughts of other men.*
> *Bill Beattie*

Whether a trend gets to the next moving average or not, it at least provides a target. It can be seen in Fig. 3-6 the Brightpoint Inc. chart, if price breaks through an important level, such as we see in late July, and starts pulling back, at least it can be anticipated the moving average might act as a support level. The pullbacks of early August and early September clearly reveal the 50-day moving average acted as an important support level. The Bullish Engulfing pattern in early September, followed by strong buying now makes the 200-day moving average the new potential target.

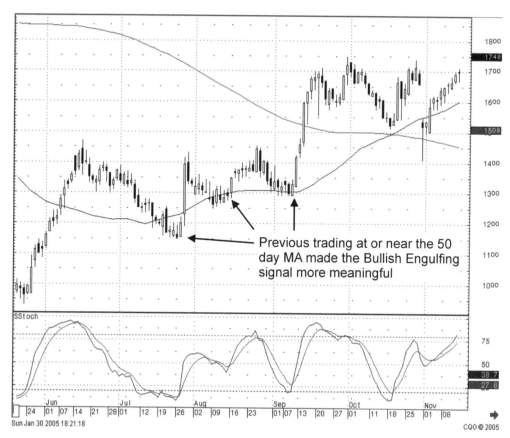

Previous trading at or near the 50 day MA made the Bullish Engulfing signal more meaningful

Fig. 3-6 *Brightpoint Inc. CELL*

That target is demonstrating *not* to be a resistance level as the large bullish candle pushed right through it in mid-September. The crossing of the two averages in mid-October once again acted as a significant reversal indicator. The quick drop in late October in between the two major averages immediately revealed candlestick "buy" signals starting the next leg up. Most investors do not know what to do with this chart pattern. Candlestick investors have the knowledge to take advantage of this pattern. The gap down in late October, the strong hammer signal followed by a small hammer signal, followed by a bullish engulfing pattern in the proximity of the moving averages are all strong candlestick signals of an ensuing reversal.

When an investor can recognize that a price trend of a stock, or any trading entity, is very closely related to the moving averages, implementing high-profit strategies becomes easy. It also decreases the elements of human emotions involved in the investment decisions. Note in Fig. 3-7, Borland Software Corp.'s chart, the moving averages act as a definite influence on the price trend.

Fig.3-7 *Borland Software Corp.*

Notice that the 50-day moving average acted as a resistance level on the prices first attempt, around the 1st of August. The second attempt in mid-August succeeded as the stochastics were in the oversold area, starting to come up. The success of the second attempt now makes the 200-day moving average the next target. The Evening Star signal was a clear indication that the sellers had stepped in during the mid-September attempt at the 200-day moving average. Once it failed, where was the next target? The 50-day moving average! Notice that the Piercing pattern, at the end of September, occurred by opening right on the 50-day moving average. The additional confirmation is stochastics being in the oversold condition. This started the second attempt at the 200-day moving average. The bullish candle, that breached the 200-day moving average, clearly indicated that level was not going to be a resistance area anymore. This now puts a completely new dynamic into the potential uptrend. The candlestick analyst realizes there may be a new dynamic to the uptrend. That allows the investor to start making investment decisions based upon that knowledge.

Simple Rules for Moving Average Analysis

1. A moving average that acted as resistance but now has been breached has a strong tendency to act as support on pullbacks as the uptrend proceeds.

2. The first attempt at a moving average will usually fail; the next approach will often succeed.

3. If the SMA is trending up, trade the market on the long side. Buy when the prices pull back to or slightly below the moving average. After a long position has been established, use the recent low as your stop.

Moving Averages as Resistance

The same characteristics that are found in an up-trending stock are also found in stocks that are in a downtrend. For example, a price that breaks down through a major moving average could eventually bounce back up to test that moving average. If it fails, then the trend will be taken lower. The continued downtrend will usually breach the recent low. If the other major moving average is below the failed moving average, it now becomes the potential target. Understanding these basic movements in prices, it does not take more than a few seconds to analyze whether a price will be affected by the moving averages.

A downtrend in price can be easily monitored when a major moving average is recognized as being a resistance level. Adding another analytical element, when analyzing a trend, increases the probabilities of being in a high probability trade. Logic dictates that if a price does not seem to be able to push through an observed resistance level, the more often that occurs, the higher the probability that it will continue its downtrend. As can be observed in Fig. 3-8 (opposite), the KLIC chart, from the peak in price in January, of 2004, every time the price climbed up towards the 50-day moving average, sell signals would appear.

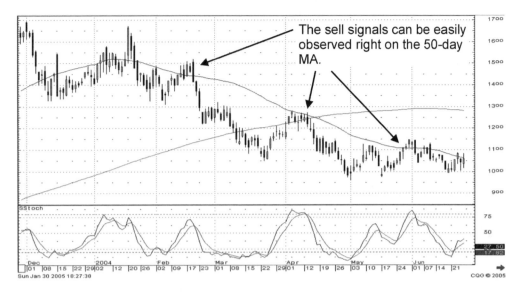

The sell signals can be easily observed right on the 50-day MA.

Fig. 3-8 *Kulick & Soffa KLIC*

This observation should not have taken too much analysis. If the stock was bought when candlestick signals and stochastics dictated, there should be the preconceived awareness that the uptrend has a high probability of running into resistance near the 50-day moving average. Being prepared for that occurrence makes viewing the candlestick sell signals, at those levels, that much more credible.

Knowing moving averages are important technical levels for many investors, it becomes important to understand what is happening at those levels. The candlestick signals provide that information. If a moving average acts as support, there should be the anticipation of a candlestick buy signal formation. Conversely, if the candlestick formations do not reveal any buying strength at those levels, it becomes apparent that the important support level was not having an effect on the downtrend. This is just simple logic. Nothing more than analyzing what is happening at supposedly important technical levels.

Illustrated in Fig. 3-9, the MPS Group Inc. chart in late May, spinning tops formed on the 200-day moving average, confirmed with a bullish candle and stochastics.

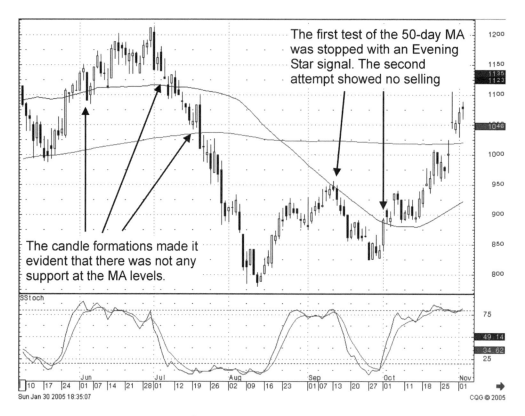

The first test of the 50-day MA was stopped with an Evening Star signal. The second attempt showed no selling

The candle formations made it evident that there was not any support at the MA levels.

Fig. 3-9 *MPS Group Inc.*

The uptrend did not stop at the 50-day moving average. A large bullish candle at the 50-day moving average indicated this to be a support level until prices topped out on the first of July. What was the first logical support area? Of course the 50-day moving average.

However, as can be seen, there were no confirmed buy signals at the 50-day moving average in early July. That should have given the indication the next support level would be the 200-day moving average. The large dark candle that came down through the 200-day moving average, in mid-July revealed that the 200-day moving average was not going to act as a support level either.

The failure of the 200-day moving average did not show any confirmed buy signals until the bullish Harami down in the $8.00 range. If the investor had been short during this downtrend or an investor was waiting to go long at important support levels, it became obvious that those support levels were not going to act as support. Simply stated, if a technical level has the potential of acting as support, it is logical a candlestick buy signal will confirm that. The lack of a candlestick buy signal will demonstrate that it is not.

Moving Averages Become Target Levels

The downtrend in MPS was finally ended with the confirmation of the Bullish Harami in early August. What becomes a logical upside target? Obviously, the 50-day moving average! As can be seen at that level, the Evening Star signal illustrated that the sellers had stopped the uptrend right on the 50-day moving average in the early part of September. The first attempt failed. The second attempt was confirmed with a strong bullish candle on the 1st of October. What is the next target? The 200-day moving average!

The more often a price fails at a particular moving average, the more confident the candlestick investor should be for finding the "sell" signals at that level. As illustrated in the Kemet Corp. chart, it had become obvious during March and April that every time this price approached the 50-day moving average, candlestick sell signals would start to appear. Take advantage of the obvious, especially when the candlestick sell signals confirm.

Fig. 3-10, The Kemet Corp. chart reveals what price reaction occur as it nears the 50-day moving average. Observing the historical tendency of a buy price move adds additional information to the chart analysis.

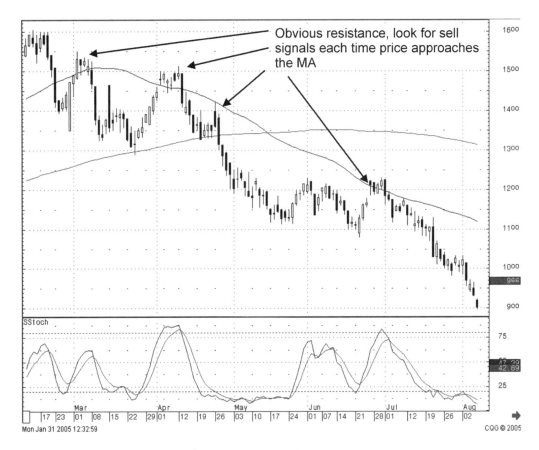

Fig. 3-10 *Kemet Corp KEM*

Observe the obvious! Simple observations are easily made when using candlestick charts. Prices move in patterns. Resistance at a declining moving average is an important pattern to add when making your investment decisions. If you are able to clearly observe what happens at those levels, assume everybody else can also. The advantage for the candlestick investor is the candlestick "sell" signals provide immediate confirmation for what is happening in the trend as it is occurring. This allows early entry and exit strategies into the trading decisions.

When the same indicators are appearing as they have been a few times before, it becomes logical that the results have a likely probability of resembling the past results. Visual analysis can be done in a matter of seconds. Once you have trained your eye to recognize what a trend has been doing at specific points, making an analysis of what should be the next future move becomes that much easier.

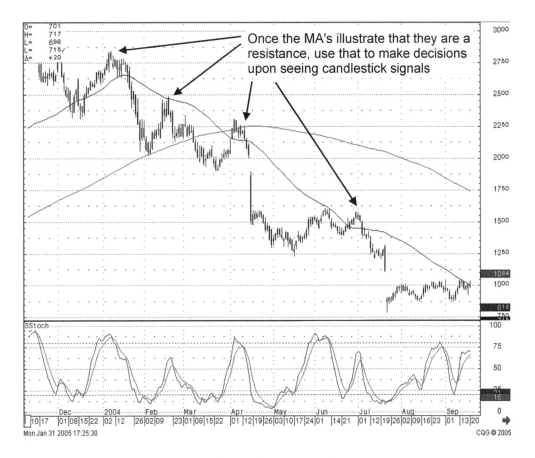

Fig. 3-10A *Advanced Energy Industries AEIS*

Keep in mind, the candlestick signals are the foremost consideration. Adding stochastics and moving averages to the analysis enhances the probabilities of being in a high probability trade.

Fig. 3-11, The Deluxe Corp. chart provides a very simple scenario. Selling, coming in after a Spinning Top, right near the 50-day moving average. This would imply that that moving average was the resistance area once again. On the other hand, witnessing additional strength would imply that the downtrend had finally been broken and the 200-day moving average could possibly be the next target.

Fig.3-11 *Deluxe Corp. DLX*

Blue Ice Failure

Prices move in patterns. Recognizing simple patterns, where moving averages act as pivotal points, is an easy mental process. The three-wave pattern: first wave breaches a moving average to the downside. The second-wave bounces back to the moving average. The third-wave fails and moves down below the previous low. This three-wave pattern has been aptly named, by David Elliott of WallStreetteachers.com as the "Blue Ice Failure." His description is that of somebody falling through the ice, bobbing back up to find the hole they fell through, cannot locate it, (thus failing the moving average), and then sinking to lower depths.

Fig. 3-12, The Cree Inc. chart illustrates a three-wave pattern, the Blue Ice Failure. The decline from the January peak down to the mid-March low came through the 50-day moving average. A bounce or the uptrend failed the first time it approached the 50-day moving average. Upon that failure, it should be anticipated that it will head for a new low.

The first target is below the mid-March bottom. The next target is probably a test of the 200-day moving average. Notice how the engulfing signal confirmed the failure of the wave-two uptrend at the 1st of April. The Morning Star signal, with the stochastics in the oversold area in the proximity of the 200-day moving average, ended down trend. Does this pattern materialize often? Often enough that it should be registered in the minds of investors to anticipate the Blue Ice Failure possibility.

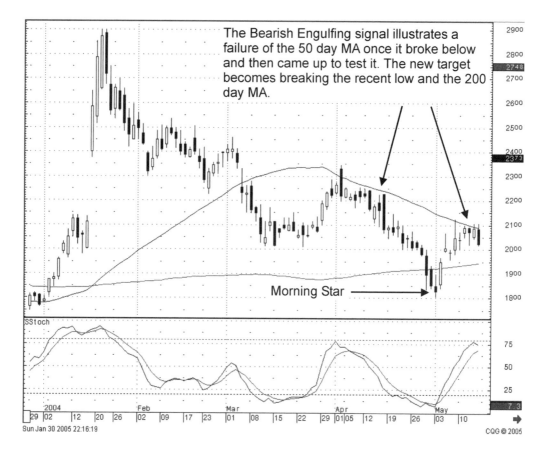

The Bearish Engulfing signal illustrates a failure of the 50 day MA once it broke below and then came up to test it. The new target becomes breaking the recent low and the 200 day MA.

Morning Star

Fig. 3-12 *CREE Inc.*

The same pattern is illustrated at the beginning of 2004 in Fig. 3-13 (opposite), the Micrel Inc. chart. The downtrend beginning in January broke through the 50-day moving average on the 1st of February. The candle formation definitely revealed no "buying" presence at that level.

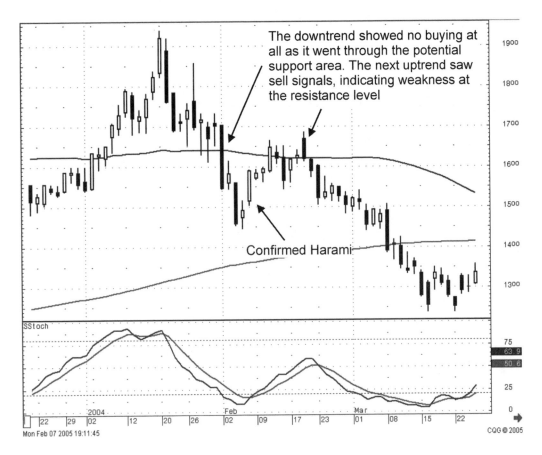

The downtrend showed no buying at all as it went through the potential support area. The next uptrend saw sell signals, indicating weakness at the resistance level

Confirmed Harami

Fig. 3-13 *Micrel Inc.*

The confirmed Harami brought the trend back up to the 50-day moving average where a Dark Cloud signal indicated the sellers had taken over again. The target now becomes a new low, below the $14.50 early February low, and probably at least targeting the 200-day moving average.

Fig. 3-14 The Ventiv Health Inc. chart provides a simple illustration for this analysis. Where the 50-day moving average acted as support during the past few months of this chart's uptrend: in late June, the moving average did not act as support. The pullback continued until a bullish engulfing signal appeared at a price in the $14 area. Stochastics indicate that this is a time to buy. But what should the target be? Obviously, what had been a support level for months now might become a resistance area.

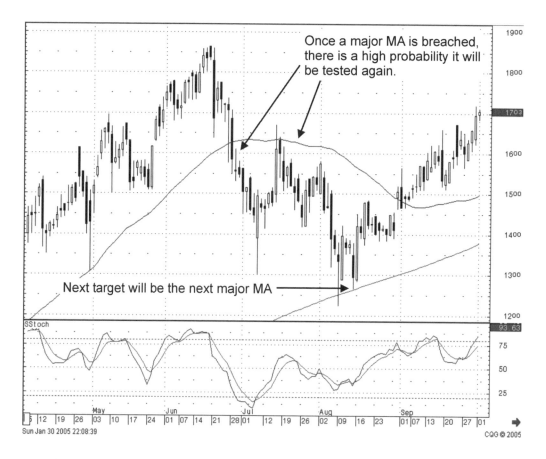

Fig. 3-14 *Ventiv Health Inc.*

Should that deter an investor from making this trade? Probably not! A purchase at approximately $14.00 with the potential move to $16.50 still represents a reasonable profit. With that in mind, at least the investor realizes what the first potential target should be and be prepared for expecting some resistance to occur at that level.

Seeing candlestick "sell" signals occurring at that level makes a selling decision at the optimal time that much easier.

As the price moves up to the 50-day moving average, the Hanging Man signal illustrated that the 50-day moving average was not going to be breached. Upon the failure of going up through that moving average, two assumptions can be made. The downtrend will continue and breach the recent low and/or test the 200-day moving average. In this illustration, both of those parameters could be accomplished at approximately the same level. Being able to visualize where to sell and when to buy provides a format for shorting stocks or buying Puts, inducing an investor to open and close trades at the optimal points.

Fig. 3-15, The Aspect Telecommunication Inc. chart illustrates a clear Blue Ice Failure pattern. It also demonstrates the effectiveness of being able to analyze what is happening to a trend based on the results of candlestick signals. Notice how the price traded relatively flat through February and the first few days of March. The Doji, appearing right at the 50-day moving average, becomes an alert, especially for the candlestick analyst. A period of indecision, as the Doji indicate, provides the "alert" of the possibility of something major happening to the price movement at this important juncture.

Fig. 3-15 *Aspect Telecomm Inc.*

This is the state of investor sentiment after two months of indecisive action. The first wave of the downtrend becomes obvious. The wave two tends to move up, stall out exactly where the candlestick "sell" signals appear. The overbought stochastics and the 50-day moving average would indicate the probable end of that move. The failure at that level provides us with two likely assumptions, the lows of mid-March should be breached. The 200-day moving average becomes the potential target.

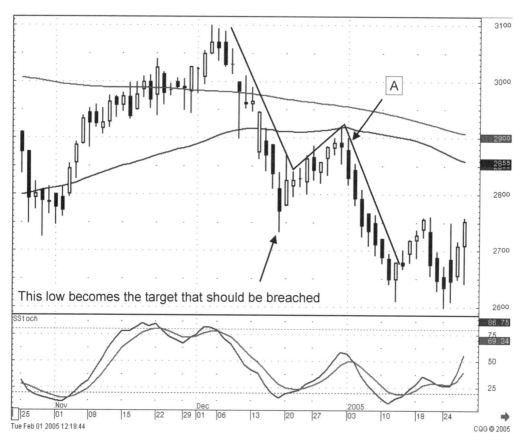

Fig. 3-16 *Crane Company CR*

Familiarity of a Blue Ice Failure allows a candlestick investor to pinpoint targets for putting on or taking off trades. Fig. 3-16, The Crane Co. chart illustrates the Long-legged Doji at Point A as a high probability trade for shorting the stock or buying the puts. The first target becomes the recent low. In this case, the 200-day moving average is above the 50-day moving average. A candlestick buy signal should be the expected termination of the downtrend. The first major candlestick buy signal appears when the stochastics are in the oversold area becomes a signal to cover the short trade.

Patterns for Daytraders

The ability to recognize high probability chart patterns is highly productive for the daytrader. Trading the index futures, which requires much greater accuracy for entering and exiting trades, is better formulated when knowing if a high probability pattern is forming. Successful intraday trading can be accomplished with a few simple analytical steps. Being able to analyze the trend of the general market provides a bias to the trading, analyzing market direction should dictate a heavier bias for the long side or the short side during any given day. That analysis may be formulated when analyzing the daily charts, then extrapolating that information into the intraday chart analysis.

Fig 3-17 *S&P one-minute chart*

Simple logic dictates that the analysis for the market in general is in a downtrend, then the one-minute, five-minute, and fifteen- minute chart analysis should be viewed with more emphasis on the moving averages acting as resistance. As illustrated in the S&P one-minute chart, if a downtrend is the predominant bias for the day, the candlestick investor's eyes should be oriented toward failures at specific moving averages. This is not high-tech analysis. This is using commonsense and then applying the candlestick signals, along with stochastics and moving averages, to enhance your entry and exit decisions.

Resistance, then Support

Moving averages that have shown to be resistance previously and are breached will now become support in a new uptrend. This basic rule works very well with the moving averages. The candlestick signals help with a visualization of that phenomenon. The analysis of what is happening at a moving average becomes a function of which signals are occurring at those levels. This makes trading in the moving average area very simple to analyze visually.

Another common technical analysis rule is that the first time a resistance level is touched, it will usually fail. The only subjective word in that rule is "usually". If this first attempt failure is a general rule, then being able to visually see what is happening at that resistance level produces a better insight. A candlestick signal that shows weakness at the point where crossing a moving average is first attempted creates a much different analysis than if the candlestick formation is a strong bullish candle that blasts through the moving average. Although this may seem simplistic, the signals reveal what the investor sentiment is at those levels. Improving the probability factor of this pattern can be easily applied by knowing the signals that occur at that level.

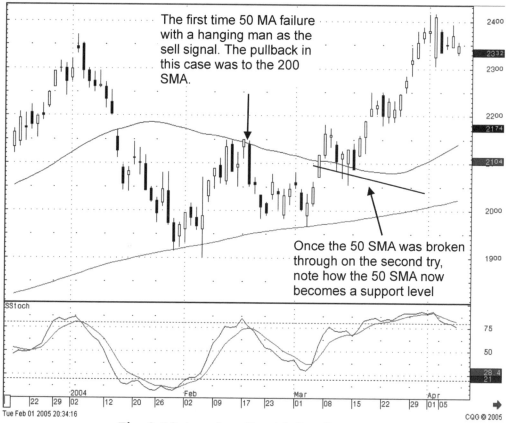

Fig. 3-18 *American Barrick Res Corp. ABX*

The probabilities are greatly enhanced when an investor can anticipate where candlestick signals should occur. For the aggressive trader, selling all or part of a position when a price encounters one of the major moving averages, anticipating that a candlestick signal could occur, creates a highly profitable low-risk trading program. Highly profitable in the sense that an investor is buying or selling right at a major support or resistance level. If the trade works as expected from that level, an optimal entry price was probably obtained. For the option trader, buying on an extended move down that just barely touches the lower major moving average allows options to be bought at a low price and probably with a minimal amount of option premium built into the price. The risk of this aggressive approach is that the downward trend does not stop at that support level. However, the point of the trade was that a downtrend stretching to that support level had the probabilities of acting as a support. If the price does not hold at that level, then the trade would be closed immediately, limiting the loss.

On the other hand, whether buying the stock or the option, it may have been bought at the most optimal price before the reversal signal appeared. Again, in the case of an option trade, this aggressive approach would have a double benefit. The price of the option will be low and the premium will have diminished. As the price starts to move back up, the premium will expand as confidence builds back up.

If moving averages are used as support and resistance levels, they will be quickly confirmed upon viewing a candlestick buy signal at support or a candlestick sell signal at resistance. The possibility of a moving average becoming a target becomes enhanced when analyzing candle formations as price approaches a target. For example, viewing candlestick bodies getting bigger, creating large black candles after a downtrend has been in existence for a good while, or seeing a gap down in price when the stochastics are in the oversold area would be good indicators that a trend is getting near the bottom. If this is all occurring when a moving average is within striking distance, then entering at a price right at that moving average becomes a better-calculated entry point.

Whether this analysis is done after an extended downtrend or after a pullback after a recent breakthrough of a moving average in uptrend, it provides a logical target for a when a trade should be entered. The more conservative approach is to wait and see if a candlestick "buy" signal is formed *after* the moving average has been touched and the time-frame has ended. Although the latter approach is more conservative, the candlestick signal analysis will usually put an investor into a trade well before the conventional technical analyst feels the support level has been confirmed.

The combination of visually being able to identify the candlestick signals and understanding which moving averages produces high probability support and resistance levels provides a powerful trading format. Through simple scan techniques, an increased number of highly profitable trade potentials can be found on a constant basis.

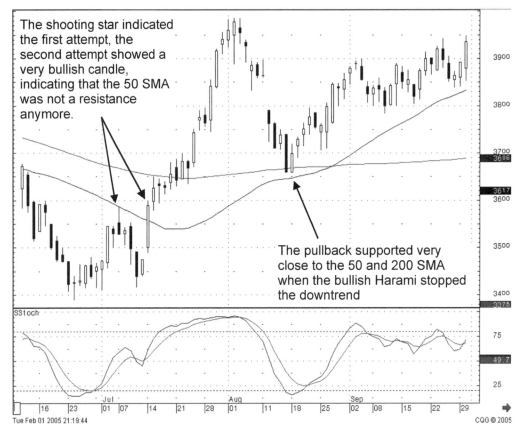

Fig. 3-19 *Apartment Investment & Management Co. AIV*

Fig. 3-19, The Apartment Investment & Management Co. chart reveals a strong buy signal after the gap up from the Bullish Harami in the beginning of the second week of July. As illustrated, the gap up bullish candle after the Harami demonstrated that there was no resistance at the 50-day moving average as seen one week prior. At that time, the Shooting Star signal just touched the moving average for the first time. The gap up from the Harami was a very strong bullish signal. The up-move remains strong until the first week of August when the Hanging Man signal was followed by a Doji/Harami. The gap-down the following day was confirmation that the uptrend was over. A pull-back should be occurring.

What would be the target for the pullback? Obviously, the moving averages! In this case, when both the 50-day and the 200-day moving average are close together, either one or both could have been the support level. The Bullish Harami confirmed this support and prices gapped up the next day.

The pullback after the initial breakthrough makes the buy signals on the support MA that much more convincing

Fig. 3-20 *Bank of New York BK*

Even if an investor did not participate in the initial up move, they can be ready for what should occur as the pullback gets near the MA.

Fig. 3-21 *Gevity HR Inc.*

Conclusion

> *We cannot seek or attain health, wealth, learning, justice or kindness in general. Action is always specific, concrete, individualized, unique.*
> Benjamin Jowett

Candlestick signals are a valuable tool for identifying reversals. Additional indicators that confirm support and resistance levels add that much more confirmation that a reversal has occurred. The moving averages act as excellent support and resistance levels. The fact that the large money managers use the 50-day and 200-day moving averages for their analysis makes those moving averages important. Identifying candlestick buy and sell signals at levels where other investors are watching for important reversal occurrences allows the candlestick investor to confirm immediately what the investor sentiment was doing at those levels.

The candlestick signals are valuable reversal signals. The moving averages are valuable support and resistance levels. Witnessing candlestick signals at the moving averages produces a very strong investment format. A candlestick signal demonstrates that a new trend has started. Having an understanding of where that trend could move is valuable information. The moving averages provide the target. Does that necessarily mean the moving averages will be the target? No, but it does give a probability of where a trend could move to. The trend will end when a candlestick reversal signal appears.

However, understanding that prices move from one major technical level to another major technical level adds valuable information to a decision-making process. When prices start moving near the next moving average, it becomes time to start watching to see what the price will do at that important level. The visual analysis becomes much easier when a price is approaching a major moving average and the stochastics are in an overbought or oversold condition. Witnessing a candlestick reversal signal in those conditions creates that much more credibility that the previous trend has stopped. Use this information to your advantage.

Chapter 4

High Profits
Using Gaps

Combining Candlestick Signals and Gaps

> *He who fears something gives it power over him.*
>
> *Chinese Proverb*

Gaps occurring at different locations in a trend have different meanings. Taking advantage of what they reveal becomes highly profitable. Dissecting the implications of a gap/window makes its appearance easy to understand. Where a gap occurs is important. The ramification they reveal in a chart pattern is an important aspect to Japanese Candlestick analysis. Some traders make a living trading strictly from gap trading.

Gaps (ku) are called windows (Mado) in Japanese Candlestick analysis. A gap or window is one of the most misunderstood technical messages. It is usually advised by a good percentage of investment advisors not to buy after a gap. The explanation being that it is too dangerous to predict what will happen next. That advice usually comes from somebody that does not know how to use gaps successfully. Gaps reveal powerful high profit trades. Candlestick signals, correlated with the appearance of a gap, provide high-probability profitable trade set-ups. The unique built-in forces, encompassed in the candlestick signals, and the strength of a move revealed by the existence of a gap produce powerful trading factors. The knowledge of what this combination of signals reveal will produce consistent and strong profits.

These are not "hidden" secret signals or newly discovered formulas that are just now being exposed to the investment world. These are a combination of widely known, but little used, investment techniques. Candlestick signals obviously have a statistical basis to them or they would not still be in existence after many centuries. Gaps have very powerful implications. Combining the information of these two elements produces investment strategies that very few investors take the time to exploit.

Consider what a window or gap represents. In a rising market, it illustrates prices opening higher than any of the previous days trading range. What does this mean in reality? During the non-market hours, something made owning a stock, or any other trading entity, tremendously desirable. So desirable that the order imbalance opens the price well above the prior day's body as well as the high of the previous day's trading range. As seen in Figure 4-1A, note the space between the high of the previous day and the low of the following day.

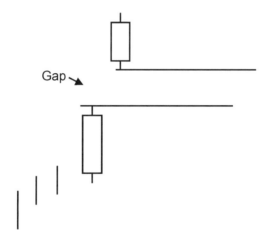

Gap

Fig. 4-1A

Witnessing a gap or window at the beginning of a new trend produces profitable opportunities. Gaps formed at the beginning of the trend reveal the buyers have stepped in with a great amount of zeal. A common scenario is witnessing a prolonged downtrend. A Candlestick signal appears; a Doji, Harami, Hammer, or any other signal that would indicate that the investor sentiment is changing. What is required to verify a candlestick reversal signal at the bottom? More buying the next day! A bullish candle indicates a reversal has occurred. A "gap up" bullish candle indicates that a reversal has occurred with extraordinary force.

Many investors are apprehensive about buying a stock that has popped up from the previous days close. A risky situation! The hesitancy is caused by the percentage move. When most investors are happy with a 10% return annually, it is hard for an investor to commit funds to a position that has moved 12% in one day. Understanding what that gap up represents eliminates fear.

A Candlestick investor has been forewarned that the trend is going to change, viewing the candlestick signal as an alert. A gap up, illustrating buyer enthusiasm, reveals excessive strength. Use the gap as a strength indicator. The fact that the initial move is substantial should act as an indication that the remaining move of this new trend could be more substantial.

Always keep in mind, the markets do not care what an investors' fears and perceptions are. A price that has moved dramatically in one day is usually cause for fear. Entering a trade for most investors becomes forbidding. They do not have the knowledge to understand what that strength illustrates for the future.

Gaps form in many different places and formations. Some are easy to see, some need to be recognized. This book will walk you through the different situations where a gap has significance. Each situation will be explained in detail, (1) to give you a full understanding of what is occurring during the move and (2) to provide a visual illustration to become familiar with the formation, making it easy to recognize. This allows the Candlestick investor to visually spot an investment situation as it is developing. The signals also make clear when to be playing the gap or trading the other side. Gaps tell when it is time to buy and time to sell. The illustrations of this chapter will clarify each situation.

A Gap up at the Bottom

A gap, appearing after a candlestick "buy" signal, has powerful implications. Knowing that a gap represents enthusiasm, getting in or out of a stock position becomes an easy identification process. The forewarning that a strong profit potential situation is about to or has occurred is established. Where is the best place to see rampant enthusiasm? At the point you are buying, near the bottom. Obviously, seeing a potential Candlestick "buy" signal, at the bottom of an extended downtrend is a great place to buy. In keeping with the concepts taught in Candlestick analysis, we want to be buying stocks that are already oversold, to reduce the downside risk. Evidence that buyers are very anxious to get into the stock is all that much better.

Reiterating the basics of finding the perfect trades, as found in the book "Profitable Candlestick Trading," having all the stars in alignment makes for better probabilities of producing a profit. The best scenario for a high-profit trade is a candlestick "buy" signal, in oversold condition, confirmed with a gap up the following day. Illustrated in Fig. 4-1, the Bombay Company, Inc. chart, the uptrend was obviously instigated after a gap up and large bullish candle following a Doji. The fact that prices gapped up was clear illustration that buyers wanted to get into this stock with great fervor.

The gap up the following the doji clearly illustrated the strength of the decision after an indecision day like the doji

Fig.4-1 *Bombay Company Inc.*

Unofficially, statistics illustrate an 80% or better probability that a trade will be successful when stochastics are oversold, a Candlestick "buy" signal appears, and prices gap up. {The Candlestick Forum will offer our years of statistical figures as "unofficial." Even though over fifteen years of observations and studies have been involved, no formal data gathering programs have been fully operated. However, currently the Candlestick Forum is involved with two university studies to quantify signal results. This is an extensive program endeavor. Results of these studies will be released to Candlestick Forum subscribers upon completion. This study has been long and difficult, but results are expected sometime in the near future.}

Having this statistic as part of an investor's arsenal of knowledge creates opportunities to extract large gains out of the markets. The risk factor remains extremely low when participating in these trade set-ups.

Many investors are afraid to buy after a gap up. The rationale being that they don't like paying up for a stock that may have already moved 3%, 8%, 10%, or 20% already that day. Witnessing a Candlestick "buy" signal prior to the gap up provides a basis for aggressively buying the stock. If it is at the bottom of a trend, the 3%, 8%, 10% or 20% initial gap move may just be the beginning of a 50% move or a major trend that can last for months.

The strength of an uptrend can be better verified when the gap in price moves up past potential resistance levels. As illustrated in Fig. 4-2, the Meridian Gold Inc. chart, the price gapped up over the 50-day moving average, what had previously been acting as a resistance area. The strength of the buyers is clearly represented. The fact that the price breached the moving average, while still forming a bullish candle after the open price, illustrates that the buying sentiment did not diminish after the dramatic increase in price.

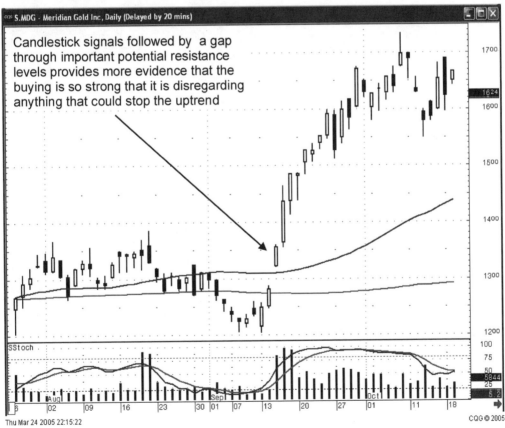

Fig. 4-2 *Meridian Gold Inc.*

The more parameters in place, confirming an uptrend, the higher the probability of being in a correct trade. Add to that the confirmation of excessive buying strength, a gap up in price, the higher the probabilities that a strong uptrend is occurring.

Fig.4-3, The Cleveland Cliffs Inc. chart reveals a Bullish Harami forming right on the 50-day moving average followed by a gap up in price. First, the Bullish Harami forming on the 50-day moving average became a good indication that the moving average was going to act as support. The gap up the following day made it evident that many buyers felt the same way. If one gap shows enthusiastic buying, two gaps reveal that much more strength. The trend is your friend, an often the spoken adage. Gaps, when used correctly, are your best friends.

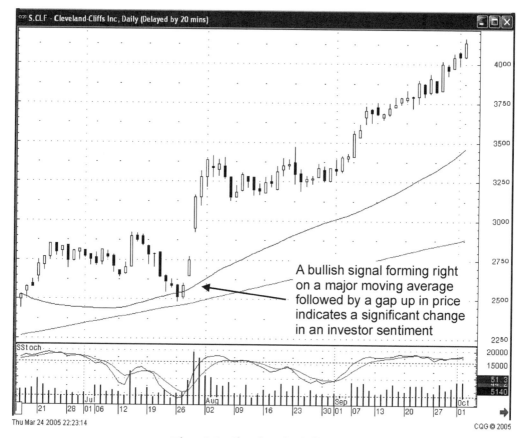

Fig. 4-3 *Cleveland Cliffs Inc.*

This is not a difficult analysis. Witnessing a candlestick buy signal followed by exuberant buying is exactly the type of trade an investor should be looking for.

Fig. 4-4, The Pride International Inc. chart illustrates how the enthusiastic buying, after a candlestick signal, provides the confirmation that a strong uptrend is in progress. Notice how the Kicker type signal, a strong bullish indication in itself, precludes the strong uptrend. The next day it gaps up on a strong bullish candle. The gap up, followed by strong continued buying, reveals a number of bullish observations.

The gap occurs at what could be considered a mild resistance level. The price appeared to have trouble closing above the $16 level. When the price gapped up through that area, it revealed that the $16 area was not acting as resistance any more. Next, the strong bullish candle went through the 50-day moving average. That average acted as a resistance level earlier. Witnessing price moving out of a trading range **and** through potential resistance should indicate that a new dynamic has come into the price trend.

Fig. 4-4 *Pride International Inc.*

Candlestick analysis can also be applied to what a price was doing before a significant buy situation. As seen in Fig. 4-5, the Premcor Inc. chart, August was a period of indecisive trading. There would not have been anything in the trading, during that time, that provided any reason to get excited about getting into that stock position. The gap up, out of the congestion area, now becomes a clear indication that new investor sentiment has entered this stock trend.

> *It is not enough to have knowledge, one must also apply it. It is not enough to have wishes, one must also accomplish.*
>
> *Johan Wolfgang von Goethe*

Once the gap up, followed by a strong bullish candle was observed, candlestick analysis of the prior month of trading becomes useful. Although the daily trading ranges were relatively insignificant, they were showing small bullish candlestick signals. Upon reviewing the trading during that time, it becomes obvious that it was forming a basing range. That information now becomes useful for analyzing the gap up.

The congestion area formed a resistance level at the $34 price. Once the price gapped up through that level, it became immediately obvious that the $34 level was not acting as resistance any more. Next, the large bullish candle went straight through the 50-day moving average without any problems. Obviously, the 50-day moving average was not going to act as resistance. Being able to analyze what happened prior to the gap up allows the candlestick investor to better evaluate what was going on in investor sentiment. Although stochastics were now nearing the overbought area when the gap up occurred, the strength with which the buyers started entering into the stock price produces a different scenario. A breakout from the congestion area meant new enthusiasm was coming into the stock price.

A gap up occurring at a top of a trend, with stochastics in the overbought area, might have a much different conclusion. In this case, the gap up did not occur at a top of a trend. As observed, the trend was sideways prior to the gap up. This observation would put a different importance on the location of the stochastics.

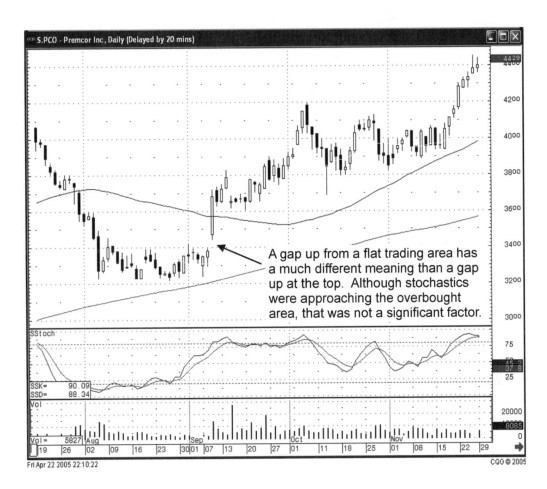

A gap up from a flat trading area has a much different meaning than a gap up at the top. Although stochastics were approaching the overbought area, that was not a significant factor.

Fig. 4-5 *Premcor Inc.*

Being able to analyze what the candlestick signals were doing prior to a gap up produces valuable information for entering high-profit trades. Preparing one's eyes for successful and powerful price-movement setups aids an investor in being mentally ready to immediately exploit a high profit potential signal. This is a simple process. Having a mental picture of how a high-profit potential trade begins helps an investor enter that trade at a very early stage. This not only benefits the profitability, it also reduces loss potential. Entering a gap up situation in the very early stages of its development, provides more effective time and price entry levels to get in and out of the trade if it doesn't reach full expectations.

Doji Followed by a Gap Up

> *He who ignores discipline despises himself, but whoever heeds correction gains understanding.*
>
> **Proverbs 15:32**

The Doji is one of the most informative signals in candlestick analysis. It appears at many significant points in a trend. In addition to it being a relevant signal at tops or bottoms of trends, it also is an important alert for gap up trade situations. An inordinate number of times a Doji will be witnessed prior to a breakout. The gap movements can occur at the top of a trend, bottom of a trend, or after a flat trading period.

One of the trading rules for a Doji is, "the trend will usually move in the direction of how prices open after a Doji." The trend strength becomes more enhanced if the open price gaps away from the Doji. A Doji followed by a gap usually produces a very strong trend.

The Japanese Rice traders say, "Always take heed when a Doji appears." It is even more important to take heed when prices gap away from a Doji. That becomes strong evidence that after a day of indecision, a decision has been made very forcefully.

Fig. 4-6, The Ultratech Inc. chart reveals a relatively sloppy trading environment in late July and early August. Stochastics are in mid-range. Notice the Doji at the end of that sideways trading is the last signal prior to a definite move to the upside. Although the gap up trading day did not show strength by the end of the day, the fact that it gapped up away from the doji, revealed important information. For some reason the buyers were coming into the stock with great strength. They did so the day after an indecision day, the Doji. As observed, buying pressure continued after that gap up day.

Fig. 4-6 *Ultratech Inc.*

The gap up day does not necessarily need to show strength after the gap up. As illustrated in Fig. 4-7, the Devon Energy Corp. chart in January of 2005, the gap up day finished at the lower end of the trading range. What should be analyzed is that when the stochastics were in the oversold condition, a Piercing

Pattern appeared. Then a Doji appeared. The gap up in price, after those signals becomes the relevant parameter for the evaluation. Would it have been better to see a strong bullish candle after the gap up? Certainly, but the fact that investors were wanting to buy aggressively the day after the Doji should be the predominant evaluation.

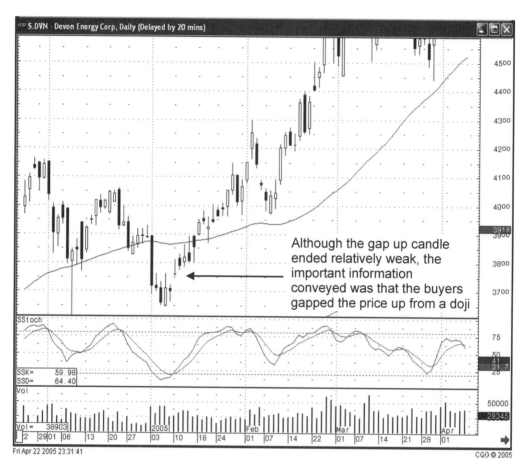

Although the gap up candle ended relatively weak, the important information conveyed was that the buyers gapped the price up from a doji

Fig. 4-7 *Devon Energy Corp.*

Fig.4-8, The American Healthways Inc. chart also demonstrates a gap up from a Doji after a relatively sloppy trading session. The strength of the initial gap up candle, going through both the 50-day and the 200-day moving average, reveals there should be more upside potential.

The strength of the gap up candle going through a trend line, the 50 day MA, and the 200 day MA should be a clear indication of the buyers are in and not worried about resistance levels.

Fig. 4-8 *American Healthways Inc.*

Should the percent move be a concern? Definitely not! A price-movement, when the proper signals are present, indicates strength coming into a trend. The message conveyed by a 5%, 10%, 20%, or greater move may just be the forewarning of a price movement that can continue up another 30%, 50%, 100%, or greater. Do not let percentages be a deterring factor. If you're going to buy with a candlestick buy signal, then sell when you see a candlestick sell signal.

Fig. 4-9, the Devon Energy Corporation chart also illustrates an indecisive trading period ending with a Doji. The last day of indecision clearly exhibited what the new decision process was on the following day. The gap up from the Doji, with trading opening above the 50 day moving average and closing with strength, provided valuable information. The buyers were stepping in and taking prices higher. It confirmed that fact again. The following day exhibited another gap up. If one gap up illustrates strength, two gap ups illustrate that much more strength.

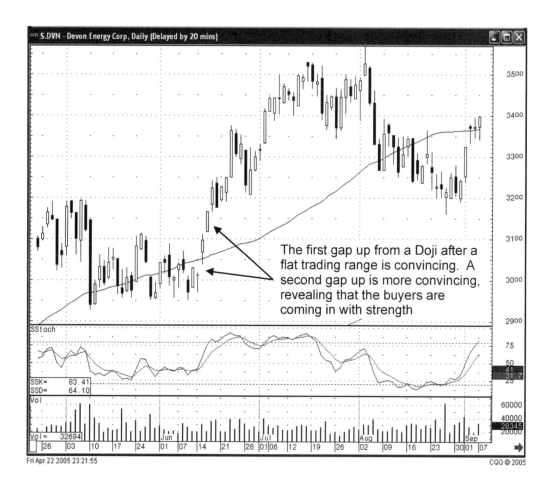

The first gap up from a Doji after a flat trading range is convincing. A second gap up is more convincing, revealing that the buyers are coming in with strength

Fig. 4-9 *Devon Energy Corp.*

The 'rules' for gapping up, after a Doji, do not have to be to the letter. The indication that the buyers are coming into a position with strength, opening the price well above the closing price of the Doji day, does not require the true gap definition. As seen in Fig. 4-10, the Magna Entertainment Corp. chart, the price gapped up the following day after a Doji/Spinning Top. Although the price did not quite open above the top of the trading range of the Doji signal, it still indicated that the buyers had moved the price significantly. Buying continued from that point.

If there is evidence of strong buying, gapping the price away from the previous days close, the message should still be the same. The buyers are coming in with much more strength than what was being traded the previous day.

Fig. 4-10 *Magna Entertainment Corp.*

The important factor in this scenario is the day of indecision was followed by a clear statement of what the investors had decided. Analyzing candlestick signals should be done with a commonsense evaluation, not a stringent set of rules! If you understand what each signal represents, the investment actions that follow can be better interpreted.

Logically, interpretation becomes much easier the stronger the indication that the buyers are coming in with force. As illustrated in Fig.4-11, the SuperGen Inc. chart, the Doji at the bottom, followed by a large gap up, produces a much easier evaluation. Stochastics in the oversold area, a gap up from a Doji, and the price going up through a major moving average, after an extended downtrend, aligns a number of the stars. These are all parameters for a high probability trade.

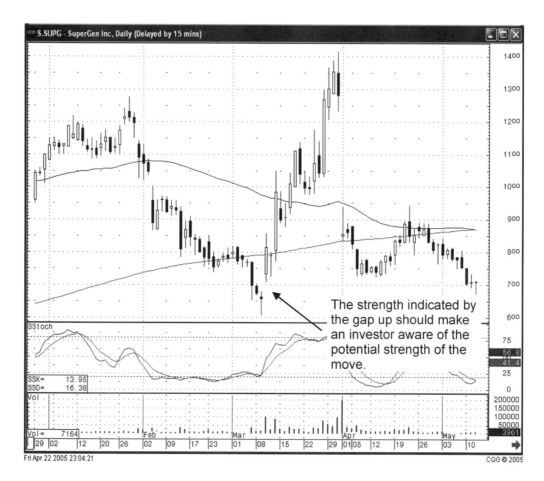

Fig. 4-11 *Supergen Inc.*

A strong trading pattern makes sitting through the day after the gap up less stressful. The strong 'buy' signal becomes the predominant investment factor. Although the selling during the day after a gap up might cause concern, knowing that a strong buy signal has been created should induce more patience. The strength of the 'buy' signal would allow sitting through the following day without panicking.

A large influx of buy orders, after a Doji, should become a clear indicator of which direction the trend will move. There is an easy method for confirming this scenario in your own mind. Scan back through charts. As you are going through the learning process, analyzing the peaks and valleys of price trends will become highly educational. When you come upon a Doji at the bottom, followed by a gap up, review what occurred in the trend if prices gapped up the next day. You'll discover that an inordinate number of strong rallies were started with a Doji followed by a gap up.

Hammers, Haramis, and Inverted Hammers with Gaps Up

If you are on the right track, if you have this inner knowledge, then nobody can turn you off no matter what they say.
Barbara McClintock, Nobel Prize winner

Although the Doji illustrates indecision and creates a high-powered move followed by a gap up, do not disregard that same effect following the other major candlestick buy signals at the bottom. The Hammer, Harami, and the Inverted Hammer signify a potential reversal when seen in the oversold condition. Confirmation of a reversal requires positive trading the following day. As with the Doji, positive trading represented with a gap up is that much more compelling evidence that the reversal has occurred. The force with which that new trend may move is demonstrated by the gap up in price the following day.

The candlestick signal is the alert that a potential change of investor sentiment may be occurring, especially when it occurs in oversold condition. As illustrated in Fig.4-12, the Marathon Oil Corp. chart, the Hammer/Harami signal gave a good indication that the 200-day moving average should act as support. This becomes better confirmed the following day when the price gaps up. It becomes more obvious that the 200-day moving average acted as the support when buyers showed great zeal to get into this position, causing the next day's gap up.

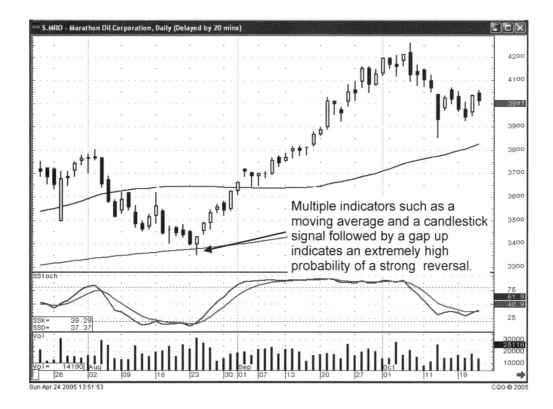

Fig. 4-12 *Marathon Oil Corp.*

Being able to use a visual analysis makes interpreting investor sentiment at important levels very easy. Utilizing the knowledge of what the signal conveys and what a gap up conveys enhances strong trend identification.

Fig. 4-13 *Skyworks Solutions Inc.*

A Gap Down at the Bottom

The basic premise of investing: buying at the bottom. Candlestick analysis provides the tools for exploiting human emotions. The fear that enters most investors investment decisions can usually be seen graphically on a candlestick chart. The evidence is usually illustrated with the candle bodies getting larger as the price enters into the oversold conditions. This is often seen after an extended decline. The further the downtrend moves, the more panic selling is observed.

The panic selling is usually fueled by the rhetoric put out by the talking heads on the financial news stations or the financial publications. Most of the time the financial news agencies are reporting what has already happened. After a stock or any other trading entity has been in an extended decline, it starts getting discussed in the news media. The discussion for why that industry/sector is in such bad condition starts getting publicized, after it has been in a three-month downtrend.

Quite often when a trend, whether positive or negative, becomes recognized by the financial news reporting media, that is usually time to start watching for reversal signals. Very rarely will you see reports from the news media stating why an industry would likely be attractive after a severe decline. They always seem to report why things are bad after the price decline has occurred. This becomes a great indicator for watching for a candlestick reversal situation. When you hear constant doom and gloom predictions for an industry, prepare for the panic selling. Then start watching for the buy signals.

> *An investment in knowledge always pays the best interest.*
> *Benjamin Franklin*

What is the ultimate indicator of the panic selling? The gap down at the bottom! A clear indication, illustrating investors wanting to get out of a position, no matter what the price! The gap down illustrates the tremendous desire (panic) to exit from that position. A gap down in oversold conditions becomes the cause for diligently watching for a candlestick 'buy" signal to occur. If most investors panic at the bottom and a gap down represents the panic selling, then the bottom is usually very near. This is purely common sense. Having this knowledge of investor psychology allows the candlestick investor to be prepared for the "buy" signal.

Does that mean a buy signal will show up immediately? Not necessarily. However it does indicate that the majority of the move in the downtrend is probably over. This creates two benefits. First, if this position had been shorted, it now reveals a time to start covering the short position. Second, it alerts in investor to start watching for a buy signal.

As illustrated in Fig. 4-14 the Powerwave Technologies Inc. chart, after an extended downtrend the selling starts escalating. This is identified with a large black candle followed by a gap down in price. That gap down forms a Doji/ Spinning Top. With the stochastics well in the oversold condition, the gap down should have been the first inkling that the bottom was near. In the Powerwave Technologies Inc. chart, the gap down Doji was the end of the majority of the downside move. About a week later, a gap up after the Hammer signal indicated the uptrend may have started.

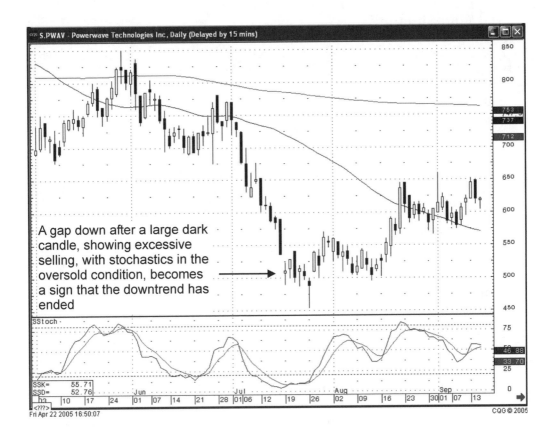

Fig. 4-14 *Powerwave Technologies Inc.*

The point of this illustration is to show that the gap down at the bottom warranted closing the short positions and watching to go long.

As witnessed in Fig. 4-15, the Raymond James Financial Inc. chart, the stochastics had indicated that the price of the stock was in the oversold condition throughout early July until early August. During that time there were a number of potential candlestick buy signals but the signals never got confirmed. Note how the ultimate bottom occurred after a gap down.

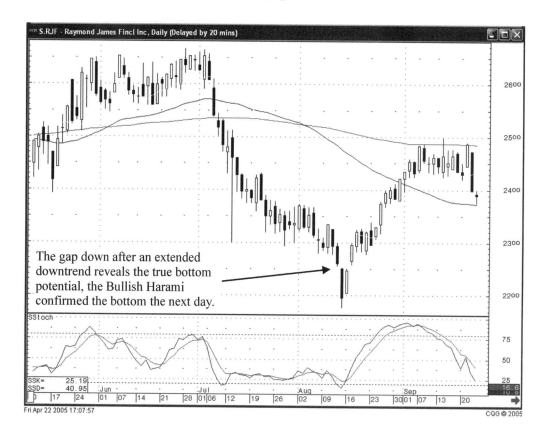

Fig. 4-15 *Raymond James Financial Inc.*

A big selling day, after a gap down when stochastics have been in the oversold condition for a lengthy period of time, becomes the alert to start watching for a candlestick buy signal. The Bullish Harami, the following day, becomes a clear indication that the last gasp selling was over and buying was starting. A gap up the following day, creating an island reversal, becomes a very strong reversal indicator. This whole sequence would have been put on watch because of the gap down.

Fig. 4-16, the Monster Worldwide Inc. chart, also illustrates the final bottom. It is not unusual to see increased volume coming into trading after a gap down. This becomes an indication that the weak are selling to the strong. Although the volume is not a necessity, the presence of a large volume day during the gap- down day, or a day or two to one side or the other, reveals that there has been a large change of ownership in a stock. The weak sellers have relinquished their stock to the strong.

Fig. 4-16 Monster Worldwide Inc.

The Spinning Top/Harami appearing during following day illustrates that the selling had stopped. The uptrend may not start immediately. There always exists the possibility of some follow-through selling from the previous down-trend. However, a gap down signifies that most of the selling occurred that day. After a few days, the rest of the selling becomes acquired by the buyers. Then the trend can get started to the upside.

The gap down at the bottom doesn't necessarily mean that a strong uptrend will occur, but it does signify that the downtrend has stopped. Fig. 4-17, The Eyetech Pharmaceuticals Inc. chart illustrates, after an extended downtrend, the gap down at the bottom revealed that the downtrend had stopped. At that point, watching for candlestick 'buy' signals becomes the strategy. Those 'buy' signals may not show up for a few weeks, but the probabilities that the bottom is near becomes extremely great when witnessing the gap down in the oversold conditions. This may not be the time to buy. However, if an investor had been short this position, the gap down would have been the signal to take profits.

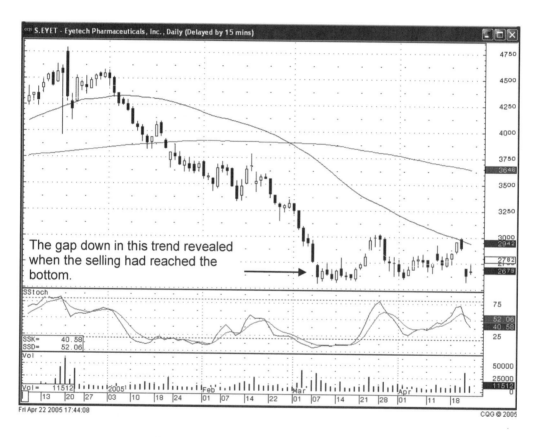

Fig 4-17 *Eyetech Pharmaceuticals Inc.*

Keep in mind, a gap down near the oversold area indicates that a bottom is near. That is why it becomes important to analyze the candlestick signals that are forming.

As in the case of Fig. 4-18, Sonic Solutions Inc., the gap down on large volume was near the bottom. It took a few more days to wash out all the sellers.

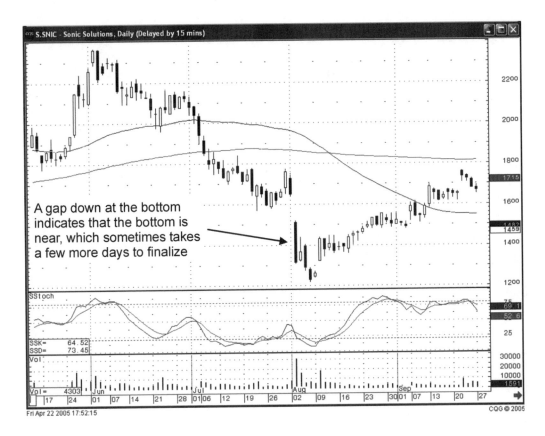

A gap down at the bottom indicates that the bottom is near, which sometimes takes a few more days to finalize

Fig 4-18 *Sonic Solutions*

The Doji/Harami, followed by the gap up bullish candle, became a 'buy' signal. After an extended downtrend, all the selling sentiment will not disappear on one major down day. Likewise, the selling doesn't always immediately disappear after a strong bullish candlestick 'buy' signal. This knowledge permits a candlestick investor to sit through a residue selling day or two after seeing a reversal situation occur.

The subtle gap downs become more apparent when a candlestick signal forms on the gap down day. Notice in Gig. 4-19, the Cleveland Cliffs Inc. chart how the gap down may not have been noticed had a Doji not formed that day. Of course, a Doji at the bottom should always be heeded. When the stochastics have confirmed the oversold condition, the slight gap down on the open of the Doji signal becomes more important.

Fig. 4-19 *Cleveland Cliffs Inc.*

A gap down on big volume should become a well recognized sign. It incorporates all the investor psychology required for identifying when investors are getting out at the bottom. It usually occurs on bad news. That news probably was known to the smart investors months before. More than likely, they were selling at the top. The information was built into the decline of that stock price months ahead of when the announcement came out.

Fundamental analysis should be used when exploiting the gap down at the bottom. Whatever bad news was reported, fundamental analysis assumes that the management of the company was aware of the problem well before it was announced. It also has to be assumed that a high percentage of management teams are relatively smart and effective

When everybody is panic selling at the bottom, the world looks terrible, who is buying?

Fig.4-20 *Charlotte Russe Holding*

This assumption is made based upon the fact that most management executives rise to their positions based upon talent. With that in mind, then it can be is assumed that by the time that a bad news announcement is made, the problem is being resolved. The management of that company had been working on the solution to the problem for at least a few months. By the time the news comes out, a resolution to the problem may already be in place.

That leads to one final question. If everybody is panic selling at the bottom, and the circumstances looks bleak for that stock, then who is buying? If you have ever found yourself selling at the bottoms because your emotions cannot stand the stress and the strain, then you should recognize where you sold in the past. Use that knowledge and the understanding of what a gap down at the bottom represents. Once you can visually identify indications of bottoming action, an investor can now establish being mentally prepared to buy when the rest of the world seems to be selling.

Gaps at the Top

> *New knowledge is the most valuable commodity on earth. The more truth we have to work with, the richer we become.*
>
> *Kurt Vonnegut*

The gap up that appears at the top of an uptrend is the one that provides ominous information. Remembering the mental state of most investors, the enthusiasm builds as the trend continues over a period of time. Each day the price continues up, the greater investors become convinced the price is going to go through the roof. The "talking heads" on the financial news stations start to show their prowess. They come up with a multitude of reasons why the price had already moved and will continue to move into the rosy future. With all this enthusiasm around, the stock price gaps up. Unfortunately, this is usually the top. Fortunately, Candlestick investors recognize it. They can put on exit strategies that will capture a good portion of the price move at the top. Consider the different possibilities that can happen when witnessing the gap up at the top of a sustained uptrend. Most of the time, the gap will represent the exhaustion of the trend, thus called an Exhaustion Gap. Or it could be the start of a Three Rising Windows formation, or big news such as a buy out or a huge contract announcement about to be announced.

What are the best ways to participate in any potential of higher prices, at the same time knowing that the probabilities are that the top is near? A few simple stop-loss procedures can allow you to comfortably let the price move and benefit from the maximum potential.

Hopefully, after a gap up is occurring, (the exuberance of an extended trend), a substantial gain is already realized in the position. The gap up is adding to an already big gain. Probabilities dictate that this is the top. However, there is the possibility of more gains.

Upon a slight to medium gap up, the Candlestick investor should put their stop at the close of the previous day. The thinking being that if the price gapped up in overbought conditions, and prices came back down through the close of the previous day, the buying was not sustained. If so, the 'stop' closed the position at the level of the highest closing price of that trend. The same rationale applied to the psychology of a gap down at a bottom of a trend can be applied equally well to the gap up at the top of a trend. Where do most investors buy? They buy when the confidence has finally built up, after the price has done well. When most investors feel safe that a price is doing well, that is usually the time to look for 'sell' signals.

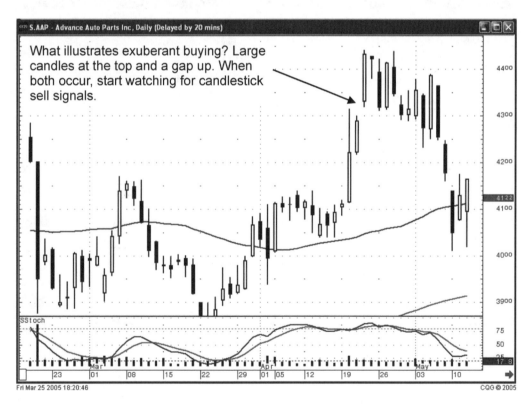

Fig. 4-21 *Advanced Auto Parts Inc.*

The gap up after a strong run up is clearly indicative of the exuberant buying. When buying gets exuberant, the smart-money starts taking profits. Fig, 4-21, The Advanced Auto Parts Inc. chart, reveals the exuberance. Large candles, in the overbought stochastics conditions, reveal that investors are piling into the stock. Finally a gap up becomes the first signal that the top may be near. This becomes more evident the following day when a Harami/Hanging Man signal appeared. Now there is the evidence of a gap up followed by a potential candlestick "sell" signal. The lower open the following day makes it more convincing that the top is here. Does a gap up at the top necessarily mean the ultimate top has occurred? Definitely not, however it produces a good indication that a top may be very near. It provides the investor with an alert to be ready to take profits and/or start shorting a position on the first signs of weakness.

Fig. 4-22 *Plantronics Inc.*

Fig. 4-22, The Plantronics Inc. chart shows a Shooting Star after a gap up. The Shooting Star at the top of a trend alone would signify that the bears are making their presence known. The fact that it occurred after a gap up is more convincing. Exit strategies can be better formulated when knowing the probabilities indicate a reversal is occurring or about to occur. Each investor can prepare exit strategies that comfortably fit their investment nature. For example, upon seeing weakness the following day after the shooting star, half the position may have been closed out. The other half might have been closed out two or three days later as more candlestick sell signals appeared. A gap up at the top has historical indications that the majority of the uptrend is over. Having that knowledge allows an investor to better analyze and shift funds from a poor probability situation back into a high probability situation.

Gaps at the Top Reveal Exuberance

Each problem that I solved became a rule, which served afterwards to solve other problems.

Rene Descartes

Exuberance at the top is depicted with the formation of long candles or a gap up. When either or both of these situations occur, be prepared for a candlestick sell signal to soon follow. This becomes a simple visual analysis. Being able to correctly interpret the investor sentiment conveyed in a gap up at the top becomes an important decision making factor. Fig. 4-23 (following page), The Nike Inc. chart reveals a gap up followed by strong buying when stochastics are well in the overbought area. The following four or five trading days indicate indecisive movement between the Bulls and the Bears at those high levels. The big trading day either revealed that something major was happening in the stock price or it was the final exuberant buying. The fact that the next five days showed indecisive trading, no bullish follow through, now provides a better picture of what is happening to investor sentiment.

Described in the "Stop Loss" chapter later in the book, effective stops can be placed upon a gap up in overbought condition. Simple techniques allow for reaping the majority of the potential returns from a trend.

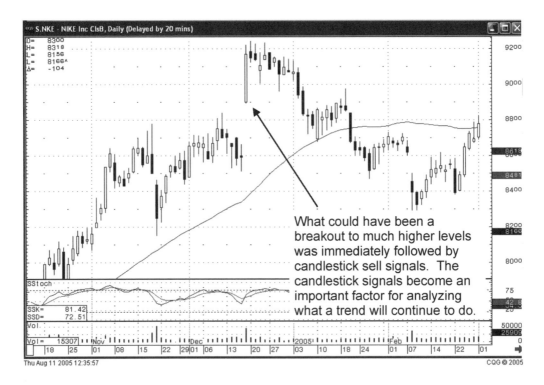

Fig. 4-23 *Nike Inc.*

When prices gap up in overbought conditions the potential for forming a candlestick 'sell' signal becomes favorable. Prices backing off from those levels can form a Dark Cloud or Bearish Engulfing signal if they continue weak for the rest of the trading day. Even if prices come back up to the top of the trading range, a signal such as the Hanging Man or a Doji could be formed.

If prices continue higher, and pull back by the end of the day, then a Shooting Star can be formed. Once a gap up occurs, the only possibility of a candlestick sell signal <u>not</u> appearing is when prices open higher and then continue to trade to the higher end of the trading range. If this is the case, the placement of stop losses, as recommended in the "Stop Loss" chapter, will not be affected. Profits will continue to be made. However, the point of being prepared for a gap up at the top is based on probabilities. The "probabilities" a trend is over is much greater than anticipating the trend going higher.

Fig. 4-24, The XM Satellite Radio Holdings Inc. chart illustrates that the sellers are ready to take over, after an extended uptrend that is followed by a gap up. Unless something dramatic is about to occur, such as an announcement of good news for the company, it is likely that the uptrend is over. This assumption is based upon the visual observations over the past few centuries. Why invest against the probabilities?

The gap up at the top, when stochastics are in overbought conditions, should be the first alert that the trend is over

Fig. 4-24 *XM Satellite Radio Holdings Inc.*

If the gap up is substantial, and it continues higher, put the stop at the open price level. On any of the scenarios described, the price moving back to the 'stops' would more than likely create signals that warranted liquidating the trade, forming Shooting Stars, Dark Clouds, Meeting Lines or Bearish Engulfing patterns. In any case, sellers were making themselves known. It is time to take profits in the high risk area and find low risk 'buy' signals at the bottom of a trend.

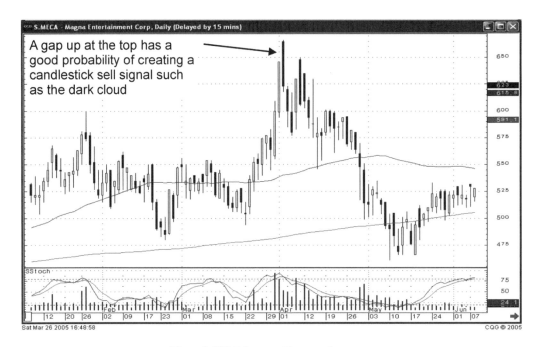

Fig. 4-25 *Magna Entertainment*

Fig.4-25a *DRS Technologies INC.*

The candlestick investor requires nothing more than the training of the eye to recognize high probability patterns. A large gap up in an overbought condition provides a definite decision-making process. As a rule, the appearance of exuberant buying is the time to be prepared to take profits. The question that should always be asked, "When prices are going through the roof, when the accompanying news appears to make the future look very bright, who is selling?"

Gaps Down at the Top

If you want to know what's happening in the market, ask the market.
Japanese Proverb

The same zeal illustrated when prices gap at the bottom is just as relevant at the top. A candlestick "sell" signal, when stochastics are in the overbought condition, followed by a gap down, clearly illustrates the sellers wanting to get out of that position aggressively. For those investors that want to find strong short positions, a gap down at the top provides strong shorting opportunities. The same confirmation that is applied to a bullish signal can be applied to a bearish signal. Prices, gapping away to the downside after a candlestick sell signal, provide the additional confirmation that the downtrend will move with good force.

Fig. 4-26 (following page), The Advanced Auto Parts Inc. chart demonstrates that investors are very anxious to get out of the stock. The appearance of the Evening Star signal produces the first indication that the sellers were stepping in. The gap down makes it visually obvious that investors wanted out of this position in a hurry. If you are planning to short positions, you want to find those positions that are demonstrating strong downside potential. A second gap down moves prices significantly below the 50-day moving average, clearly illustrated the downside selling force is reasonably strong.

Fig.4-26 *Advance Auto Parts Inc.*

Doji at the bottom are powerful indicators when followed by a gap up. The same is true when witnessing Doji at the top. Fig. 4-27 (following page), The Placer Dome Inc. chart clearly demonstrates a period of indecision with a series of Doji in the overbought condition. Notice how the gap up created the series of Doji, a flat trading range of indecisive signals. The new trend started to the downside with a gap down bearish candle that immediately breached the 50-day moving average.

This chart pattern reveals an immense amount of information. The gap down bearish candle provides information needed to make an important short decision. The sellers want out of this position with great vigor. The 50-day moving average appears not to be a support level. The two weeks of Doji type trading started after a gap up. The gap down created an island reversal which is a very strong reversal signal. Numerous indecisive trading days foretell a strong downtrend. The bigger the number of indecisive signals, prior to a gap down in a trend, the stronger the new trend will be.

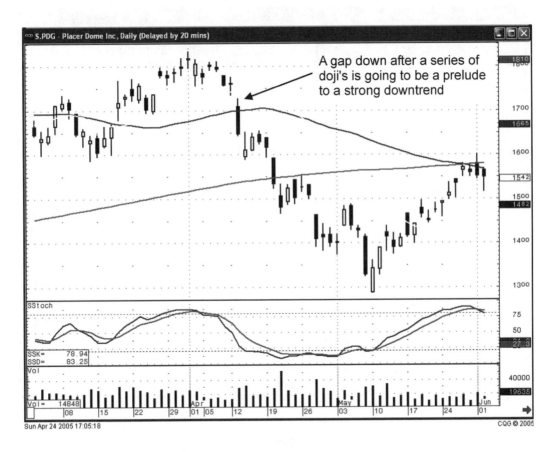

Fig 4-27 *Placer Dome Inc.*

Fig.4-28, the Legg Mason Inc. chart has the downtrend confirmed, after the Bearish Engulfing signal at the top, with the appearance of a gap down. Although the downtrend had temporary support at the 50-day moving average, there was a gap down after the candlestick reversal signal. This should have indicated the potential of additional selling. Until the stochastics had gotten into the oversold condition, an extremely strong candlestick 'buy' signal would have been required to negate the implications of the gap down.

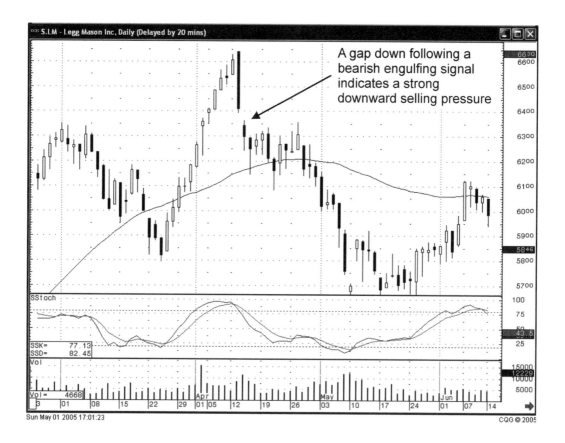

Fig. 4-28 *Legg Mason Inc.*

A gap down informs the investor that there is a selling force that is usually stronger than just a downward trend force. That information becomes built into the analysis. What will a trend do if it hits a support level soon after the gap down? As seen in the Legg Mason Inc. chart, what could be some consolidation, at what would be considered a support level, does not have any strength in the follow-through buying. A gap down indicates that the selling pressure should be substantial.

Fig. 4-29, The August Technology Corp. chart reveals the same type of pattern, a Bearish Engulfing signal followed by a gap down the next day. As illustrated in the previous chart describing a Doji, it is not unusual to see a Doji day after a reversal signal. This is the Bears conflicting with the last of the Bull buying after the signal. The fact that the open gaps down from the close of the Bearish Engulfing signal should immediately reveal that the sellers are anxious to get out of the stock.

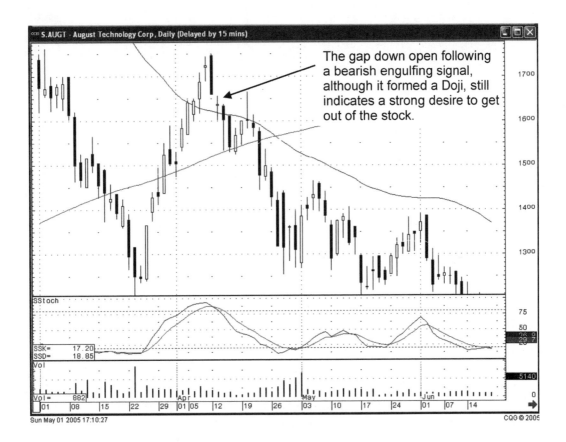

Fig. 4-29 *August Technology Corp.*

Being able to identify a candlestick reversal signal produces the visual advantage that the non-candlestick analyst do not have. Witnessing a gap down from a major signal formation provides much more confirmation.

Fig. 4-30, The Agnico-Eagle Mines Ltd. chart reveals the strength in which the sellers want to get out of the stock. The large Doji signal, followed by a gap down in price the next day, was a signal that the uptrend was over.

Fig. 4-30 *Agnico-Eagle*

Use a gap down at the top as a profitable indicator. A gap down indicates that the sellers are moving the downtrend with force. Especially when seen in over-bought conditions, a gap down produces an extremely high probability that the existing uptrend has now been reversed. The downtrend is going to move with significant strength.

Conclusion

High-profit gap trades occur in four predominant scenarios. The gap up after a bullish signal in oversold conditions! The gap up at the end of an uptrend! A gap down after a candlestick sell signal in overbought conditions! A gap down after an extended downtrend when stochastics are in an oversold condition! Each one of these gap situations can be exploited for high profit potential utilizing candlestick analysis. Simple scanning techniques as found on The candlestick forums training CDs make identifying each gapping scenario easy to find.

Once an investor becomes acquainted with gapping patterns, analyzing and implementing potentially high profit trades becomes an easy process. Applying the knowledge that a gap is an indication of investors wanting to enter or exit a trade with extraordinary force is the format for finding high profit situations. Utilize this knowledge to your advantage. When other investors may be hesitant to enter a trade after a gap, the knowledgeable candlestick investor can take advantage of the trade set up immediately. Utilize the statistical performance that is inferred when a candlestick signal is followed by a gap.

Chapter 5

Candlesticks with Technical Patterns

> *To steal ideas from one person is plagiarism; to steal from many is research.*
>
> *Wilson Mizner*

The simplest technical indicators can become powerful tools. Applying candlestick signals to the analysis of very simple indicators has beneficial ramifications. The easier an indicator can be identified visually, the more likely a large number of investors are watching what will happen at that level. The ability to identify candlestick signals at those important levels gives the candlestick investor immediate, valuable information.

A bullish candlestick signal forming right on a major trend line does not require the additional confirmation that most technical investors are waiting to see. Use simple patterns to your advantage. Use simple technical indicators to your advantage.

The Three-Wave Pattern

Prices move in patterns. This is a function of the multitude of investment criteria of the investment community. An investor places money into a position, based upon their individual investment goals. Whereas one investor may be buying for the long-term, the next investor may be in the position for a short term trade. Whatever the reasoning for an investor to commit funds to a trade, the price movement of any trading entity will be predicated upon the emotional sentiment of how that price movement reacts. Simply stated, the magnitude in which a price moves will create changes in investor sentiment.

A price that moves up too fast for normal expectations will cause profit taking to occur. A price that moves in a slower consistent fashion will have a different result in investor sentiment, causing a different pattern. The fact that prices move in patterns/waves is evident in the existence of technical analysis. Stochastics, Fibonacci numbers, Elliot Wave theory, trendlines and a host of other technical methods have been developed as a result of prices moving in predictable fashions.

The most predominant study of wave patterns comes from the Elliott Wave theory. Over 50 years ago, R.N. Elliott observed that price movements move in a series of dramatic patterns. He analyzed that these patterns were based upon the natural progression of the sentiment shift in mass investor psychology. These patterns or WAVES illustrated the oscillations between investor fear and greed.

Elliott observed various types of wave patterns. His research formulated two basic types of wave patterns. The impulse waves, waves which moved in the direction of the predominant trend of the market consisted of five smaller ways. The corrective waves, waves that moved counter to the main trend consisted of three smaller waves. Unfortunately, these two wave patterns are just the basic wave counts. The major difficulty of Elliot wave analysis is analyzing and correctly labeling which wave count is currently occurring. It is always difficult to define which wave count is in progress. Wave patterns can occur inside other wave patterns.

The wave patterns in the Elliot Wave analysis can also have variations to the basic wave patterns, having seven or nine wave counts. Even R.N. Elliott admitted that with the numerous variations of wave counts that could be applied to a trend, each trend could be analyzed differently, depending upon the initial wave analysis. He admitted that the interpretation of the wave counts could not always have a stringently defined set of rules.

Apparently there are students of the Elliot Wave analysis that have been able to convert their knowledge of how the waves perform. They can produce very good profits for their trading programs. The one consistent factor that successful Elliot wave analysts reveal is that to become successful at analyzing the waves profitably takes many years of experience. This is all well and good for those that want to spend many years in learning how to invest successfully.

For those investors that want investment methods that can be learned and used effectively in a much shorter period of time, there are aspects of waves that are much easier to utilize. Using candlestick signals in a three-wave pattern becomes much more productive. A three-wave pattern can be defined as any wave pattern that starts from a point where a new wave or trend becomes apparent. This approach makes the wave pattern a projection element versus an anticipatory element.

The candlestick signals remained the main analytical tool for identifying a trend reversal. The three-way pattern becomes a projection tool for how that new trend may perform. A three-wave pattern has a few different identifiable moves. As illustrated in Fig.5-1, a trend can move up and then pullback. The third leg of the trend now moves back up to test or exceed the previous high.

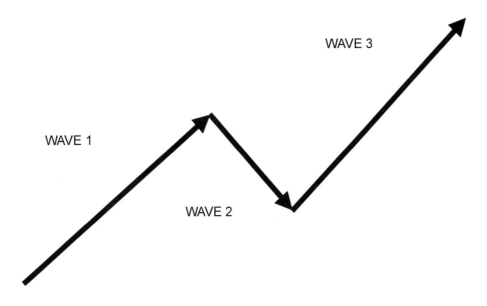

Fig 5-1

A trend can also move up, with the following leg 2 moving sideways until leg three begins the final leg of the pattern as seen in Fig. 5-2. This sideways movement, once observed, can have some timing elements built into it. That timing can be a result of the stochastics retracing to the oversold area and curling back up. Then a candlestick 'buy' signal appears at the end of a flat trading period. The end of the flat trading can also be correlated to the intersecting of a major moving average. Most importantly, being able to visually identify the three-wave pattern set-up allows the candlestick investor to exploit the proper timing of getting back into a trade.

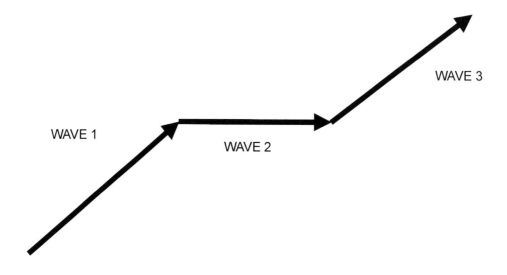

Fig 5-2

The same analysis can be made on trends in a downward direction. A downward leg will be followed with a bounce upwards. Then the final leg continues down to test or breach the recent low, fig. 5-3.

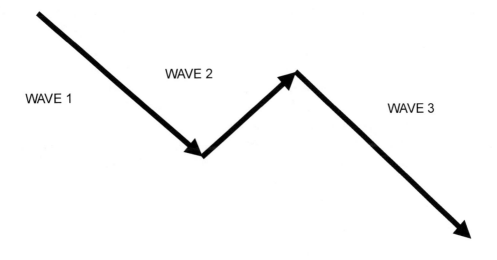

WAVE 2

WAVE 1

WAVE 3

Fig. 5-3

As in the upward trend, a three-wave pattern can be a down leg, a flat trading area, followed by the next leg to the downsideas shown in Fig. 5-4.

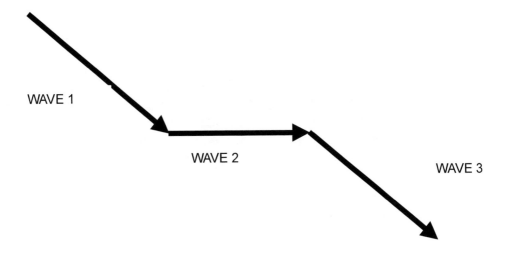

WAVE 1

WAVE 2

WAVE 3

Fig. 5- 4

Anticipating how a wave pattern is developing provides the candlestick investor with valuable information. It allows for the potential viewing of candlestick signals at specific times, knowing that a leg of a wave pattern is forming. This may seem very elementary. However, with the well-established knowledge that prices move in waves; then being prepared for a candlestick signal and a new leg of a wave pattern creates excellent timing characteristics.

Does a three-wave pattern always perform clearly? Not always, but often enough to know to start looking for the next pattern. Keep in mind, the candlestick signals are the main parameter for entry or exiting a trade. The wave pattern is to provide a game plan for when those signals could appear. The advantage provided by candlestick signals is the more defined reversal points. Whereas Elliot wave analysts may want to hold a position through wave one to five, the candlestick investor has the advantage of selling at the top of wave one, then buying back at the end of wave two, etc. This produces much better use of the invested funds, not losing equity during the pullbacks.

> *"Think simple"* as my old master used to say – meaning reduce the whole of its parts into the simplest term, getting back to first principles.
> **Frank Lloyd Wright**

Keep your wave count simple. Profits are not made by being able to proficiently count wave counts. Profits are made by effectively buying at the proper time and selling at the proper time. Utilizing candlestick signals, then evaluating what the wave movements might be, will greatly enhance your profitability.

Fig. 5-5, the Arch Coal Inc chart illustrates a three-wave pattern. Wave 2, the pullback in early June has a clear support level probability, the 50-day moving average. The Bearish Engulfing signal forming on June 2 becomes the obvious sell signal as the stochastics have finally climbed into the overbought area.

The 50-day moving average becomes the obvious target. That target experiences some indecisive candlestick signals at mid-June. The Doji/Harami, a small hammer that goes below the 50-day moving average, then closes above the 50-day moving average, and the Inverted Hammer/Doji, all trading at the 50-day moving average, provides a visual evaluation that the Bears are having

a difficult time pushing the price below that level. The buying confirmation the following day provides an excellent trade entry indicator. The low for that day also touched the 50-day moving average before revealing that the Bulls had stepped in.

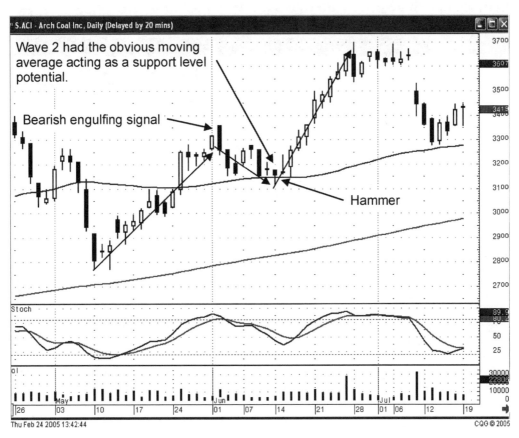

Fig.5-5 *Arch Coal Inc.*

These signals, followed by a bullish trading day, caused the stochastics to turn up, and provide a good visual picture of investor sentiment. This becomes a 'buy' area when analyzing that leg-three of a three-wave pattern could be developing. The analysis becomes the anticipation that if there is no resistance at the recent high, a good strong move could be occurring from these levels. The upside potential is good. The downside risk is minimal. A close below the 50-day moving average from this point would be the 'stop.'

Fig. 5-6, The Biosante Pharmaceuticals Inc. chart demonstrates a three-wave pattern with a sideways movement. The series of Doji illustrate that although the buying had stopped, the selling pressure was not overwhelming. An investor may not want to sit through this period, having money exposed to a possible pullback. However, the bullish candle after the final Doji reveals which way investor sentiment wants to go after a flat trading period of indecision. If the position had been closed during the Doji, then buying back upon seeing the new buying strength, becomes a good decision anticipating that the third-leg of a three-wave pattern is starting.

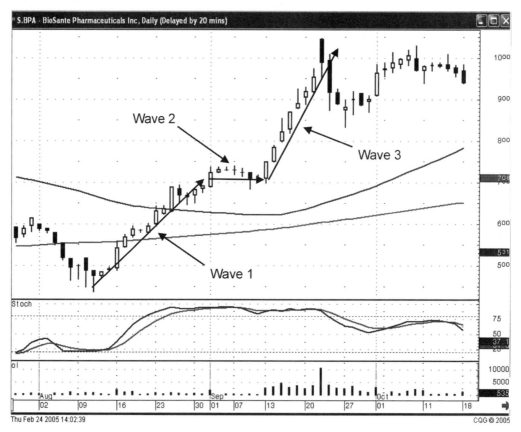

Fig. 5-6 *BioSante Pharmaceuticals* Inc.

Being able to analyze a sideways movement, after viewing a series of Doji, allows for an intelligent decision to be made. The end of the series of Doji was going to either reveal investors selling, creating a top, or a bullish signal would begin the formation of a three-wave pattern.

In either case, an investment decision could be made with a high probability outcome. This analysis is nothing more than being mentally prepared for what could occur. Having been mentally prepared creates the opportunity to take advantage of the next price move. The execution of the next trade can be done quickly and decisively.

Using Trendlines with Candlestick Analysis

One of the most commonly used indicators is the trend line. Trend Lines are visually apparent levels where support or resistance has been occurring. Technical analysis is built upon the premise of identifying trends. They are one of the most important tools for both identifying a trend and confirming the existence of that trend. They are the simplest indicators to place on a chart. When analyzing any chart, the eye can usually distinguish an area where a line could be drawn across the bottoms or the tops.

The basis of a trendline is that it is formed when connecting at least two points. The more points that fall upon that line, whether actually drawn or visually evaluated, the greater the confirmation that the trend is being affected by that trendline. Many of the principles that are applied to other support and resistance indicators can also be applied to trendlines.

Many technical analysts require that a trend line be confirmed by at least three points touching that line. A rising trend line is identified with successively higher low price points. The rising slope is now considered a support level. The Bulls are in control, providing demand every time prices come back to test the trendline. As long as the prices remain above the up trending trendline, the uptrend is considered intact.

As illustrated in Fig. 5-7, the March crude oil chart, a Bearish Engulfing signal appeared when the stochastics still indicated more upside potential. The trendline drawn from the top of the October high through the recent top at the January high can now be viewed as an important resistance. The candlestick "sell" signal provides an 'alert' for selling to appear at this level when the stochastics indicated that there was still more upside to this trend.

Fig. 5-7 *March Crude Oil*

Had this trendline not been acknowledged prior to the Bearish Engulfing signal appearing, going back to analyze the chart after the Bearish Engulfing signal appeared provides an additional technical parameter for evaluating what the price of crude oil may do from this point. This is a case of using the trend-line to add credence to a candlestick signal.

This falling trendline acts as the resistance level. The Bears are in control, stepping up their selling every time the price comes up to the resistance area.

As long as prices remain below the declining trendline, the downtrend is considered to be in affect.

The use of computers has refined the use of trendlines in recent years. The accuracy of drawing trendlines on a computer screen is much greater than using a pencil and a ruler on a printed chart. The width of the pencil lead versus a slight change of angle of a manually drawn line could dramatically alter a trend lines relevance. Today's computer generated charts can establish a trend line using the exact tops and bottoms of price moves. This would become very important for those investors that were anticipating a breakout of a trendline support or resistance level.

The strength of a trend becomes a function of how many times prices bounce back up above the trendline. As mentioned, a trendline can start by drawing a line between two points and extending that line into the future. If that trend is to continue, then future prices should support or resist at that line. That becomes the primary basis for trend analysis. The candlestick signals dramatically increase the evaluation potential at the support or resistance line. Where most investors are "anticipating" a result at that trendline, the candlestick analyst can get an immediately clear picture of what investor sentiment is doing at the trendline. This not only provides valuable investment information, it provides that information much earlier than what other investors are able to glean from the trading at that level.

The disadvantage of using trendline analysis on its own is the different interpretations of which trendline is most relevant. Establishing that a trendline can be formed by two, three, and more points being used to develop a trendline, there is the possibility that different combinations of those points can create a short-term trend, medium-term trend, or long-term trend. The question now becomes which trendline is providing the correct analysis for support and resistance. Utilizing the candlestick signals assists in recognizing which trend-line is the prominent trendline.

Developing a trading strategy utilizing the candlestick signals at the trend lines becomes much more decisive. If a trendline is anticipated to be acting as a support, and that is being confirmed by a candlestick buy signal, purchasing the trading entity at that level produces a couple quick distinctions. The candlestick signal allows the investor to enter a trade at a highly opportune time. It also provides a logical stop loss strategy. If the buy signal occurs on a trendline, implying that the uptrend is going to continue from that point, then prices immediately coming back down through the trendline, the support level, alerts the investor to close out the position immediately. This should not be a difficult concept. If the indicators that had been working previously appear to work once again but immediately reverse and fail, then a major support level has been breached, immediately indicating the buying that showed support is not present where it is supposed to be seen.

Fig. 5-8, The Hansen Natural Corp. chart illustrates an ascending trendline. After two or three times of coming back to a level that appears to be in a straight line, the eye can start to visually detect what would appear to be a trendline forming.

Fig. 5-8 *Hansen Natural Corp.*

Drawing a line from those points now becomes a potential target for each pullback that occurs. Being that the visual analysis is easy for most investors to perceive, a trendline becomes an important technical factor. As viewed in the Hansen Natural chart, any future pullbacks to the trendline become an obvious spot to watch for candlestick signals. Having the mental image of where support might occur and being able to visually recognize candlestick buy signals allows the candlestick analyst to make better decisions for entering a trade.

Trendlines can be developed by using points in the past that all appear to be lining up. If a number of points line up from two different time frames or more, the chart might have different trendlines that could be relevant. Which one of those trendlines should be heeded? The candlestick signals make the answer very easy. If there is more than one trendline to be considered, then the candlestick signals will help identify which trendline has importance. This is just a simple function of seeing where a candlestick 'buy' signal has formed. Fig, 5-9, The General Cable Corp. chart illustrates a couple of trendlines that have been created from previous bottoms. Which trendline will work effectively for the period we are looking at right now? The signals will tell you which trendline should be currently considered.

As seen in the General Cable Corp. chart, during an expanded time frame, there are two trendlines that appear to act as support levels.

Fig. 5-9 *General Cable Corp. longer-term chart*

Once the long-term chart, Fig.5-10, has established important trendlines, the analysis of what to do currently is better visualized by shortening the timeframe of the chart. This better illustrates what is currently occurring in the price pattern.

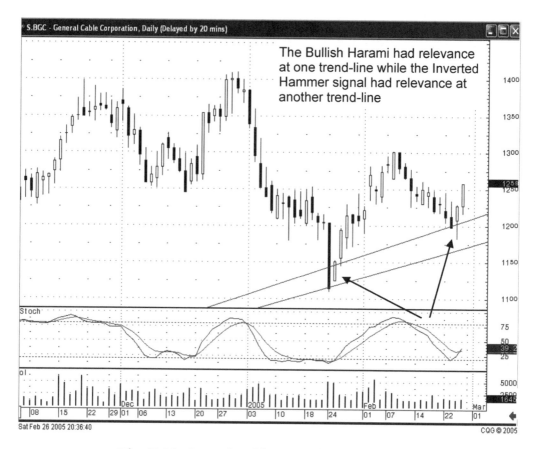

Fig. 5-10 *General Cable Corp. short-term chart*

Making the chart bigger for better visualization, it can be clearly seen which trendline is affecting the current price. In this case, the Inverted Hammer is being confirmed at the upper trendline.

This may seem very elementary, but it is what is occurring at trendline levels that are being observed by many investors. The candlestick signals confirm immediately what is happening at an observed level.

Trendlines also become important factors when acting as resistance levels. Fig. 5-11, The Magnum Hunter Resources chart provides a simple illustration of what occurs every time prices approached a specific trendline. It became apparent that every time a peek was reached in June, July, and August, candlestick sell signals appeared. Mid-September revealed candlestick formations that did not show weakness at the trendline. This becomes important information for the candlestick investor. The fact that a bullish candle formation breaches what had obviously been a resistance trendline reveals that there is new investor sentiment.

A bullish breakthrough as revealed by the candle formations demonstrates that the trendline resistance has now become a non-factor. If this position was purchased, based on bullish candle signals forming at important moving averages, the decision process should be to take profits at the obvious resistance level. That decision now becomes different once the resistance level is broken. Simply stated, the lack of a candlestick 'sell' signal where a 'sell' signal is expected provides a new evaluation.

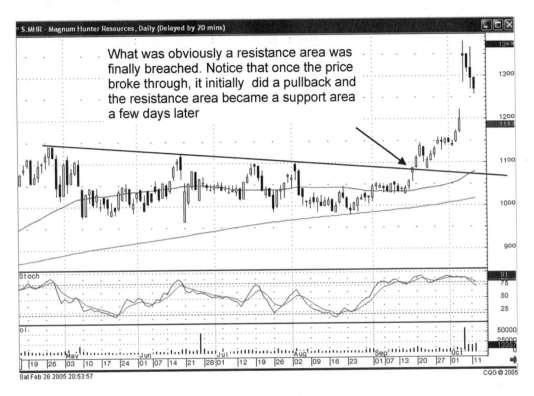

Fig. 5-11 *Magnum Hunter Resources*

If trendlines are creating obvious formations, such as pennant formations or ascending triangles, etc., then a breakout from those patterns can be better analyzed when viewing the candlestick formations. This is not a complex procedure. This is using the simple visual analysis of investor sentiment at previous levels that would indicate buying and selling.

Fig. 5-12 The DJ Orthopedics Inc. chart illustrates a Triangle formation that is breached to the upside. When viewing the longer term chart, it becomes relatively clear that there is a triangle pattern forming. If those trendlines are brought forward into a shorter term chart, the analysis is easy to formulate once one of those trendlines is breached.

Fig. 5-12 *DJ Orthopedics Inc. long term chart*

In the short-term chart Fig. 5-13 (following page), it becomes apparent with the large bullish candle that the trendline is now no longer a resistance level. The fact that the Bulls pushed through that trendline with great force reveals important information. That information now creates a new evaluation of what the trend might be for the future of this stock. Although a sell signal was created the day after the break through, with a Bearish Harami, a pullback stopped at what had been the resistance trendline, with it now becoming a support level. The fact that the trading was now above the descending trendline should bring a different evaluation into this stock. The candlestick signals are still the most relevant factors for trading decisions, but the overall trend analysis will have changed.

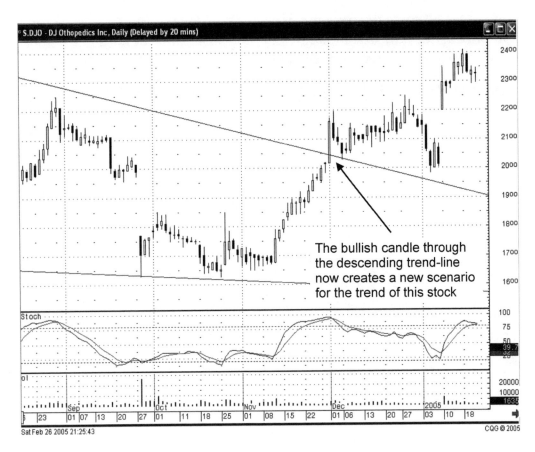

Fig. 5-13 *DJ Orthopedics Inc. short term chart*

Keep in mind, when everybody is watching to see what will happen at important technical levels, the candlestick analyst has the advantage of immediately seeing what the investor sentiment is doing at those levels.

Fig.5-14, The Phelps Dodge Corp. chart reveals a bullish candle that broke out through what had been a resistance trendline. The bullish candle of the previous day, followed by a bullish candle with a gap up becomes very revealing. What is the future of the price of this stock? Who knows! But the evaluation of this price move now becomes different, knowing that a trend line resistance congestion area has now been broken.

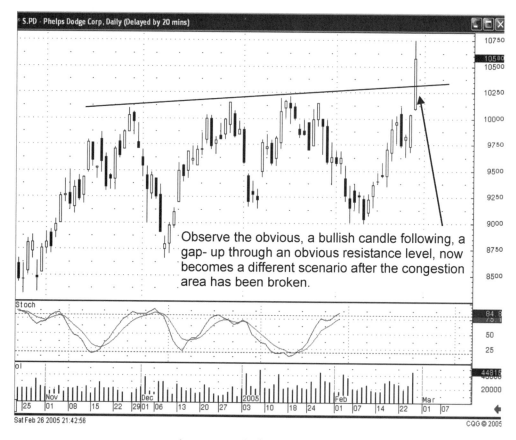

Fig. 5-14 *Phelps Dodge Corp.*

Trendlines can be used to analyze what candlestick signals "might" be occurring in the near future. As seen in Fig. 5-15, the Warnaco Group Co. chart, the price move has become extended up to one of the obvious trend lines. The price closed remarkably close to that trendline on a big bullish candle day. This alerts the candlestick investor to a couple of possibilities. Seeing strength the following day should reveal that the next trendline might be the target. A weaker open on the following day may reveal this trendline as the resistance level. A Bearish Harami would signify that the buying had stopped. This, occurring at that trendline, would be more confirmation to take profits.

Fig. 5-15 *Warnaco Group Corp.*

An ascending triangle chart, as seen in Fig. 5-16, the KCS Energy Inc. chart provides important information. The trendlines being drawn across the top and the bottom of the trading pattern should reveal the simple patterns in which that this stock characteristically trades. Once that trading pattern has been breached, a new evaluation can be made for the price movement. Having the advantage of knowing that the trend is now in a new stage of development, in this case a bullish move, the use of candlestick signals becomes more effective. They can be used knowing that an uptrend is in progress. The potential of the trend should continue until a definite candlestick 'sell' signal appears. Or a pullback could occur, testing the recent resistance level. Having the knowledge of what could potentially happen after a breakout allows the use of candlestick signals to enhance the probabilities of being in the correct direction of the trade. This is nothing more than putting the probabilities more into the investors favor.

Fig. 5-16 *KCS energy Inc. long-term chart*

Fig. 5-17 *KCS Energy Inc. short-term chart*

Fibonacci Numbers

Leonardo de Pisa, Fibonacci to his friends, was a 12th century monk that discovered a fascinating reoccurring sequence that appeared in both mathematical formulas and nature. While studying the Great Pyramid of Gizeh, he discovered a unique ratio of numbers. The series of numbers 1, 1, 2, 3, 5, 8, 13, 21, 34, 55, 89, 144, 233, 377, 610 etc. is created a by adding the first two numbers together to get the third and that process continuing in sequence.

For example: 1+1=2, 1+2=3, 2+3=5, 3+5=8, 5+8=13, 8+13=21, 13+21=34, etc. A very interesting ratio is produced with this numbered sequence. If each number is divided by the number following it in the sequence, it produces a remarkably constant ratio. That ratio value is 0.6180345. It has been referred to as "the golden ratio". These ratios have been found in many studies whether in mathematics or in nature's natural series of events. A large majority of leaf patterns involve ratios of space that correlate exactly with the Fibonacci numbers.

How these numbers are derived is not nearly as important as knowing that they do work consistently in nature, which includes human nature. The application of this number to technical analysis has become an important determinant of support and resistance levels. The common Fibonacci numbers are 38.2%, 50%, and 61.8%. The repetitious results that have become apparent through centuries of investment habits indicate that these numbers are significant when applied to human emotions.

These numbers have become important pivotal points when analyzing retracement of a trend. How these numbers were derived is much less important in understanding that they do have great relevance to many technical investors. The Fibonacci numbers are the crucial numbers for the Elliot wave analysis. Realizing that many technical investors use these critical levels to anticipate reversals, it makes sense to utilize these potential reversal levels when applying candlestick signals.

Fibonacci Retracements

- Fibonacci Retracements are based on a trendline drawn between a sustained trough and peak.
- If a trend is rising, the retracement lines will descend from 100% to 0%
- If a trend is declining falling, the retracement lines will move up from 0% to 100%
- Horizontal lines can be drawn at the common Fibonacci levels of 38%, 50%, & 62%
- As the price retraces, support and resistance occur at or near the Fibonacci Retracement levels with a high degree of accuracy.

If the 38%, 50%, and 62% area are known to be retracement levels that many technical investors are watching, then it makes sense to analyze what candlestick signals might be occurring at any one of those levels. The advantage of being able to read the candlestick formations is very beneficial. It allows an investor to evaluate immediately which one of these levels is going to act as support or resistance. That knowledge allows the candlestick investor to position themselves ahead of other technical analysts that need confirmation that a specific level has held. For the daytrader, utilizing this knowledge can be highly profitable when trading the index futures. Being able to enter a trade at the exact optimal level provides a very high-profit, low-risk trading platform. Utilizing the Fibonacci number levels can be used as a primary trade entry system or it can be added as an additional entry parameter. Where will a pullback stop? If a trend pattern can be recognized, then watching for the candlestick signals at support levels that other investors are watching can prepare the investor for when a reversal should occur.

As seen in Fig. 5-18, the PLX Technology chart, a strong uptrend was followed by a pullback. To identify where that pullback should stop, applying the obvious technical indicators increases the probabilities of being in a correct trade. The PLX technology chart illustrates the effective use of candlestick signals with the Fibonnacci numbers. After an extended uptrend, a pull back occurs.

Fig. 5-18 *PLX Technology Inc.*

Where can a pull back be expected to stop? The moving average becomes a possibility. Putting Fibonacci numbers on the chart becomes a logical target.

Witnessing a Doji just barely touching the 38% retracement level becomes the point to start watching for a reversal. A Doji, followed by a Bullish Engulfing signal, reveals that buying started right at an important technical level.

Is the 38% Fibonacci retracement level a place to watch for a reversal? Not necessarily! The candlestick reversal signals are the primary decision making factors. Placing the Fibonacci retracement levels on the candlestick chart adds another element for indicating that a reversal has occurred.

Increase Your Probabilities

Utilizing the candlestick signals in conjunction with any other technical indicator increases the probabilities of being in a correct trade. The simple and obvious technical indicators are the most productive. When the least experienced investor can identify important levels on a chart, it has to be obvious to everybody. Knowing that a candlestick reversal signal demonstrates immediate information on investor sentiment, a candlestick investor is provided with a very efficient analytical tool. A major candlestick reversal signal, occurring right where everybody is watching for a reversal, allows an investor to take immediate advantage of a trend change. Observe the obvious.

Chapter 6

High Profit Patterns Enhanced with Candlestick Signals

> *To him that watches, everything is revealed.*
>
> *Italian Proverb*

The effectiveness of candlestick signals stem from one basic factor. Human emotions! When applied to investment decisions, human emotions produce signals. Technical analysis, in general, is the result of price patterns forming recurring patterns. The ebb and flow of investor decision-making processes have produced a multitude of technical indicators. The utilization of these indicators is the result of recognizing statistically favorable price movements. Indicators, such as stochastics, Fibonacci numbers, Elliot Wave, and many other technical analytical tools exist because they identified recurring price patterns.

Most technical analysis is the anticipation of price behavior at specific levels. The Fibonacci investor is expecting something to occur at the 38% retracement, 50% retracement, or the 62% retracement level. The 'stochastics' investor will buy when the slow stochastics and the fast stochastics cross each other in the oversold condition. An investor, utilizing trend-lines, will buy or sell when a price confirms a reversal at those levels.

A major benefit of candlestick signals is the illustration of what investors are doing right at that time. Applying candlestick signals to other technical methods dramatically increases the probabilities of being in a correct trade. Instead of anticipating, then waiting for confirmation of a trend reversal at a major technical level, an investor can immediately analyze what investor sentiment is doing right at that level. This allows for entry and exit strategies to be implemented at opportune times or levels.

An additional benefit of the candlestick signals is the ability to recognize a high-profit pattern in the process of forming. Having the ability to visually analyze a high-profit pattern formation allows for the preparation of entering a trade at a low-risk level. Entering a trade in the early stages of a reversal pattern makes the stop-loss strategy easier to implement. A failure of the pattern permits an investor to close out a trade with minimal losses.

Recognizing the components of a high-profit pattern allows an investor to take profits when it is time to take profits. It also allows the investor to re-enter the trade when the pattern indicates further profitability. This ability greatly reduces the risk factors.

J-Hook Pattern

A J-hook pattern (J-hook) is a variation of a wave 1 — 2 — 3 pattern. It becomes an easy pattern to identify with the use of candlestick signals. The problem most investors have is understanding when to sell after a price has made a strong move. The J-hook pattern demonstrates some easily identifiable attributes. First, it starts with a strong uptrend that usually produces "stronger than normal" returns in a very short period of time. This strong up move is significant enough to create the normal wave pattern. A reversal caused by profit taking, followed by a declining trajectory of the pullback, then the continuation of the uptrend. The J-hook pattern is the description of the pullback that starts to round out at a bottom and starts moving back up, thus forming a 'hook.'

This pattern provides the candlestick investor with some very simple profitable applications. The first uptrend will usually show clear candlestick 'sell' signals when it comes to an end. The top may be formed with the stochastics in the overbought, or very close to the overbought area. Because of the strong initial uptrend, the first evidence of 'sell' signals should be acknowledged. Even if it is suspected that the uptrend could be forming a J-hook pattern, why risk remaining in the trade? When a sell signal becomes evident take your profits.

What criteria makes a candlestick investor suspect a J-hook pattern will form? The analysis of the market trends in general should provide that information. For example, if a stock price had a strong run up while the market indexes had a steady uptrend, and the market indexes do not appear to be ready for a significant pullback, then a strong stock move could warrant some profit taking before the next move up. The benefit of being able to identify candlestick signals is being prepared for some candlestick 'buy' signals after a few days of pullback. These signals would also alter the trajectory of the stochastics that will be pulling back.

Witnessing Doji, Hammers, Inverted Hammers or Bullish Harami after a few days of a pullback becomes an alert that the selling is starting to wane. If the stochastics are flattening out during that same timeframe, then a set-up for a J-hook pattern is taking place. Taking profits when the first sell signals occur in the initial uptrend eliminates the downside risk. Those candlestick 'sell' signals indicate that it is time to get out of the trade. Even though the strength of the initial move would warrant suspecting a J-hook pattern to form, there is no guarantee that the pullback could not retrace 20%, 40%, 60%, or even greater of the initial move up.

This creates a trading strategy that allows an investor to utilize the common sense built into the candlestick signals. When it is time to get out, get out! If after four days, small candlestick buy signals start forming, there is nothing wrong with buying back into the position. The second entry of this trade now has some targets that can be clearly defined. The first target should be the test of the recent high. Although it may not be a huge percentage return moving to that level, at least the probabilities indicate that it should be profitable.

The benefit of candlestick signals once again can be applied if and when that recent high is tested. Witnessing another sell signal, as the price approaches the recent high trading level, would be a clear indication that the recent high was going to act as resistance. This would induce taking quick profits and getting back out of the trade. On the other hand, if strong signals are seen as the recent high is breached, that would be a clear indication the high was not going to act as a resistance level. A new leg of the trend may be in progress.

Note the J-hook pattern in Fig. 6-1, the Loews Corporation chart. Once the trend started up, the pattern formed when the price pulled back for a few days.

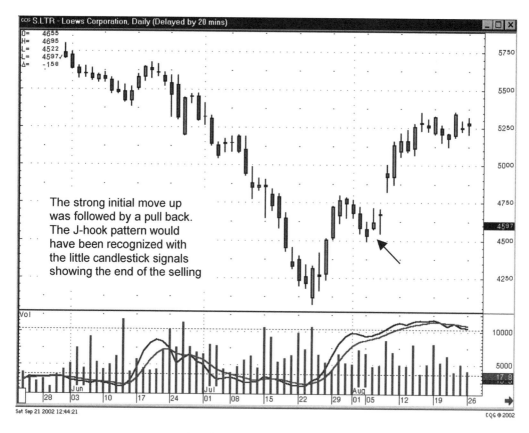

Fig. 6-1 *Loews Corporation*

However, the stochastics never reached the oversold area and they came down only part way before hooking back up. The signals indicated buying before it pulled back too much, showing the buyers were going to test the high of the previous week. The gap above the recent high indicated that the buyers were very anxious to see prices go to much higher prices. Recognizing this pattern and the elements that form it allows an investor to move decisively at the right points of a trend. Being prepared for the pattern and knowing what signals to look for, creates opportunities to participate in a profitable trend while greatly reducing risk.

Where will the pullback move to? Sometimes that is obvious, sometimes it is not. Yet there are indicators that can at least provide a target for a J-hook pullback.

In the example of the Diamond Offshore Drilling Inc. chart, Fig. 6-2, the 50-day moving average becomes the obvious support level. Although the stochastics have not moved back down to the oversold condition, it becomes apparent with the Bullish Engulfing pattern, followed a few days later by a Doji and a gap-up day, the potential of a J-hook pattern is starting.

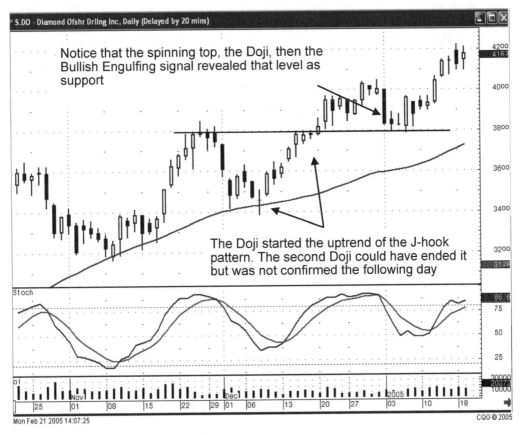

Fig. 6-2 *Diamond Offshore Drilling Inc.*

Some patterns become very easy to recognize and things do not have to be made complicated. "Buy" signals, occurring at a major technical support level, even though the stochastics are only part way down toward the oversold area, should be recognized for their potential. Buying in the $35 area should be done with the anticipation that the price could reasonably test the recent high at the $38 area. Once again, the benefit of candlestick signals is being able to determine whether the $38 level will become a resistance level or not. The Doji could have been the resistance signal had the prices opened lower the following day.

Seeing prices move higher the following day would have been an indication that there was no selling at the recent high level. More upside from that point now became a good probability.

As a side-note, the uptrend, at $40 a share, indicated the potential pull-back, but notice how the recent resistance level, the $38 area now becomes the support level. The Spinning Top, the Doji, and then the Bullish Engulfing signal provided the visual information that the $38 area was now acting as support.

Fig.6-3, The Valero Energy Corp. Inc. chart is an illustration of a potential J-hook pattern move. As the candlestick buy signals appear, the Hammer, followed a few days by later the Piercing signal, and the stochastics start curling up, the recent high becomes the first potential target.

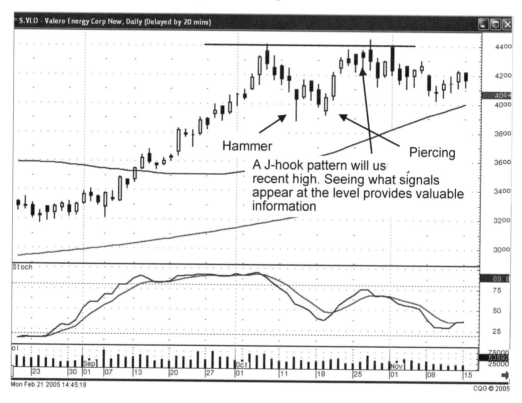

Fig. 6-3 *The Valero Energy Corp. Inc.*

In this case, the candlestick sell signals make it apparent that the $44 area is not going to be broken. The Spinning Tops, Hanging Man, and Dark Cloud signals, as stochastics are starting back down, revealed that the buyers have run out of strength. The evidence of buying strength would have been revealed with more white candle bodies. The presence of the black candle signals becomes our message that the buying strength is waning at the $44 area.

Fig. 6-4, The Excel Maritime Carrier chart provides an opportunity to take advantage of a J-hook pattern. Whether an investor was involved in the initial move or not, the fact that a potential J-hook pattern could be forming can produce calculated profits in the next move. Buying into this stock at about the $12.50 area still has a viable probability that the $15 area will be tested once again.

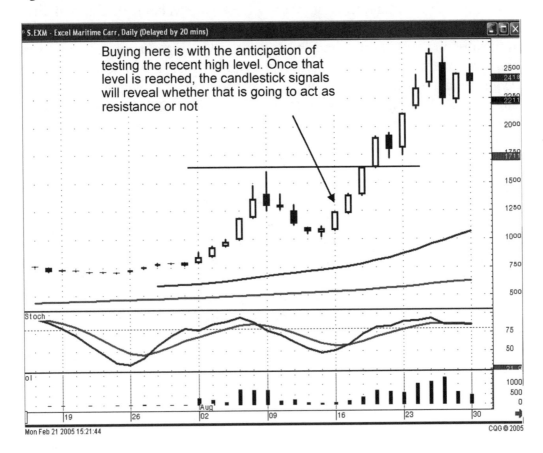

Fig. 6-4 *Excel Maritime Carriers*

A $2.00 to $2.50 move is still worth the attempt. If prices gap back up to the $15 area and candlesticks sell signals started appearing, then it would be a logical deduction that this move was not heading to new highs. However, a $2.00 move on a $12.50 price is still a reasonable percentage return. But, as illustrated in the EXM chart, the resistance level at the $15 area was breached with a large bullish candle. This should reveal immediately that new high levels were going to be attempted. This makes participating in a J-hook pattern very rewarding. Somewhat rewarding, even if it fails at the recent highs, with additional explosive return potential if the recent high is breached.

Does the J-hook pattern always allow an investor to sell at one level and buy back in lower? Not always! However, keep in mind that the point of investing is to maintain the practice of maximizing your profits for your account, not necessarily maximizing profits for each individual trade.

As illustrated in Fig.6-5, the Audible Inc. chart, the high-probability trade was taking profits on the confirmed selling after the Bearish Engulfing signal. Buying back, upon the formation of the J-hook pattern being established, may have been done at a higher price. Candlestick analysis does not attempt to buy at the absolute lowest point and sell at the absolute highest point. Candlestick analysis illustrates when it is time to buy and when it is time to sell. That definitely eliminates the possibility, most of the time, of buying in at the absolute bottom. The 'buy' signals indicate a high-probability 'time to buy' in a trend. The time to sell does not come at the absolute top. The time to sell comes in the top "range".

Understanding the mechanics of a J-hook pattern allows an investor to take profits after the initial move. This has the investor out of a trend that "potentially" could pullback to much lower levels. When the signals indicate the pullback is over, establishing a new position has the investor in a trend that should be moving in the anticipated direction. Not participating in all of a move that a trend offers reduces investor risk dramatically. Selling at one level, when the candlestick signals indicate that is time to sell and buying back when the signals/pattern tells the investor it is time to buy, even if at a higher price, is the cost of insuring that your investment funds are always participating in high probability trades.

Why own stock if the signals show a high-probability that it could be heading back down? Sell it! If a J-hook pattern forms, buy it back.

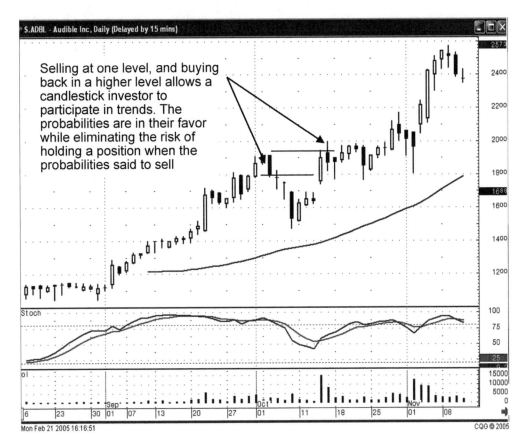

Fig. 6-5 *Audible Inc.*

The benefit of the candlestick signals is that they reveal when a pullback is not occurring with great enthusiasm. When an uptrend moved with inordinate force, a pullback with greater magnitude can be expected. Viewing small candlestick "buy" signals, a few days after a pullback has occurred, at least provides the inkling that the pullback may just be profit taking. As the downward trajectory of the pullback starts flattening out, watch for more buy signals. When the trend starts moving up, a new position can be established.

Fig. 6-6 (following page), The Affiliated Managers Group Inc. chart demonstrated a good strong move to the upside, followed by a week of trading that lacked decisiveness. The Bullish Engulfing signal, correlating with the stochastics curling back up, would have been a signal that the sellers were getting out of the way. The strength of the candle following the Bullish Engulfing signal would have revealed that the uptrend should now be continuing.

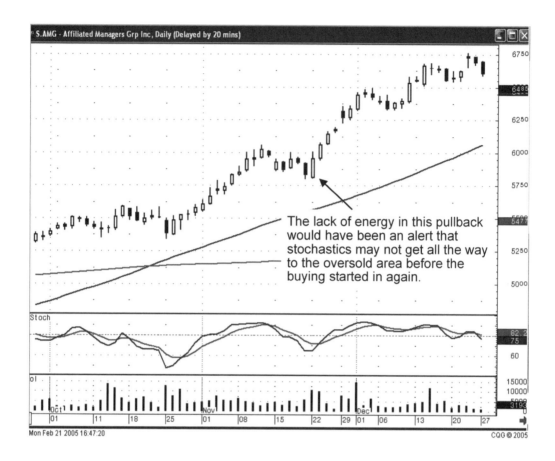

The lack of energy in this pullback would have been an alert that stochastics may not get all the way to the oversold area before the buying started in again.

Fig. 6-6 *Affiliated Managers Group Inc.*

The J-hook pattern should be analyzed in conjunction with what the markets are doing in general. The market indexes can be analyzed by themselves. After a strong rally, a profit-taking period is to be expected. Having the benefit of the candlestick signals allows an investor to better decipher whether the rally has ended. A full-scale reversal may have occurred. However, seeing some candlestick buy signals after a few days of pullback allows the candlestick investor to formulate a strategy. That strategy should involve deciding whether to short heavily in that market or be prepared to re-establish long positions.

Once candlestick buy signals start appearing in a market index chart, giving the indication that a J-hook pattern could appear, prepares the investor mentally to move one way or the other. If short positions were established at the first sell signals in the trend, being prepared for the covering of those positions can be better executed when a J-hook pattern formation is anticipated.

Individual stock positions have the additional benefit of the market trend itself in evaluating the potential J-hook pattern. If during the market uptrend, a stock price has moved up with greater magnitude than the market trend in general, that becomes the first alert. Simply, that stock trend is inordinately strong. A pullback occurring in that stock, when the market trend appears to be continuing, also gives rise to watching for a J-hook pattern to occur.

Fig. 6-7 The Cameco Corp. chart illustrates a J-hook pattern that is confirmed with a Bullish Engulfing signal. The continued buying, the following day, provides a good indication that they are going to test the recent high.

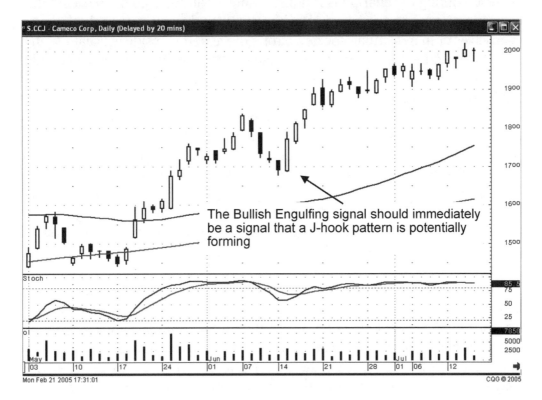

Fig 6-7 *Cameco Corp.*

This may not result in a very large percentage return if the sell signals appeared at the recent high. However, the probabilities could be better justified if the market trend in general was moving in a slow bullish fashion. It makes entering a trade more appealing when market conditions do not show any severe selling and a strong moving stock is about to break out to new levels on a J-hook pattern.

This may seem very elementary, but this allows the candlestick analyst to make some very simple, quick evaluations. The whole point of candlestick investing is exactly that; making high-probability trade evaluations in a very short timeframe, within minutes every afternoon.

J-Hook Summary

The J-hook pattern should be remembered as a high profit trade potential. As discussed during the chart illustrations, a J-hook pattern is going to occur after witnessing a very strong move in price. Whether that price is in the indexes themselves or in individual stocks, a strong move to the upside is usually going to be followed by some profit taking. Being able to analyze whether that pullback is profit taking or a true reversal is easily analyzed when applying the candlestick signals.

The J-hook pattern is more often going to be found in market conditions where the trend is moving steadily in one direction. The stronger than normal percentage move is the first major criteria for a J-hook pattern to occur. Once a candlestick sell signal appears, after an extended strong move, the candlestick investor wants to watch for candlestick 'buy' signals to begin appearing. The signals do not necessarily need to be big, strong signals. Small volatility days of Doji, Hammers, and Inverted Hammers or Bullish Engulfing signals provide the indication that the selling is losing strength. As they occur, the stochastics should start showing a flattening of the downward trajectory.

Upon seeing the downward trajectory in the price flattening out, an investor can now start watching for the next candlestick buy signal that starts moving price in an upward direction. When that occurs, establishing a position is based upon the price testing the recent high, prior to the pullback. At that level, a decision can be made. If candlestick sell signals start appearing near the recent high, it becomes obvious that the recent high is going to act as resistance. The trade can be closed out immediately. On the other hand, if the candles indicate buying, going through the recent high, it becomes a clear indication that the recent high will not act as resistance. The move into a higher ground can now be expected. This move will usually produce a move up with the same magnitude as the first move up before the J-hook pullback. The likelihood of a

J-hook pattern is a function of the market conditions in general. The longer and more steady an uptrend in the general markets, the more likely J-hook patterns will become present.

The Fry-Pan Bottom

The Fry-Pan Bottom pattern is aptly named. It does not take a high degree of technical analysis to figure out the investor sentiment that forms a Fry-Pan Bottom. This pattern gets its name because it looks like a Fry-pan bottom. The pattern is a slow curving pattern to the downside, flattening out at the bottom, and then slowly coming up out of the other side of the pattern. The analysis for the investor sentiment is very easy to understand. Initially after a downtrend, the selling sentiment starts to wane, making the trajectory of the downtrend a slow inactive bottom trading pattern.

After a lengthy period of time, the sentiment almost becomes neutral, forming a flat area. This lack of interest eventually starts to incorporate a very slow change of investor sentiment to the plus side. The new positive outlook shows the same lack of enthusiasm on the buy side as it did on the sell side. However, the difference now becomes that the selling interest has disappeared. The buying interest is slowly coming back into the price. This pattern, unlike other patterns, utilizes the condition of the stochastics in an opposite manner. It is when stochastics are approaching the overbought conditions that investor sentiment can be gauged.

The alert for this pattern is activated when stochastics get up in the over-bought area. The price now shows that confidence has built back up into the price in the form of a large bullish candle or a gap up coming out of the positive side of the Fry-Pan Bottom pattern. This buying indicates that investor senti-ment has now produced confidence for being back in the position. A gap up becomes a signal to buy even though the stochastics are approaching or are in the overbought area. That enthusiasm, coming out of a long bottoming action, will usually create a strong buy trend.

Notice the long four-month period of time in Fig. 6-8, the Isonics Corp. chart that the investor confidence shifted. The telling factor for the potential breakout was the subtle Fry-Pan Bottom formation. A couple of simple ele-ments can be added to Fry-Pan Bottom analysis. The first being the very bottom of the Fry-Pan is approximately one-half the distance from the time the Fry-Pan Bottom started until it will break out. This is not anything that is set in stone. A simple observation is that the very bottom occurs in the middle of the Fry-Pan

Bottom. Having this knowledge allows the investor to estimate when the breakout might occur.

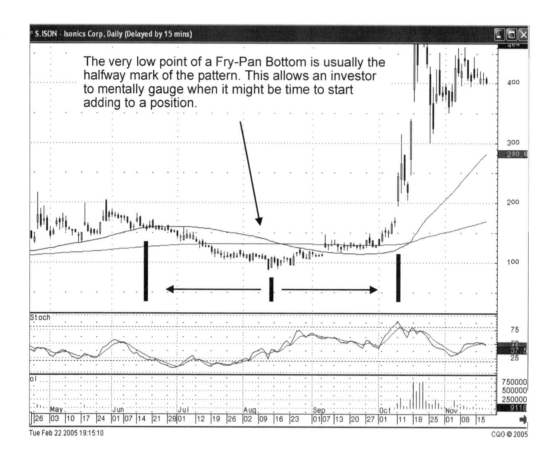

The very low point of a Fry-Pan Bottom is usually the halfway mark of the pattern. This allows an investor to mentally gauge when it might be time to start adding to a position.

Fig. 6-8 *Isonics Corp.*

This calculation does not need to be exact. Visually the buying can be seen as the confidence starts building back up. When the buying level starts approaching the same level as when the pattern started to develop, that is when to start taking action. In early October the Isonics Corp. chart started revealing some bullish candlestick formations. The volume started expanding. This now becomes evidence that the buyer's confidence could create a breakout situation.

The confirmation of the breakout, after the Fry-Pan Bottom, comes as a large bullish candle or a gap up. This will usually occur near the high point of the beginning of the Fry-Pan Bottom formation. Whether you decided to buy this stock in the first few days of October or after the breakout occurred, does not really matter. After the extended period of time it takes to form this pattern, buyer confidence has built up a lot of steam. The percentage move out of the pattern should be very large.

These patterns do not occur very often. Fortunately, when they do occur, they can be found and then followed without too much difficulty. That allows an investor to become well-prepared for taking advantage of the potential results.

Fig. 6-9, The W. R. Grace & Co. chart illustrates a very slow decline, followed by a 'dimple' at the very bottom of the pattern. Once it was interpreted that the buy signal was not creating the immediate buying one would hope for, the slow build-up of confidence could be seen. The Fry-Pan Bottom pattern creates a different analysis versus a stock price that is starting to get to the overbought area, then seeing some exuberant buying. The breakout occurring after a Fry-Pan Bottom formation reveals a completely different scenario.

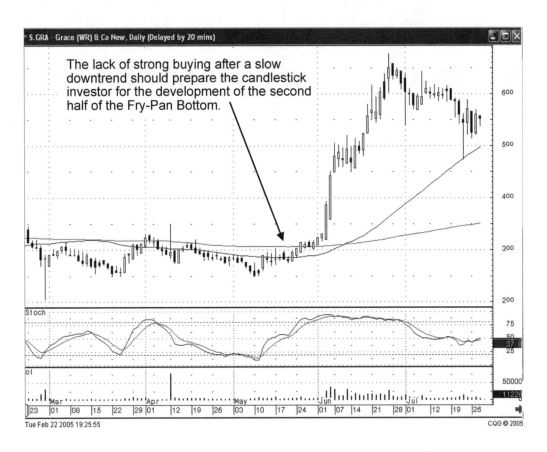

Fig. 6-9 *W. R. Grace & Co.*

Training the eye to recognize how a pattern is setting up creates the opportunity to participate in a big profit move. The slow downtrend, followed by a slow uptrend, will have different results. When the trading gets close to completing the Fry-Pan Bottom formation, funds can start to be committed.

Because of the length of time the pattern takes to develop, they should not be a primary source for a trading strategy. However, this pattern can be used when the timing becomes apparent. Although they do not occur with great frequency, the percent return produced makes the pattern well worth being able to recognize the formation.

Fig.6-10, The Regeneron Pharmaceutical, Inc. chart demonstrates analysis of a Fry-Pan Bottom pattern correctly. Whatever bad news generated the big sell-off in late March, the investor sentiment remained negative going into the latter part of April. Although the sentiment was not severely negative, it still was negative. A small bullish signal occurring approximately April 24 was the first sign of negative sentiment reversing.

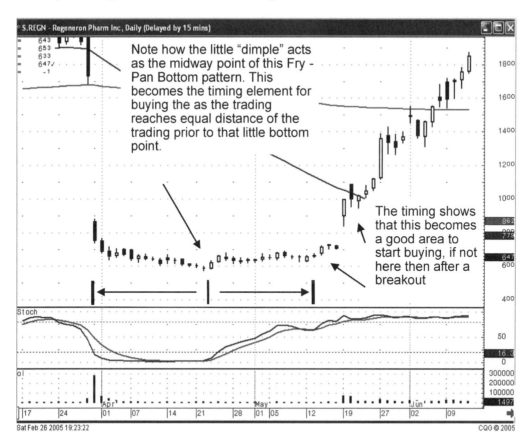

Fig. 6-10 *Regeneron Pharmaceutical Inc.*

This could have caused buying of that position. However, the lack of follow-through for the next few days would have revealed that no new extensive buying was coming into the stock. That may have produced a decision to move money elsewhere. The indecisive period continued, with very slow upward movement. That is what visually revealed a Fry-Pan Bottom formation.

As we have learned, a basic rule of a Fry-Pan Bottom is that the bottom usually occurs midway from the time the pattern starts to the time that a breakout occurs. The little "dimple" occurring approximately April 24 now becomes a timing factor. As the formation approaches the same timeframe after that dimple, it becomes time to look for a potential breakout. The second week of May becomes a good time to start adding to this position. The breakout, on big volume in mid-May, is definitely the time to be buying.

> *Every man who observes vigilantly and resolves steadfastly grows unconsciously into genius.*
>
> *Edward G. Bulwer-lytton*

Although the breakout occurs with the stochastics in the overbought area, the breakout clearly illustrates that investor sentiment has grown. Everyone is confident, once again, to be in the stock.

Fig. 6-11 (following page), The Dynamic Materials Corp. chart may not clearly reveal a Fry-Pan Bottom until the latter stages of the formation. Buying in the second week of January, upon the formation of a Morning Star signal, or buying in mid- February after the three indecisive days formed right at the 50-day moving average pullback, may have been based on other factors. As the chart pattern moves into late February, the gap up has a different connotation to it, after being able to view the whole pattern, starting from the peak of late November.

What might have been analyzed as a Shooting Star at the top of a trading range in normal circumstances now should be analyzed as the potential breakout from a Fry-Pan bottom formation. This analysis, along with the stochastics not quite being in the overbought area, would provide more reason to hold the position, expecting more buying.

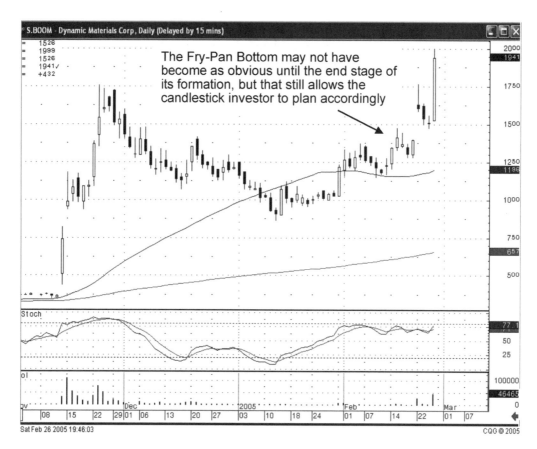

The Fry-Pan Bottom may not have become as obvious until the end stage of its formation, but that still allows the candlestick investor to plan accordingly

Fig. 6-11 *Dynamic Materials Corp.*

The Fry-Pan Bottom formation is not a difficult formation to analyze. It should be kept in your mental arsenal of potentially large trade results. Identifying its formation changes the basic rules of how to use stochastics with candlestick signals. Where most buy signals work effectively, when stochastics are in the oversold area, that rule does not necessarily apply in a Fry-Pan Bottom formation. The slow buildup of confidence, witnessed in the slow uptrend, should be considered like the coiling of a spring. As it gets close to the same level as the beginning of the pattern, the potential for that spring's energy to let loose becomes greater.

If a purchase of a position was not made in the latter stages of the pattern, the majority of the move can still be exploited once the breakout occurs.

> *A man has no ears for that to which experience has given him no access.*
> *Nietzsche*

The Scoop Pattern

The Scoop pattern works effectively and can be easily recognized. The candlestick signals allow an investor to exploit it properly. The explanation of how and why it works is subjective. The pattern is formed after a lengthy period of flat trading, known as the 'handle.' The handle is usually comprised of small, indecisive trading days. After a recognized flat trading timeframe, the price starts to back down. The term "recognized" is visually determining a flat trading area. That flat trading will usually maintain for a longer length of time than what is usually seen in the price movement of that trading entity. It becomes obviously lengthy, to the point where it becomes boring to be in that position.

It may be the boredom that finally makes the price move down. Investors get tired of waiting for it to do something. However, after a few days the small buying signals start showing up. The price starts moving back up toward the flat area creating the scoop. An inordinate percentage of the time when the price comes back up to the flat trading area, the trend continues in a strong upward direction. This may be the result of everybody that was bored with the trading sees it is finally moving and start adding to their positions again.

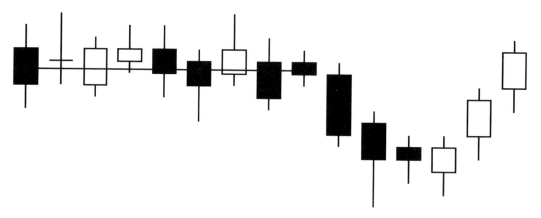

Fig. 6-12 *The Scoop pattern*

The visual recognition of the handle, being followed by the pullback should be the 'alert.' Upon seeing new buying, after a few days a pullback is a set up for a low risk trade. Buying near the bottom of the scoop allows the stop-loss area to be at the low of the scoop. The first test from there should be the flat trading area. A breakout through that area indicates that a good trend is in the making.

Fig. 6-13, The Affiliated Computer Services chart reveals a flat trading period, followed by the price breaking down. After just a few days of pullback, bullish candlestick signals start to appear. Being able to visualize the handle, followed by a pullback, then witnessing candlestick buy signals should alert the candlestick investor to the potential of a scoop pattern forming.

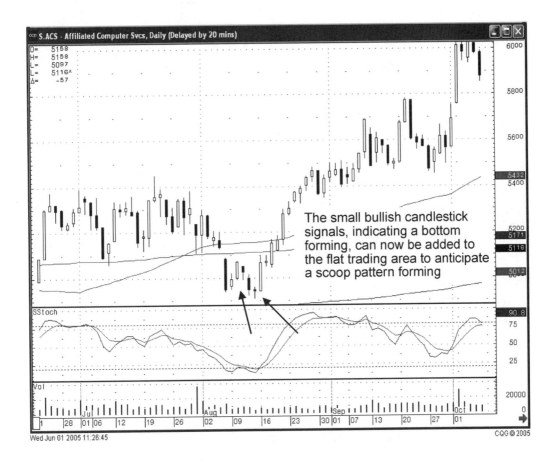

Fig. 6-13 *Affiliated Computer Services*

Additional technical indicators such as moving averages can help anticipate a support level. The trading support at that level after a relatively long flat trading area adds more visual credibility to the scoop pattern development.

As seen in Fig. 6-14, the WCI Communications chart, the 50-day moving average is a logical support level.

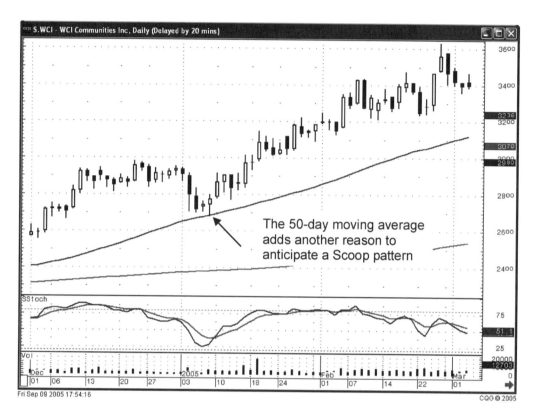

Fig. 6-14 *WCI Communications Inc.*

What is the key element forewarning a Scoop pattern? As can be seen in Fig. 6-15, the FuelCell Energy chart, the long flat trading area, the handle, followed by a pullback has the makings for a Scoop pattern. Notice how the force of the selling is depicted by the smaller candlestick bodies until a little star formation appears. That should suggest watching for new buying.

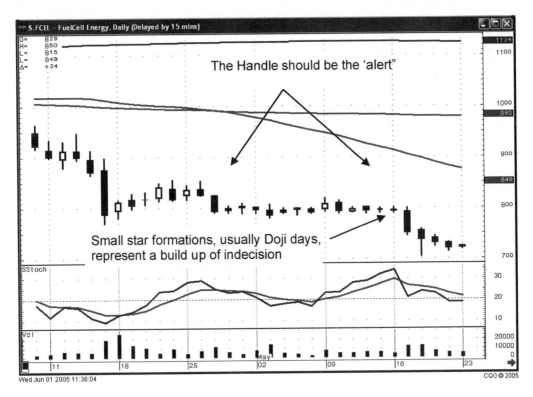

Fig. 6-15 *FuelCell Energy*

The trajectory of the downtrend, created by small trading days, is an alert to expect bottoming action. Once buying is witnessed at this level anticipate the first price test to be back at the 'handle' level. The appearance of a large bullish candle after the Star/Doji provides a better visual confirmation that a Scoop Pattern is about to form. The analysis from that point is anticipating a test of the recent flat trading area. A successful scoop pattern will be the stimulus for a long and steady uptrend.

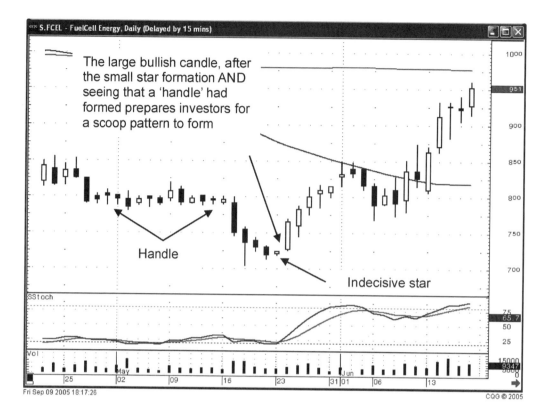

Fig 6-16 *FuelCell Energy*

The uptrend can continue for an extensive period of time, keeping the stochastics waffling in the overbought area. It is not unusual to see the uptrend coming out of the scoop pattern last for four to six weeks. This makes identifying the scoop pattern in its early formation an extremely profitable trade

Once the price has tested and then breached the previous flat trading level, upside targets can be projected. FuelCell Energy hit its first target, the 50-day moving average. Once an uptrend comes through the handle area, the stochastics become less of an influence.

The Scoop pattern, the same as the Fry-Pan Bottom pattern, is going to be more effective when the stochastics are in the overbought area. Also, developing a scan for a scoop pattern is going to be difficult. The only recognition of the pattern comes from reviewing the chart once a buy signal occurs at the end of a pullback. Recognizing the flat trading period prior to the pullback prepares the investor for a high profit trade.

As seen in Fig. 6-17, the Global Industries, Inc. chart, the buy signals forming in an oversold condition was the first alert. Those signals forming right on the moving averages added more credibility to the trade. Was this a worthwhile trade? That becomes an easier evaluation when understanding that a Scoop pattern possibility should at least test the 'handle' area. If the handle area was breached, then the likelihood of a strong trend after that was good.

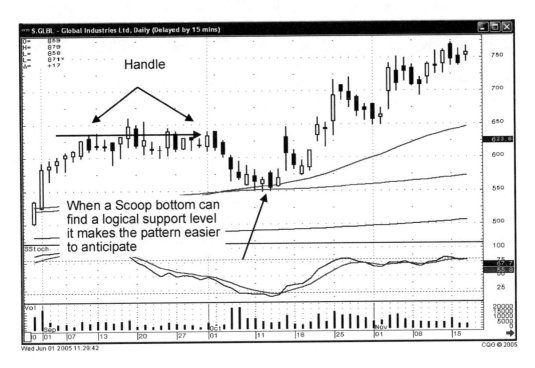

Fig. 6-17 *Global Industries Inc.*

The Scoop pattern can produce big profits. Buying at the bottom of the potential scoop makes for a small stop-loss set-up. The first test is the handle. The upside potential if breaching the handle will provide good profits.

Breakouts

One of the most powerful investment techniques is to exploit the explosive nature of a breakout. The term "breakout" should be relatively self- explanatory. It signifies a price move that is dramatically out of the ordinary for the normal trading pattern of a trading entity. How do candlestick signals and formations benefit in breakout trading? Being able to evaluate what the continuing move will be after a significant price move becomes very important. Is the price move a one-day fluke? Did severe short covering affect the price? Will the trend continue after a significant percentage price move? These are all questions that can be answered by simple evaluation of the candlestick formation at the end of a trading day.

There is a significant difference of a breakout where the price starts low and ends near the top of the trading range. This creates a large white candle. A price that opens up significantly higher and closes at the lower end of the trading range is a completely different scenario. Although the price may be dramatically up for the day, the type of candlestick formation produced on that day provides significant investment information.

Fig. 6-18, The INVN chart clearly illustrates a change in investor sentiment when an outside event affects a stock price. Notice how the stock jumped from $2.50 a share to $8.00 a share during the 9/11 attacks on the World Trade Center. The large volume breakout, although impressive, did not have any major significant price move for two months after the breakout. The fact that the breakout day opened at around $11 a share and closed near $8.00 affected the price trend. The buying started three days later after a small Morning Star signal formed but overall the price of this stock was almost the same as where it opened on the breakout day in mid-November

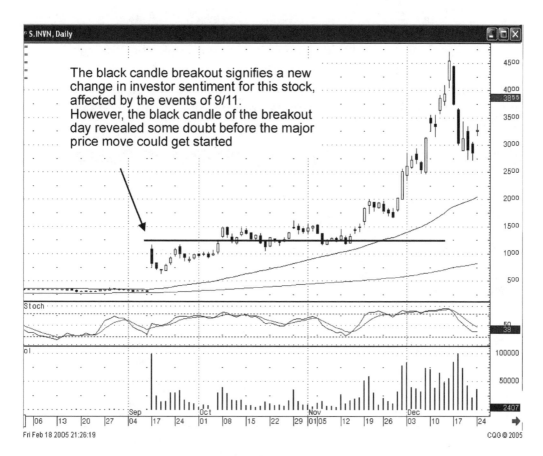

The black candle breakout signifies a new
change in investor sentiment for this stock,
affected by the events of 9/11.
However, the black candle of the breakout
day revealed some doubt before the major
price move could get started

Fig. 6-18 *INVN*

As seen, the price started moving significantly after the breakout. But the large
black candle on the breakout day indicated there was still some doubt in investor sentiment at the end of the day. This was reflected in the stock price for a
few months.

The fact that a breakout has occurred in the first place reveals something.
That something may be a new dynamic coming into the stock price. That dynamic may have been created by internal improvements of a company. The
new investor sentiment may also be caused by an external event that changes
the outlook for a company's fundamental potential or a commodity supply or
demand potential. Whatever the cause for the breakout, an investor wants to
be able to analyze whether a dramatic price move is a one time shot or if it's the
beginning of a huge price jump. Candlestick analysis greatly enhances the ability to evaluate the potential move.

The common sense that is incorporated into candlestick analysis makes interpreting a breakout situation relatively easy. The signals are still the impor-

tant criteria. The analysis of what the signal represents, in correlation to the trend, is greatly enhanced with simple explanations of what the candlestick formations are illustrating. Fig. 6-19, The Applied Digital Solutions Inc. chart revealed important information. The breakout opened and continued to move up, closing on the high. It moved through the 200-day moving average with no problems. This becomes a significant message.

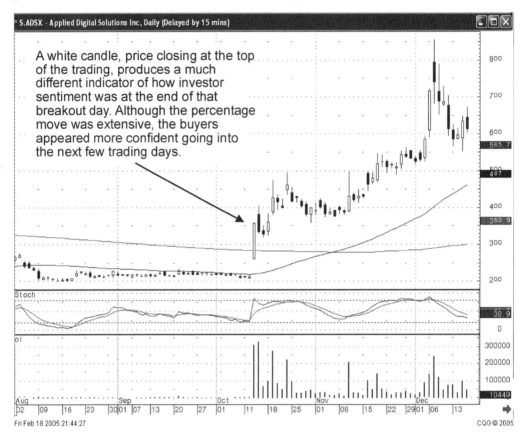

Fig. 6-19 *Applied Digital Solutions Inc.*

The term breakout can be applied to stocks that have traded in a flat range for an extended period of time. A giant move to the upside, based on any news announcement or world event, becomes an important 'alert' system. Simple logic dictates that if a substantial price move takes effect after a particular event, the price move becomes a beacon for analyzing what a company's potential should be in view of that event.

The development of other formations, after a breakout, becomes very revealing as far as what the next potential move will be. The evaluation, of what the reaction should be from investors after an extensive move, is easily analyzed when understanding candlestick analysis.

Fig. 6-20, The Air T, Inc. chart illustrates additional buying enthusiasm, even after a 50% move in the price on the breakout day. The fact that the slight gap up the following day was followed by continued buying indicated that the buying pressure had not diminished. This creates a much different evaluation versus seeing a gap open, followed immediately by selling, or an open that occurred back down in the previous days trading area.

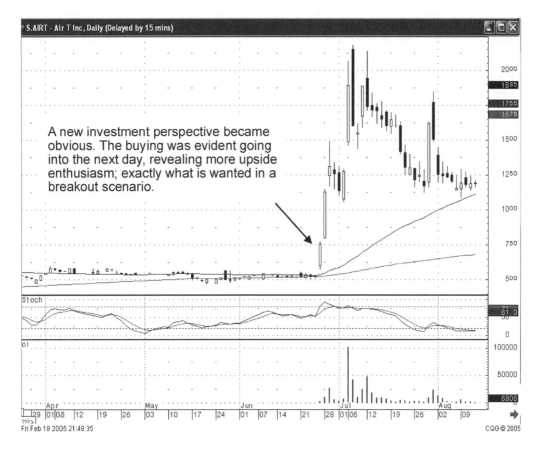

Fig. 6-20 *Air T Inc.*

Having an immediate visual graphic of what investor sentiment is producing is paramount when debating whether to hold a position or take profits. When prices increase dramatically, percentage-wise, in very short period of time, human emotion factors have to be analyzed very quickly. The greed factor, the fear factor, or the profit taking aspects have to be accounted for as quickly as possible. Buying and selling decisions become quicker on the trigger. The fear of not getting in fast enough or getting out fast enough becomes exaggerated in the price movement.

The elements of a breakout pattern can involve other technical indicators. As seen in Fig. 6-21, the W. R. Grace & Co. chart, the 50-day moving average began acting as support. Witnessing a big price move becomes the alert.

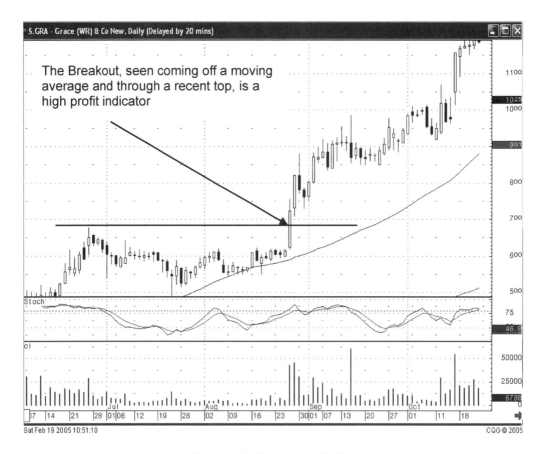

Fig, 6-21 *WR Grace & Co.*

The fact that the price move was created on big volume is another indicator. A large price move, accompanied with high volume trading and breaking through the top of an established price range, is a significant message. It clearly illustrates that a new dynamic has entered this stock price.

The combination of a gap up and a large candlestick body, with expanded volume, and the price breaking out through a resistance level, is a clear message. The bullish candle formation left little doubt at the end of the day that the bullish bias was still present. Had a significant shadow been viewed at the end of the day, to the upside, then a different analysis would have been applied.

The question arises as to whether this may not be demonstrating exuberance at the top. That observation would have been more crucial had this been a day of large buying at the end of an uptrend. In this case, this was a breakout from a flat trading area, definitely a different trading mode than witnessed in the prior month and a half.

Breakouts can also occur in an established trend. If they can clearly be observed in a price pattern, such as a trading channel, and a large-volume price movement breaches that trading area, that breakout now reveals new investor sentiment coming into the price. How a price moves out of the norm, in a trading pattern, is illustrated by the candlestick formation. The information revealed in that formation can be used to great advantage for entering very profitable trades.

Does a breakout always immediately signify massive gains? Not always! However, a breakout from an established trading area should at least be the shot across the bow. Notice in Fig. 6-22, the Catalina Marketing Corp. chart, the breakout was obvious. Yet the main thrust of the uptrend did not occur until three weeks to a month later. The gap up from the breakout day now becomes an important factor. The pullback, after the initial breakout, appeared to stop at the bottom of the bullish breakout candle. The fact that the 50-day moving average and the 200-day moving average crossed as the price came back to the bottom of the breakout candle adds significance.

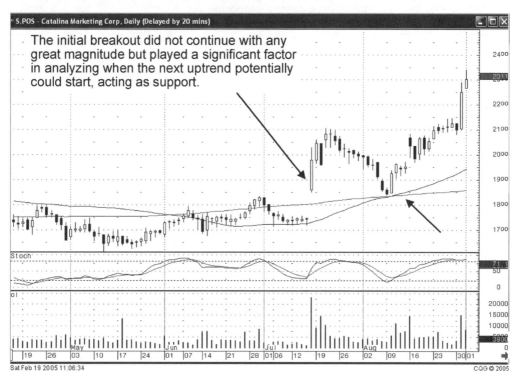

Fig. 6-22 *Catalina Marketing Corp.*

The candlestick signals provide relevant information in a breakout situation. Notice in Fig. 6-23, the AVII chart how a breakout, that more than doubled the price of the stock, was followed the next day by a Bearish Harami. That information provides a completely different scenario than if the buying was still present the day after the breakout. This is nothing more than utilizing what the Japanese Rice traders have observed for centuries.

Will the price of this stock eventually recover to the high of the breakout? More than likely. That provides the candlestick investor with an alert system to watch for new activity in this stock. Keep in mind, the basic element of a breakout situation is that a new dynamic has entered into the stock. The probabilities indicate that the new dynamic will not disappear after one day of trading. Whatever news or event that affects the price greatly is probably going to be revisited within a reasonable amount of time.

Fig. 6-23 *AVII*

A huge move? What do the candlestick formations tell you is happening at the end of the trading day? This information is valuable. The proper evaluation of a breakout candle can produce very large profits.

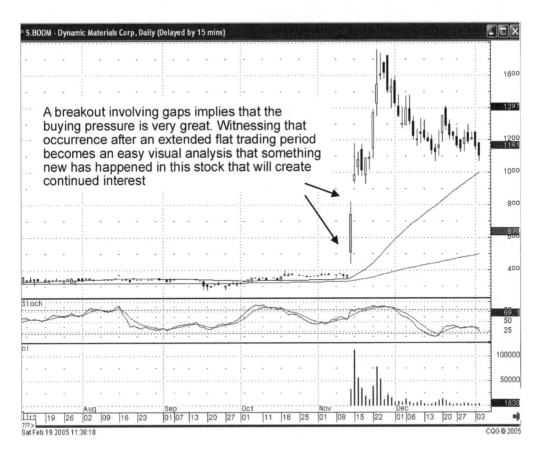

A breakout involving gaps implies that the buying pressure is very great. Witnessing that occurrence after an extended flat trading period becomes an easy visual analysis that something new has happened in this stock that will create continued interest

Fig. 6-24 *Dynamic Materials Corp.*

Breakout Summary

How do you find a breakout situation? This is a very simple scan. It involves finding the stocks that have the biggest percent move during a given timeframe. Breakouts are usually news-driven. They can be found in all-priced stocks. Volume will have a great important also. Volume should be significantly greater than a normal trading day. Some common sense still needs to be applied when evaluating volume. A stock that normally trades 3200 shares a day that has a big moves on 40,000 shares a day should not have as much relevance as a stock that normally trades 200,000 shares a day and moves up to 4 million shares in one day. Logic dictates that a low-volume stock can be moved around by one purchaser.

Breakouts are the result of something significantly different happening for the future potential of a company (or any other trading entity). That result can be visually analyzed in the candlestick bodies following the breakout move. Simple analysis wants to identify whether the buyers are still involved. The presence of more 'buy' signals, such as gaps up, acts as an efficient analytical tool. The strength of an up move will be predicated upon the candlestick formations appearing during or very soon after a breakout candle appears. As with all analysis of candlestick signals, a black candle following a breakout does not necessarily reveal a reversal if that black candle does not portray a candlestick 'sell' signal.

The same rules for analyzing candlestick signals in a normal trend should be applied in a fast-moving breakout situation. A Shooting Star on a second day of a breakout still requires confirmation the following day. A Bearish Harami reveals a different scenario.

The elements that form a breakout situation can produce extremely large profits for the investor that takes the time to analyze what the candlestick formations are revealing. Is it worth chasing a stock that is already up 40% on the day? If you can interpret what the chart pattern is revealing, using candlestick formations, the fear of chasing can be eliminated. The confidence that comes with understanding what that chart formation can produce allows the candlestick investor to participate in analyzed and calculated trades.

The Cradle Pattern

A variation of the series of Doji at the bottom is the Cradle pattern. The Cradle pattern is aptly named. It looks like a cradle hanging at the bottom. This reversal pattern is easy to identify. It begins with the same visual alert as found in most candlestick bottoming signals; a large bearish candle at the bottom of a downtrend. This illustrates the extensive selling at the bottom. The following day shows a candlestick signal such as a Doji, Spinning Top, Harami, Hammer or Inverted Hammer, indicating that the selling had stopped. What will a candlestick investor be watching for? Confirmation of the buy signal! However, for a number of days, small indecisive trading days occur. The indecisive trading occurs in a relatively flat trading area.

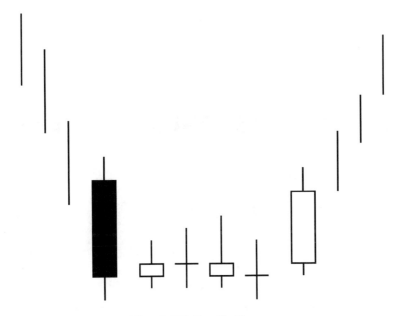

Fig. 6-25 *Cradle Pattern*

The Cradle Pattern Description

After an extended downtrend, a large dark candle forms,
1. A candlestick signal such as a Harami, Hammer or Doji signal indicates that the selling has stopped.
2. The next three, four, five, or more days reveal indecisive trading.
3. The confirmation of the Cradle Pattern is a large bullish candle. The large bearish candle acts as the headboard. The large bullish candle acts as the footboard.
4. The indecision days in between become the 'sleepy' days.
5. The signal pattern is very symmetrical. It illustrates a definite change of investor sentiment after an indecisive trading span. It is a derivative of the series of Doji at the bottom

A bullish candle reveals what investor sentiment decided after the indecisive trading period. If the large dark candle is considered the headboard, the bullish candle becomes the footboard. The cradle formation is now hanging at the bottom, implying that the trend should move up from this level.

Fig. 6-26, The Marchex Inc. chart reveals the indecision occurring at the end of an extended downtrend. Notice the stochastics remained in the oversold area for a number of weeks prior to this pattern demonstrating a change of investor sentiment.

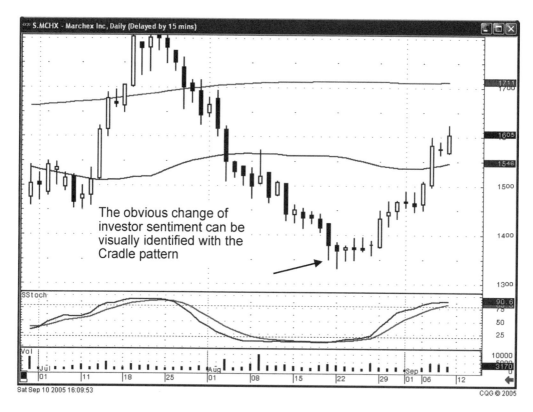

Fig. 6-26 *Marchex Inc.*

Fig. 6-27 (following page), The JDA Software chart exhibits a Cradle pattern. It should be noted that from the appearance of the long dark candle, a head-board, to the appearance of the long bullish candle, numerous candlestick signals could be identified. Doji's and Spinning Tops illustrated the lack of conviction by both the Bulls and the Bears. The important visual aspect of the indecisive trading was that price traded completely flat for approximately a two-week period.

Recognizing there was no definitive direction, after the last large dark candle, the candlestick investor can be prepared for the large bullish candle. If watching closely, a position could be established upon seeing strength coming in the day the footboard was forming.

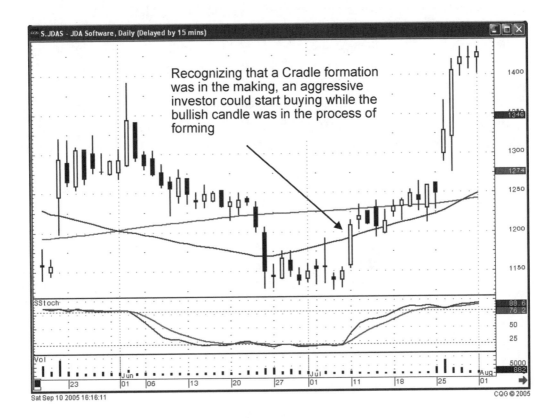

Fig. 6-27 *JDA Software*

The Cradle pattern, the same as the series of Doji's at the bottom, demonstrate that the Bulls and the Bears cannot figure out what to do with prices at the bottom. A large bullish candle, completing the Cradle formation, immediately declares where investor sentiment has moved. This is a high probability reversal pattern. Any time a series of indecisive trading signals can be identified, the likelihood of a strong trend occurring afterwards is very strong. Once the direction is disclosed, the price move will usually be significant. The elements for making this a successful trade are already in place. After an extended downtrend, the stochastics will be in the oversold condition. A bullish signal, forming after the indecisive signals, becomes your 'buy alert.'

The Methods Rising Pattern

The Methods Rising Pattern is a derivative of the Three Methods Rising pattern. The Three Methods Rising pattern is a candlestick continuation pattern. Although the continuation patterns are not addressed in this book, the Methods Rising pattern occurs frequently enough to include it in the High Profit Patterns chapter.

　　The Three Methods Rising pattern consists of a large bullish candle during an uptrend. The following three days are indecisive bearish candles. The Methods Rising Pattern consists of three or more indecisive bearish trading days.

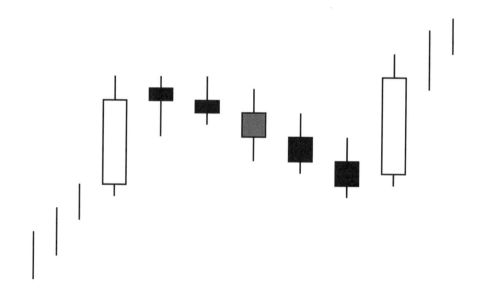

Fig. 6-28 *Methods Rising Pattern*

The Methods Rising Pattern

1. Usually considered the Three Methods Rising pattern, where once a bullish candle is formed, three pullback days are seen before the next bullish candle.
2. The Methods Rising Pattern is an extension of a Three Methods Rising pattern, having 3, 4, 5, or 6 indecisive pullback days before viewing the next bullish candle.
3. The pullback days are usually indecisive days, Doji's or Spinning Tops, demonstrating that the sellers are not acting forcefully.
4. The final pullback day does not close below the open of the last bullish candle. This discourages the Bears.
5. The final day opens higher than the close of the previous day and finally closes above the close of the last bullish candle. This illustrates that the Bulls are now back in the trend. The trend should continue upwards.

An important aspect of the pattern is the 'pullback' days. Witnessing indecisive bearish trading days divulges crucial information. The selling is occurring without any great conviction. There will usually be Spinning Tops, Doji, small Hammers or small Inverted Hammer signals. Another important factor is that the final bearish day does not close below the open price of the previous bullish candle. The fact that the Bears could not move the price below the open of the last bullish candle makes them discouraged. It also gives the Bulls confidence.

The following day should open higher. The buying, seen from the confidence of the Bulls, will take the closing price above the closing price of the previous bullish candle. This illustrates that the Bears have stepped out of the way. The Bulls are back in control. The uptrend has an extremely high probability of continuing from these levels, provided the stochastics indicate more upside.

Fig. 6-29 (following page), The F5 Networks Inc. chart demonstrates how the Bulls overcame the Bears when they could not reverse the trend after six days. The Bulls, with new confidence, start taking the trend up to much higher levels. The significant factor was that the Bears could not close the price below the open of the last bullish candle.

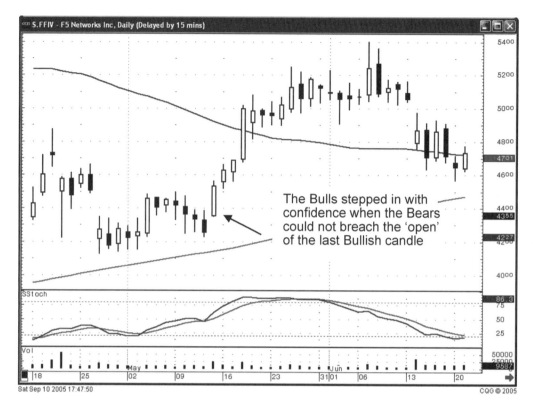

Fig. 6-29 *F5 Networks Inc.*

Kicker Signals at Moving Averages

The Kicker signal, the most powerful candlestick signal! As described earlier, the Kicker signal is formed when something dramatic has changed the investor sentiment. The Kicker signal should never be ignored. It has the capability of producing extremely large profits. The news event or announcement, that creates the signal, changes investor sentiment so greatly that the trend will probably move in the new direction for a lengthy period of time.

The Kicker signal does not require the evaluation of the stochastics. However, a Kicker signal, formed at or near major moving averages, increases the significance of the signal. What is the reasoning behind this phenomenon? It could be the added implication that the price is not going to remain at the normal price area, the moving averages.

Additionally, the gapping of the price movement up through a moving average implies that the moving average will not act as resistance. As seen in the Micromuse Inc. chart, a Kicker signal gaps up through the 50-day moving average. This becomes relevant information. Massive buying strength at an important technical level!

What is the common reaction to a stock price that may have gapped up 10% to 20% in one day? Most investors will shy away after a price move of that magnitude. That is unfortunate! The information conveyed in a Kicker signal, moving through or away from a moving average, will produce powerful results.

Recognize the signal. When you see it, take advantage of it. Technical analysis is the utilization of previous price movements. Candlestick analysis exploits patterns that have produced significant profits in the past. Kicker signals, witnessed at major moving averages, will produce huge profits for your account.

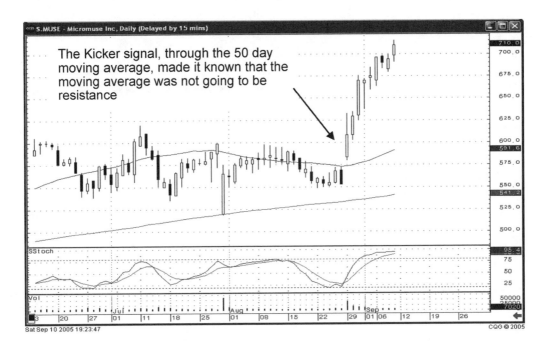

Fig. 6-30 *Micromuse Inc.*

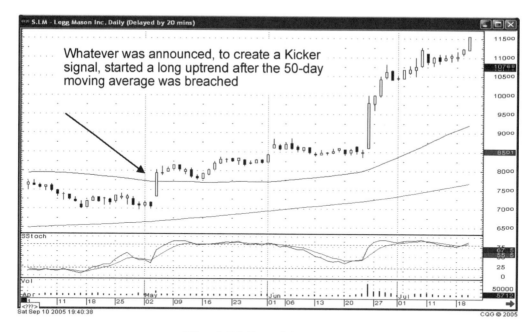

Fig. 6-31 *Legg Mason Inc.*

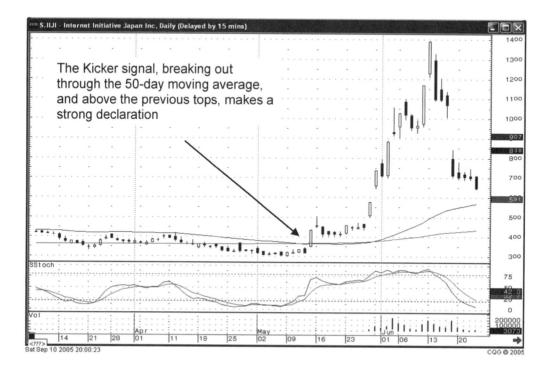

Fig. 6-32 *Internet Initiative Japan Inc.*

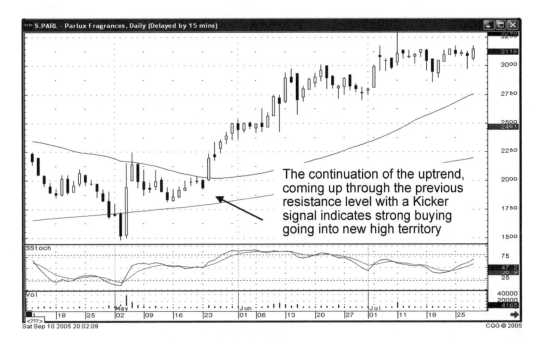

Fig. 6-33 *Parlux Fragrances*

Utilizing High Profit Patterns

> *Could everything be done twice everything would be done better.*
> *German proverb*

The basis of technical analysis is utilizing past chart information. Prices move in patterns. An investor that can recognize a pattern developing will achieve a huge advantage. Candlestick signals increase the visual recognition of pattern development. If a projected pattern requires certain buying elements, the candlestick signals will confirm that information immediately.

Creating inordinate profits is nothing more than recognizing when to take advantage of recurring price movements. Applying the information that candlestick signals convey expedites the recognition of potential patterns and early execution of profitable trades.

If an investor knows what a specific pattern should produce, they can get early confirmation when witnessing the right signals. Knowing what that pattern should do also provides exit strategies for when the signals demonstrate non-confirming trend signals.

The candlestick signals and high-profit patterns are based upon the probabilities of expected results. Profitable trading is greatly simplified when identifying whether the signals are performing in the manner they were supposed to. Profitable investing involves exploiting the probable percentages of a trading method. The combination of candlestick signals, incorporated into high-profit pattern potentials, puts investors' funds into trades that should work a high percentage of the time. When they do not work, it will be revealed immediately by what the candlestick signals are telling. When they do work, the upside results will be better than most investment results.

Chapter 7

Option Trading With Candlestick Signals

> *Good judgment comes from experience, experience comes from bad judgment.*
>
> *William Saroyan*

Huge profits can be made trading options. It is easy to do. At least that is what a multitude of option trading services preach. "Use our program and watch your profits soar," is promoted on option trading web sites over and over. Unfortunately, reality finds that there are a few investors that have been made wealthy from these sites.

Why shouldn't it be easy to make big profits with options? All you have to do is find stocks that are going up and buy the calls. Find stocks that are going down and buy the puts. The sites or programs that are doing well for demonstrating how to use options successfully stand out like sore thumbs. Everybody knows about them. When something is working well in investing, everybody becomes instantly aware. Oops, you don't know about these easy-to-learn programs for successful option trading? If they were out there, you would know about it! Everybody would know about it. Option trading is like any other investment program. If an investor wants to be successful at trading options, they need to learn their own program.

Candlestick analysis becomes an integral part of formulating a successful option trading program. Options strategies, just like any other investment strategies, require proper application of correct strategies in different market conditions. One trading program that may work successfully in today's markets may not work in the trading atmosphere 90 days from now.

Understanding the different elements of successful option trades is the first step. Options have many parameters involved in their successful applications. Unlike most investments, where direction is the main criteria, options require the analysis of a number of criteria.

What make options attractive to investors? Leverage!!! The following explanations may appear to be relatively elementary. However, most investors approach trading options without realizing all the criteria that need to be fulfilled to make a successful option trade. Having a full understanding of what makes for a successful option trade will make the utilization of candlestick analysis, for option trading, much more clear.

What is the intriguing element of trading options? A small amount of investment funds in control of a large amount of assets. Essentially a small amount of money controlling a larger asset base, timed properly, can produce huge profits. The dream of every investor!

Option Trading Criteria

Unlike investing in stocks, options have a time element involved. The infusion of a timeframe to an investment creates dramatically different dynamics. The time factor creates three crucial criterion: DIRECTION, TIME, and MAGNITUDE.

As has been experienced through the centuries, most investors have difficulty in mastering the direction of a price move. Implementing candlestick analysis greatly increases the probabilities of analyzing price movement in the proper direction. Knowing the direction of a trend's move, with a relatively high degree of probability, allows an investor to produce high-profit option strategies.

The direction of a price move is only one key element to a successful option trade. The amount of time available for that price to move is also an important factor. The strategy for a trade will have a vast difference when considering a trade that will expire in one week versus a trade that will expire in two months.

Evaluating what the candlestick signals are demonstrating makes establishing a very short-term option trade much more feasible. Establishing longer-term option trades can be implemented with more sophisticated risk/ reward strategies when the direction is visualized with the signals. The fact that the candlestick signals illustrate what investor sentiment is doing right NOW permits an investor to incorporate the direction of a move for any time period.

Magnitude is a third key element. Magnitude or volatility! Just because a price moves in the correct direction does not guarantee that an option will make money. Bill Johnson author of "An Investors Guide to Understanding and Mastering Options Trading," "The Single-Stock Futures Revolution," and " 10 Biggest Mistakes in Option Trading" provides valuable instructions for investors that want to master profitable option trading strategies.

Option trading usually implies high risk. Utilizing candlestick analysis can eliminate a lot of the risk implication. The same analytical approach for putting all the probabilities in your favor for a stock trade can easily be assembled into a successful option trade. Stop-loss procedures can easily be incorporated. Evaluating price movement with candlestick signals at potential targets provide improved exit strategies.

Bill Johnson's 14 years of option trading background has helped with the creation of many successful trading strategies. Applying that knowledge with candlestick analysis makes for some high-probability, high-profit trade potentials while utilizing commonsense risk management procedures.

The following chapter, written by Bill Johnson, not only describes how direction, time, magnitude/volatility are important factors, but another major criterion needs to be considered. The value of the option as measured by the remaining time and past volatility of the underlying trading entity needs to be evaluated. When putting all the probabilities in one's favor, evaluating whether an option price is over valued or undervalued becomes part of a successful option trade.

Using Candlesticks with Options

In the mid-1700s, a man named Munehisa Honma had a prominent rice farming estate and, consequently, had considerable influence over the rice market. Through years of trading the rice markets, Honma discovered that, while supply and demand played a role in determining price, the markets were also strongly influenced by the emotions of traders. In other words, traders' emotions could cause significant changes in supply and demand. Honma found that traders could benefit from understanding emotions. Through his analysis, Honma brought to us one of the most important insights to trading: There can be a vast difference between the *price* of rice and the *value*. Hundreds of years later, the legendary investor Warren Buffett came to the same realization when he said, "Price is what you pay. Value is what you get."

While the words "price" and "value" are often used interchangeably in everyday communication, there is a big difference between them when it comes to investing or trading – as Honma and Buffett have figured out. The *price* of a financial asset can be found by looking at the current market quote but the *value* is a subjective measure. Value is something that exists in the trader's mind and is an assessment of whether the price reflects a good deal.

Here is an example that demonstrates the difference between price and value. Assume you are a currency trader and think the yen will rise against the dollar and you wish to buy one million yen to capitalize on your outlook. Another trader offers you one million yen in exchange for 7,000 British pounds. Should you take the trade? Note that 7,000 pounds is the *price* for one million yen – it is what you have to give up in order to buy the yen. However, it should be evident from this example that it may not be a good deal since the *value* between the two currencies could be vastly different. In order to check, we can convert the two currencies into dollars and then make comparisons. At the time of this writing, 7,000 pounds were equal to $13,440 and one million yen were equal to $9,615. Now it is easy to compare the two currencies and we can see that it is not a good deal to give up something worth $13,440 in exchange for something worth $9,615. In other words, 7,000 pounds is too high of a price to pay for one million yen since there is not an equal amount of value between the two currencies.

But there is something more troubling about the trade than the fact that price is higher than the value. Notice that if you pay 7,000 pounds for one million yen you could still end up losing money – even if your outlook is correct and the yen rises against the dollar. You could lose on this trade because the rise in the yen may not be enough to offset the high price paid to acquire the yen.

When it comes to trading stocks, there is only one thing that a trader needs to know to determine if a particular stock is a good value; that is, the future direction of the stock's price. That is exactly what candlestick charting helps a trader identify. Unfortunately, most option traders take this same approach when it comes to trading options. They see an option as nothing more than a leverage substitute for stock. If they think the stock will rise, they buy calls; if they think it will fall, they buy puts.

But option trading cannot be reduced to this same simplistic approach. The reason is, while an option's price is sensitive to the direction of the stock's price, it is also sensitive to the volatility of the underlying stock. Volatility is simply a mathematical measure of the price swings exhibited by the closing prices. In mathematical terms, volatility is the standard deviation of stock price returns[1]. If there are large price changes from day to day, we say that is a volatile stock. If the price changes are relatively small then the stock is not volatile. It is not important to understand the mathematics involved in measuring the volatility of a stock but the ability to interpret those numbers is of utmost importance for an options trader.

As odd as it may sound, knowledge that a stock is moving higher is of little use to an options trader. In order for that information to become useful, we must also know how quickly the stock will move.

Why Volatility Matters

Many option traders choose to ignore volatility and trade options based solely on directional beliefs. However, this approach ignores the value of options in terms of volatility and large losses can occur – even if you are right on the direction – as the following real-life example shows.

---

1. Technically, the volatility is the annualized standard deviation of the logs or stock price changes. But that definition clouds the important concept in that volatility is simply a type of standard deviation.

On December 16, 2004, VimpelCom (VIP) was trading for $31.41 as shown by
the quotes in Figure 1:

| VIP (NYSE) | | | | | | | | | | | 31.41 +0.62 |
| Dec 16,2004 @ 16:39 ET (Data 15 Minutes Delayed) | | | | | | | | Bid 18.80 Ask 18.81 Size 14x6 Vol 29728 | | | |

Calls	Last Sale	Net	Bid	Ask	Vol	Open Int	Puts	Last Sale	Net	Bid	Ask	Vol	Open Int
05 Jan 31.625 (VIP AU-E)	3.00	+0.80	3.00	3.50	392	645	05 Jan 31.625 (VIP MU-E)	3.50	pc	2.40	3.60	0	249
05 Jan 33.375 (VIP AV-E)	2.10	+0.45	1.75	2.50	12	1348	05 Jan 33.375 (VIP MV-E)	3.30	pc	3.40	4.60	0	175
05 Jan 35 (VIP AG-E)	1.65	+0.45	1.15	1.75	48	977	05 Jan 35 (VIP MG-E)	5.20	+0.30	4.50	5.70	20	618

Figure 1 *VIP Option Quotes*

Most option traders who were bullish on the stock might be tempted to buy a
call option to leverage their outlook. Figure 1 shows that the $31.625 calls
were asking $3.50, the $33.375 calls were asking $2.50, and the $35 calls were
asking $1.75.

On December 29, just thirteen days later, the stock rose significantly from
$31.41 to $34, which is a healthy 8% increase (over 200% on an annualized
basis). This certainly sounds like it should leave the trader with a nice profit on
the leveraged calls but Figure 2 tells a different story. The $31.625 call was
bidding only $2.90 thus leaving the trader with a 17% loss for being correct on
the direction of the stock.

| VIP (NYSE) | | | | | | | | | | | 34.00 +2.50 |
| Dec 29,2004 @ 12:56 ET (Data 15 Minutes Delayed) | | | | | | | | Bid N/A Ask N/A Size NA/NA Vol 1845000 | | | |

Calls	Last Sale	Net	Bid	Ask	Vol	Open Int	Puts	Last Sale	Net	Bid	Ask	Vol	Open Int
04 Jan 31.625 (VIP AU-E)	3.20	+1.20	2.90	3.30	269	1515	05 Jan 31.625 (VIP MU-E)	0.90	-1.15	0.75	1.05	13	305
04 Jan 33.375 (VIP AV-E)	2.00	+0.95	1.80	2.25	217	1630	05 Jan 33.375 (VIP MV-E)	3.30	pc	1.20	1.65	0	186
04 Jan 35 (VIP AG-E)	1.25	+0.65	1.00	1.40	60	1396	05 Jan 35 (VIP MG-E)	2.30	-2.60	2.00	2.45	11	661

Fig. 2 *VIP Option Quotes (13 Days Later)*

What would have happened if you purchased either of the other calls? If you
had purchased the $33.375 calls, you would have a 28% loss (paid $2.50 and
sold for $1.80) and a massive 42% loss (paid $1.75 and sold for $1.00) had you
purchased the $35 calls. No matter which call you may have chosen in Figure
1, you were left with a substantial loss in Figure 2 even though the stock's price
rose substantially. This example clearly shows that understanding stock price
direction is not enough to trade options profitably.

Options are Two-Dimensional

What happened? How did these VIP call options lose money even though the stock's price went up? The reason the VIP options lost money is because options have two main factors that affect their price: *direction* and *speed*. Because of this, we say that options are two-dimensional. In order to be profitable, you must correctly guess the direction of the underlying stock along with the speed at which the stock's price will move. Option traders must correctly guess the direction (up or down) of the underlying stock as well as how quickly it will move (will it move today or next week?). Stock traders, on the other hand, only trade in one dimension. They only need to correctly guess whether the stock's price will rise or fall. They do not need to account for the speed.

It is the volatility of the underlying stock that determines the speed component. If you are trading options on a highly volatile stock then that stock's price must move quickly in order for that option to become profitable. The reason has to do with the fact that there is a direct relationship between volatility and option prices. If volatility rises, so do call and put prices. But if volatility falls, then call and put prices fall in response. Volatility, however, is a hidden component to option prices. It is easy to see if the stock's price goes up or down but it is not so easy to get the same information about volatility. It is certainly possible for the stock's price to rise but for volatility to fall enough so that there is an overall decrease in the call option's value. This is exactly what happened with the VIP calls in Figures 1 and 2. In this example, the option trader got the stock direction right but not the speed; it took too long for the stock to rise. If the stock had moved to $34 in a shorter time, say a day or two (rather than thirteen), the calls would certainly have made money. It is this second dimension of speed that makes options trading so much more difficult than stock trading. Notice that a one-dimensional stock trader would have made money by purchasing at $31.41 and selling for $34. The speed at which the stock rises does not matter. Therefore, while a stock and option trader may both have guessed that VIP was moving higher, only the stock trader made money since he does not need to account for speed at which the stock gets to a certain price.

This example shows that call options are not necessarily a direct substitute for stock. If you think a stock is moving higher, you cannot just buy a call in place of the stock and expect to make money if you are correct. (Similarly, put options are not a direct substitute for shorting stock.) Yet most option traders mistakenly apply this one-dimensional stock trading technique to options and, consequently, end up losing money.

Understanding candlestick charts will take care of the directional aspect. Understanding volatility will take care of the speed aspect. Only when we have correctly identified both direction and speed can we expect to make money with options.

You must be convinced that the speed of movement in the stock's price matters. So before we get into the details of how to identify both direction and speed, let's look at a quick analogy to convince you that speed matters.

The Need for Speed

What causes an option to have a speed component to its price? The quick answer is that it has to do with the fact that options have a time premium. The bigger the time premium, the further the stock must move to recoup the cost. But that begs the question why do options have a time premium? In order to understand why options have a time premium, consider the following similarity of a football bet.

Imagine that you are betting on this year's Superbowl between the New England Patriots and Philadelphia Eagles. You do your homework and find that all of the analysts are predicting that New England will win. To the unwary, this high probability outlook sounds like it is too easy to make money; all you have to do is bet big on New England and you'll walk away richer. But if you attempt this, you'll quickly find it is not that easy. The reason is that *everybody* is reading and acting on the same information and the crowd will want to bet on New England too. That means you now have a problem since you cannot find anybody to take the other side of the bet.

How can you entice someone to take the other side; that is, to bet on the Eagles? One of the easiest is to offer a point spread. While nobody is willing to bet on the Eagles in actual points (or "even up"), people will take the bet if you create a point spread. For instance, if you offer someone a 7-point spread that means you must subtract seven points from the Patriots' score before comparing it to the Eagles' score (or, equivalently, anybody betting on the Eagles gets to add seven points to their score). This acts as a handicapping system thus making it more difficult for the Patriot bettors to win. If the Patriots win 21-14, there is exactly a 7-point spread (the difference in scores) and no money is won or lost. A bigger difference in scores results in a win for the person betting on the Patriots while a smaller spread results in a win for the one betting on the Eagles.

How is the spread determined? It is determined by the market. If a bookie posts too low of a point spread then nobody will be swayed to betting on the Eagles. If the point spread is too large, then everybody will wish to bet on the Eagles. It's only when the point spread is just right – the market price – that bookies will find an equal number of buyers and sellers and all bets can be placed. Only when you have a balanced number of buyers and sellers can the bet be viewed as fair; the crowd is indifferent between betting on one side or the other.

Now, if you just think of an option as a directional bet on the stock, let's see how this football analogy relates to the options market. If everybody thinks that VIP stock's price will rise, then everybody would want to buy call options. In other words, nobody would be willing to sell those calls. That is, nobody will sell the calls unless you offer a point spread on the bet. The spread on an option is somewhat hidden but it is easy to show that it is there. Figure 1 shows that the $31.625 call was asking $3.50. Any trader who buys this option and exercises it will have a cost basis of $31.625 + $3.50 = $35.125 on the stock. However, the trader could have elected to buy the stock at the current price, which gives him a cost basis of $31.41. So the trader who buys the call needs the stock price to move to $35.125 just to break even at expiration.

In essence, anybody buying this call is really betting on something more than that the stock will rise. The buyer of this call is really betting that the stock's price will be above $35.125 by expiration since that is the breakeven point on the option. The stock buyer is really betting that the stock's price will be above its current price of $31.41 whereas the call buyer is betting that the stock's price will be above $35.125. And those are two very different bets.

Since the current stock price is $31.41, there is effectively a $35.125 - $31.41 = $3.71 spread on the "bet" at this time. This spread acts in the same way a point spread does for our earlier football example bet. It is only because of this $3.71 point spread that a market between buyers and sellers could be created. If the time premium was higher than $3.50 on that call then we would have too many people wanting to sell the bet and the price would fall. If the premium were less than $3.50 then we have too many people wanting to buy the bet and the price would rise. At a price of exactly $3.50, the number of buyers and sellers is balanced at that point in time and the bet can be viewed as fair.

Notice that, at expiration, if the stock rises to $35.125 *or less*, any trader who paid $3.50 for the $31.625 call loses the bet – even though the stock's price rose. Using the football analogy, you would lose the bet if the Patriots win by less than the spread. Even though you picked the correct team to win, you still lost the bet since they did not win by a big enough spread. And this is exactly what happened to the traders who bought any of the VIP calls in Figure 1 and tried to sell thirteen days later. Although traders buying the call were correct on the stock price direction, they accepted too big of a point spread on the bet.

Hopefully, you are now convinced that volatility matters. Yet most option traders do not take it into account when assessing the value of a trade. So how does a trader account for the volatility? That is where the Black-Scholes Model comes into play.

The Black-Scholes Model – A Scientific way to Value an Option

When we value a football bet, there is no way to say for certain if it is valued other than by the fact that the crowd seems to think so. The spread we end up with is a result of broadcasting different point spreads until all bets have been made. Prior to 1973, this is exactly how the options market worked. Traders had to throw out bids and offers based on what they felt a trade was worth. Because nobody really had a means to quantify the numbers, traders tended to bid low and offer high, which creates very large bid-ask spreads. Large spreads mean low volume so the market became very inefficient and never quite got off the ground.

Fortunately, that all changed in 1973 when Fisher Black and Myron Scholes created the Black-Scholes Option Pricing Model, which allowed traders to get a more scientific idea of what an option's price should be. It is no surprise that this was the very year that the Chicago Board Options Exchange (CBOE) was created since there was now an objective way to readily determine the fair price of an option. And with this knowledge, traders were willing to bid higher and sell for less.

Despite the importance of the model, most option traders do not use it. They pick all their option trades based on directional beliefs. They feel the model is only a theoretical tool that has no place in the real world of option trading. Unfortunately, that is far from true. The Black-Scholes Model allows traders to gain access to one of the most important pieces of information before jumping into a trade – it allows traders to judge whether the price of an option reflects a good value.

Before we can appreciate the significance of the Black-Scholes Model, it is necessary for us to take a little detour at this point in order to understand the mathematical concept of fair value. Once we understand the meaning of fair value then we can put the Black-Scholes Model to use and show you how to create a winning trade from the quotes in Figure 1.

Fair Value –
How Much is a Bet Worth?

Let's say you are offered the chance to play the following game indefinitely: A coin is flipped and you win $1 if it lands "heads" but lose your bet amount if it lands "tails." How much should you be willing to wager on this game?

In order to solve this, you must understand that the value of any bet is determined by the reward and the probability of winning that reward. As the reward or probability of winning increases, so does the value of the bet. In this coin-tossing problem, we know that the reward is one dollar so all we need to determine is the probability of winning.

We can probably guess that the coin will land heads and tails about equally often so we might decide to use 50% as the probability of winning (which implies there is a 50% chance of losing since the total probabilities must add up to one). Now that we know the reward is $1 and the probability of winning the reward is 50%, we can figure out how much to pay for this bet. We will show you a mathematical way shortly but first let's see if we can figure it out intuitively. What would happen if you paid $1.50 for the bet? Since we reasoned the probability is 50%, we can guess that you would win $1.00 half the time and lose $1.50 half the time. This results in a loss of 50 cents every two flips, or 25 cents on average. Although you might win an occasional bet here and there, we can be sure that you would end up on the losing side after hundreds of flips. So $1.50 is too high of a price to pay.

What would happen if you paid 50 cents? We would now expect that you would win $1.00 half the time and lose 50 cents half the time, which means you should make about 50 cents every 2 flips or 25 cents on average. You could certainly lose some bets but, over the long run, you would be sure to end up on the winning side.

Well, if $1.50 is too high of a price to pay and 50 cents is too low, then there must be a price in between that is neither too high nor too low. That price is called the *fair value* of the bet. If a bet is priced at fair value then neither player will sustain a long-run advantage. Both players are expected to just break even over the long run.

You may have guessed that the fair value of this bet is $1.00. If you wager $1.00, then you would win $1.00 half the time and lose $1.00 half the time thus making you no richer or poorer over the long run. At a price of one dollar, the bet is fair to both gamblers.

Fair Value Formula

We can find the same answer mathematically by multiplying the probability of winning by the reward and adding that to the probability of losing multiplied by the amount wagered. In this example:

$$(0.50) * +\$1.00$$
$$\underline{+\ (0.50) * -\$1.00}$$
$$\text{Net} = \$0$$

This top line of this calculation is saying there is a 50% chance of winning $1.00, which means that has a value to you of 0.50 * +$1.00 = 50 cents. But the second line shows you also have a 50% chance of losing $1.00, which has a value of 0.50 * -$1.00, which equals -50 cents. The positive and negative 50 cents cancel out and you're expected to walk away with nothing after many flips. We can even run a computer simulation to see if we are right. Figure 3 shows a computer model with the total profit or loss on the vertical axis and the number of tosses on the horizontal axis:

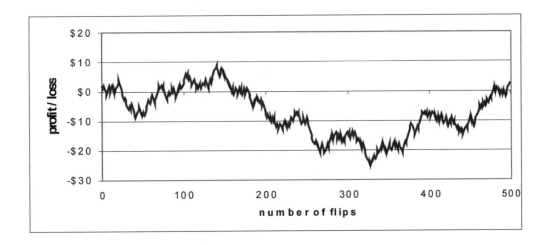

Fig. 3 *Computer simulation of fair value: Paying $1 to win $1*

The $0 mark on the vertical axis represents the break even point since that is the point where zero profits or losses are incurred. You can see that after 500 tosses, you are about back at break even. However, prior to that, you can certainly end up winning or losing due to chance. But in the long run, you would just expect to just break even. The $0 horizontal line acts like a magnet for a fairly valued bet. The profit and loss line does not get too far above or below break even without being pulled back toward zero. Although the profit or loss line can stray from zero, it cannot move away from it indefinitely. The profit and loss line just tends to oscillate sideways around zero if the bet is fairly priced.

Let's use the fair value formula to see what it says about paying $1.50 for the $1 reward:

$$(0.50) * +\$1.00$$
$$\underline{+ (0.50) * -\$1.50}$$
$$Net = -25 \text{ cents}$$

The formula shows that we are expected to lose 25 cents per flip, which is exactly what we reasoned earlier. Paying $1.50 for this bet is therefore too high of a price. Figure 4 (following page) shows that a computer simulation agrees with the formula:

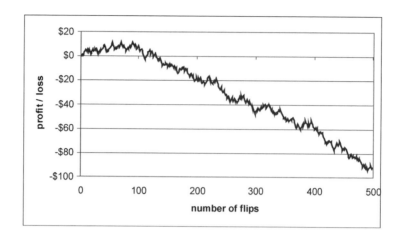

Fig. 4 *Computer simulation above fair value: Paying $1.50 to win $1*

After 500 flips, we are down roughly $90. Mathematically, we would expect to have lost 25 cents per flip multiplied by 500 flips for a total of $125. Of course, there will be fluctuations around that $125 figure and the chart shows that we are not too far off.

Notice that even though we are paying $1.50 for this bet (above fair value) that it is still possible for us to end up on the winning side in the short run. Figure 4 shows that we ended up on the winning side even after 100 flips. But after hundreds more, the profit and loss line does not tend to get pulled toward zero. Instead, it moves into a definite downward path and never returns.

Let's see what the formula has to say about wagering 50 cents for the $1 reward:

$$
\begin{array}{r}
(0.50) * +\$1.00 \\
\underline{+\ (0.50) * -\$0.50} \\
\text{Net} = +25 \text{ cents}
\end{array}
$$

As we found before, wagering only 50 cents to win $1.00 at the flip of a coin is a good deal as you would expect to win about 25 cents per flip. Figure 5 shows a computer simulation of this arrangement:

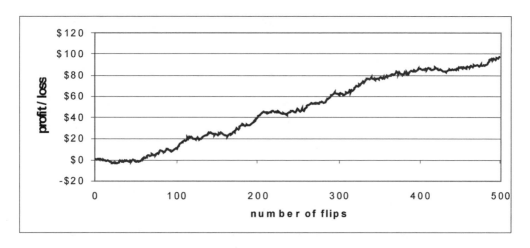

Fig. 5 *Computer simulation below fair value: Paying 50 cents to win $1*

Notice that the profit and loss line is not pulled toward zero in the long run. Instead, it heads into unlimited gains. Mathematically, we would have expected to be up 25 cents * 500 flips = $125 and Figure 5 shows that we're up about $100 so, once again, the computer simulation is not too far from what we'd expect.

Figure 5 shows we actually lost money after about 50 flips even though the odds were on our side. So even though we could certainly lose in the short run, we will end up on the winning side after hundreds of flips, which is confirmed in Figure 5.

Only when the price of the bet is $1.00 can we say that it is "fair" for both parties. As a reminder, just because the bet is fair does not mean that someone cannot end up on the winning side (and the other on the losing side). The fair value just means that, *over the long run*, neither side is expected to end up on the winning or losing side.

Fair Value Depends on Perspective

In the coin toss gamble, we calculated that $1.00 was the fair value of the bet. However, that result is due to our assumption that the chance of winning (and losing) is 50%. Obviously, if we used different probabilities, we would get different results. This means that the fair value of any bet depends on our perspective; it depends on our views of the future probability of winning.

For example, let's assume that somebody offered to pay $1.50 for this coin toss game. There are two ways we could look at it. First, we could assume there is a 50% chance of winning and losing and say that it is too high of a price since that results in an expected loss of 25 cents per flip:

$$
\begin{array}{r}
(0.50) * +\$1.00 \\
+\ (0.50) * -\$1.50 \\
\hline
\text{Net} = -25 \text{ cents}
\end{array}
$$

However, we could also look at this bet another way. We could assume that the $1.50 price is a fair price since nobody should intentionally pay more than what they think is fair. If we could assume that it is a fairly valued bet, we would need to adjust the probabilities so that they balance to zero. It works out that if there is a 60% chance of winning the dollar (and therefore a 40% chance of losing your wager) then $1.50 is a fair price to pay for the game. If somebody were willing to pay $1.50 to play this game, we would say that the gambler is *implying* that his chances of winning are 60% (and the chances of losing are 40%) since those probabilities result in a fairly valued bet:

$$
\begin{array}{r}
(0.60) * +\$1.00 \\
+\ (0.40) * -\$1.50 \\
\hline
\text{Net} = 0
\end{array}
$$

Although the gambler may not specifically state that he believes the probability of winning is 60%, the mere fact that he is willing to pay $1.50 for such a bet implies a 60% probability of winning if we assume the bet is fair.

This shows that there are two ways of looking at any bet. First, if we believe there is only a 50% chance of winning then paying $1.50 is too high of a price. Second, we can assume the $1.50 is a fair price and adjust the probabilities to make the bet fair. So is $1.50 a fair price to pay for this game? It all depends on how we view the future probability of winning.

Now, as the gambler, it is up to you to decide which viewpoint is more realistic. Should you assume the future chances of winning are 50% and only be willing to pay $1.00? Or is a 60% chance of winning more realistic? Notice that if you assume that 50% is the correct probability that you will be outbid by another gambler if he feels 60% is the more realistic probability. You would only be willing to bid up to $1 for the bet while he would be willing to pay up to $1.50. It is critical that we are confident in our assessments. If 60% sounds like too high of a probability, we're probably better off not taking the bet. It's better to miss out on some reward rather than to lose some or all of our money.

You can see from this example that your probability assessment of 50% or 60% (or something else) to value this coin flip game is an important assumption if you are to make money. It is even more important when valuing options. However, as we said before, very few option traders ever check to see how the price of the option compares to their assessment of value. In order to do that, option traders need to use the Black-Scholes Model before stepping into any trade.

Using the Black-Scholes Model

The Black-Scholes Model is an option pricing model that takes six inputs and calculates what the call and put prices should be. The six factors are:

- Stock price
- Exercise price (strike price)
- Risk-free rate of interest
- Time to expiration
- Dividends
- Volatility

You can find Black-Scholes calculators at many websites but one of the best is available, free of charge, through the Chicago Board Options Exchange (CBOE) at the following link:

http://www.cboe.com/LearnCenter/RCTools.aspx

Let's run through an example of how to use it. Assume that the underlying stock is $50, the strike price is $50, there are 60 days to expiration, volatility is 30%, the risk-free interest rate is 2%, and no dividends are paid during the life of the option. If we put these values into the calculator (as shown in Figure 6, following page) and hit the "calculate" bar, we find that the call should be priced at $2.50 and the put at about $2.35 as shown by the circles in Figure 6:

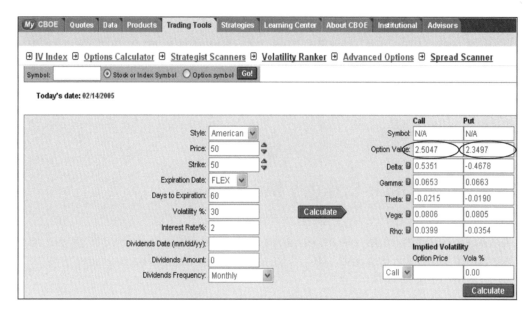

Fig. 6 *Call and put values based on the six inputs on left hand side:*

Those circled values are not just some ambiguous values. They are the *fair values* of the option "bets" based on the six inputs given on the left hand side. In this example, if you pay more than $2.50 for the call option (or $2.35 for the put), you are expected to just break even in the long run. If you pay less, you'll end up on the winning side and if you pay more you'll end up on the losing side. This assumes that you are able to make this exact bet hundreds of times, which is an unrealistic assumption. In the real world, you are probably only going to get one shot at any given option scenario. Still, understanding the fair value of such a bet over hundreds of trials gives us a benchmark for what we should be willing to pay for only one shot.

Black-Scholes Input Explanations

Style
The "style" pull down menu asks you to select either "American" or "European" style options. An American style option is one that can be exercised at any time prior to expiration while the European counterpart may only be exercised at expiration. All equity (stock) options are American style while most index options are European (the OEX is about the only major exception – it is an American style option). If you are valuing stock options, make sure you select the "American" style.

Interest Rate

The interest rate is always the annualized risk-free rate over the time period of the option. In this example, we need the risk-free rate for a sixty-day investment (expressed as an annual rate). However, the CBOEs calculator automatically looks this up for you based on the "days to expiration" field you provide. So the risk-free rate is not an input that you need to worry about finding if you are using this calculator.

Volatility

This is the most important number in determining an option's value. We used 30% for this example but, in the real world of trading, that number could be anything from a low of about 10% to a high of 300% or more. The volatility number is simply the standard deviation of stock price returns, which we will talk about shortly. The volatility number gives us an idea of how large we expect the future price swings to be.

Dividends

The "dividends" field requires us to type in the amount of any dividend that will be paid during the life of the option.

Of the six factors, volatility is the most critical since it is not directly observable in the market. In other words, if you asked 100 traders to fill in the six fields in the Black-Scholes Model for a particular option, they would all use the same current stock price, the same exercise price, the same risk-free interest rate (or at least very close), the same dividend amount, and the same time to expiration. Those five factors are fixed at each moment in time. However, it is possible that no two traders would use the same volatility since there is no way to say for sure what the correct answer is. This is why volatility is so important to understand.

Valuing an Option

According to the Black-Scholes Model, the key ingredient in valuing an option is the future volatility – the volatility of the stock's prices that will occur over the life of the option. We do not need to know anything about the direction of the stock (notice that the model does not ask you for a prediction on the direction of the stock). The reason for this is that stock price changes follow a bell-shaped curve. Once we have the volatility (the standard deviation) we can determine many probabilities since we know the following properties must hold for bell curves:

1) 68% of the data fall within one standard deviation
2) 95% of the data fall within two standard deviations
3) Essentially all of the data fall within three standard deviations

As an example, if we have a $100 stock with 30% volatility, we know that in one year:

1) There is a 68% chance the stock's price will fall between $70 and $130 (one standard deviation, or 30% on either side of the current $100 price).
2) There is a 95% chance the stock's price will fall between $40 and $160 (two standard deviations, or 2* 30% on either side of $100)
3) There is virtually a 100% chance that the stock's price would lay between $10 and $190 after one year (three standard deviations, or 3 * 30% on either side of $100).

Once we have a standard deviation (volatility), the Black-Scholes Model can then find the probabilities and payoffs of the option and that means we can find the fair value of the bet. If we are faced with low volatility, then there are only a few possible stock prices that can occur and the option has only a few possible small payoffs. Consequently, the option has a low price. But if there is a lot of volatility then there are a lot of possible stock prices underneath that bell curve and the bet becomes more valuable (the option has a much higher price). For option trading it is important to remember the following: High volatility equals high-priced options (true for both calls and puts). Low volatility equals low-priced options.

   Of course, we will never know what the true volatility number is until after the fact but we can get an idea based on past volatilities. There is one more concept that we need to grasp before putting all of this information together. That is, volatility tends to move sideways over time. Let's take a closer look at why this statement is true.

Volatility Moves Sideways

In order to use the Black-Scholes Model to your advantage, you must understand an important characteristic of volatility. That is, volatility tends to move *sideways* over time. For example, Figure 7 shows an 18-year history of the Volatility Index, or VIX, which measures the volatility of the S&P 500 Index. Although the index has risen substantially over this time period, notice that the volatility did not – it just moved sideways.

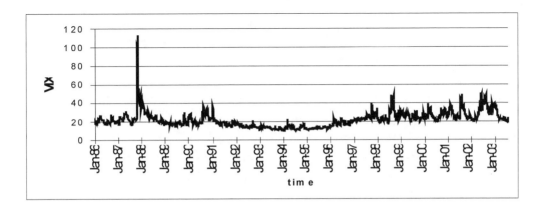

Fig. 7 *Volatility Index (VIX)*

This sideways characteristic of volatility is about the only constant in options trading and, consequently, is an important observation we can use to our advantage. When volatility rises significantly above the long-term average, there is a tendency for it to fall and vice versa. The tendency for volatility to fall toward the long-term average is called *mean reversion*. That is, volatility tends to revert to the mean (average). Anytime an extreme event happens, chances are that following events will be less extreme, not more. Mean reversion is easy to understand by looking at a real-world example – one that is often explained by a jinx.

Mean Reversion –
The Sports Illustrated Jinx

The *Sports Illustrated* jinx states that if a professional athlete makes the cover of Sports Illustrated; his or her performance has now been jinxed and will slip the following season. There is a long (and quite convincing) history of this phenomenon ever since Sports Illustrated was first published. In fact, in January 2002, nobody would even pose for the cover and it hit the newsstands with a picture of a black cat and the caption "The Cover that No One Would Pose for: Is the SI Jinx for Real"?

But let's take a look at this "jinx" from a mean reversion standpoint. In 1998 baseball superstar Mark McGwire set an all-time record when he hit 70 homeruns. This is a remarkable feat that had never been done before in history – that is the reason he made the cover. The next season we should not expect him to outperform that record but, instead, fall back toward his long-term homerun average. He did, in fact, hit 65, 32, and 29 homeruns in the following three years. This is simply mean reversion at work and not an apparent jinx, as many believe. People who believe in the Sports Illustrated jinx are simply confusing cause and effect. McGwire's homeruns did not fall *because* he made the cover of Sports Illustrated. Instead, he made the cover because the number of homeruns was abnormally high and we should have expected his subsequent homeruns to fall.

If you look back at Figure 7, you'll see that the VIX tends to bounce back and forth between 20% and 40% most of the time suggesting that the long-term average may be around 30%. When it moves significantly above or below 30%, it is a rare feat and we should expect it to fall back toward the 30% mark rather than continue in one direction or the other.

Putting it all Together

Now that you understand about fair value along with the fact that volatility tends to move sideways, let's see if we can use this new knowledge to help us check the value of an option.

Let's go back to the VIP trade we discussed at the beginning of the chapter. To make the example easier to follow, let's just pick one of the call options.

Since most option traders are tempted to buy the out-of-the-money strike, we will assume that we are interested in buying the $33.375 call.[2]

Figure 1 shows that the $33.375 call was priced at $2.50 on December 16. But we also said that there can be significant differences between an option's price and its value. *Before we buy this (or any) option, we need to check the value by checking the past volatility of the underlying stock.* Once we get a feel for how the past volatilities have behaved then we can gauge how much we should be willing to pay for the option.

By checking the historical volatility, we are gaining an idea of the possible payouts from the option. In other words, if VIP closes at $34.375 at expiration, that call is worth $1. If the stock closes at $35.375 it is worth $2 and so on. How likely is it that the call is worth either of these values? How likely is it that it's worth more? To answer that, we need to know the standard deviation of the bell curve representing the stock price changes and that's exactly what the past volatilities show us.

One of the simplest ways to check the past volatility is to view a long-term chart, perhaps one year or more, of the volatility on the underlying stock. Because we are trying to determine the value of the $33.375 call, it is usually best to match the expiration with the moving average. For example, the $33.375 call expires in about 30 days so we should use a 30-day moving average for the historic volatility. Figure 8 shows a one-year chart of the 30-day moving averages for the volatility of VIP stock:

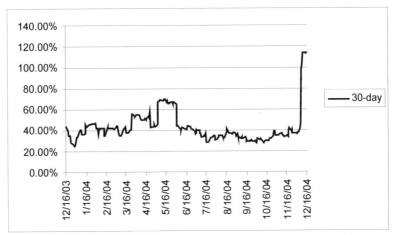

Fig. 8 *One-year historic volatilities for VIP stock*

---

2. Technically, the $31.625 call is out-of-the-money too but that would probably be considered the at-the-money strike by most traders since it is pretty close to the current stock price.

If you look at Figure 8, you will see that the average has just moved between a low of 30% and high of about 70% with the exception of the spike at the end of the chart approaching the 120% level.

Now we have a decision to make. Which volatility level will be correct for the next thirty days until expiration of the calls? While we will never know the correct answer until after the fact, we do know the long run history has been between low of 30% and a high of 70% so our estimate should probably lie in this region. Figure 8, however, shows that the current level of volatility is near 120%. If we use this volatility to price the option we will probably be fighting a downward pull on the option's price, as the volatility will most likely fall back to the average. Remember, the price of an option is directly tied to the volatility. If the volatility is high then so is the price. But if we are expecting volatility to fall, then the price of the option will fall as well if our expectations are correct.

Prior to the large spike in Figure 8, the 30-day volatility had just crossed the 40% so that might be an estimate for future volatility over the next 30 days. Although 40% is one estimate, it is not the only one we could use. Remember that volatility is the only true unknown in the Black-Scholes Model and now you see why – volatility does not stay constant. However, most option traders would agree that the future volatility estimate should be fairly representative of the moves we observe in the chart. If we were to ask many option traders for their opinion on future volatility, we might obtain estimates in the shaded area of Figure 9:

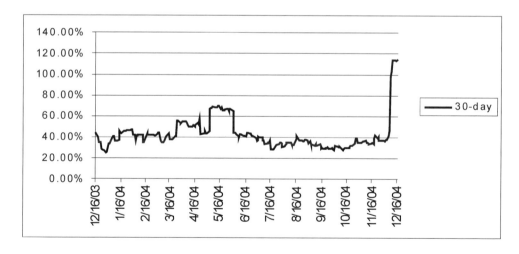

Fig. 9 *Range of volatility estimates we might expect to receive from many traders*

Traders with a strong bullish conviction may be willing to buy the option with a volatility level at the high end of the shaded area, say 60%. Traders less convinced of a large price move in the stock may only be willing to buy the option at the lower end of around 40%. But very few traders should be willing to pay the current level of 120% since that is a very rare volatility level. This shows why it is not a good idea to rely on software that compares a single point (such as the 30-day average) to the current price. Under this system, the software would tell you that an option priced at 120% volatility is fairly priced even though that's far from true based on historical standards.

Let's assume we split the difference between the 40% and 60% levels and use 50% for our future volatility estimate. What does the Black-Scholes Model says about the value of this option?

We know the current stock price is $31.41, we're interested in buying the $33.375 strike, there are 39 days until expiration, no dividends are paid on the stock over the life of the option, and we just decided to use 50% as a future estimate of volatility. (Remember, this calculator automatically finds the risk-free interest rate for you.) Figure 10 shows that the fair value of a call option with these inputs is only about $1.30:

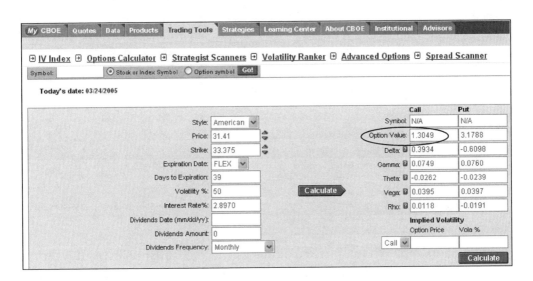

Fig. 10 *Fair value of the $33.375 call option assuming 50% volatility*

There is clearly a discrepancy between what we think the call is worth when compared to the $2.50 market price. In other words, the $2.50 market price of the option is far greater than the $1.30 value to us.

We said earlier that there are two ways we can view a bet and now it's time to take a look at the second way. Let's assume that the market is correct and that the $2.50 asking price is a fair value for this bet. Which volatility must the market use to come up with a price of $2.50? We can find out by simply entering the $2.50 asking price into the "implied volatility" section in the lower right hand corner of the calculator, which is circled in Figure 11. (Make sure you also select "call" from the drop down menu.) After we hit the "calculate" bar in the same circle, the calculator shows that the market is using a volatility estimate of nearly 80% (79.64%).

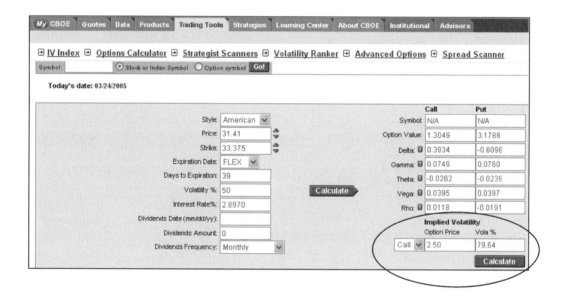

Fig. 11 *Implied volatility of the $33.375 call*

The implied volatility shows us the volatility level that must be used in order to make the current market price true. The market does not agree with our 50% estimate and is, instead, using a volatility of nearly 80%. If you type 79.64 into the "volatility %" box on the left hand side of the calculator, the price of the call would show $2.50. Just as with our coin toss example, the market does not need to specifically think that the future volatility is 80%. The mere fact that traders are willing to pay $2.50 for the call implies that they are using 80% as an estimate of future volatility. It is for this reason that the 80% figure is called the *implied volatility*. What likely caused this high level of volatility is the fact that traders continued to buy up these call options without consulting a pricing model.

Now, as option traders, we have a decision to make: Does 80% seem like a reasonable estimate of future volatility? After checking the volatility over the past year we find that it does not seem to be in line with any of the volatilities we've seen in the past with the exception of the recent spike. This does not mean that it's impossible to make money with this option if we were to pay $2.50. Instead, it shows that the odds appear to be stacked very much against us. It is a trade we're better off avoiding. In our opinion, this appears to be a losing proposition if we were to make this exact trade hundreds of times.

Why does $2.50 appear to be an unfair price? If you pay $2.50 for this option, there is a very good chance that volatility will revert to the average – dragging down the option's price with it. And that is exactly what happened with the VIP calls in Figure 1.

Figure 12 shows an overlay of the stock's price (shaded line) and the 10-day historical volatility (bold line). You can see that the stock's price did rise after December 16 but that volatility also fell right back to the average as we expected. The net result between these two forces was an overall loss. It was the falling volatility that was the culprit of the call losses.

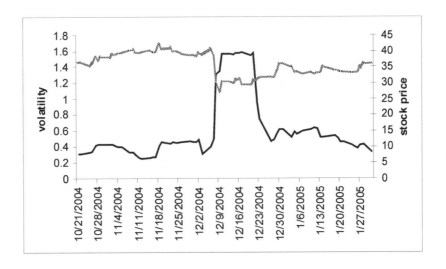

Fig. 12

Time Decay?

Many traders believe that the VIP calls lost money simply because of time decay. Time decay means that time has been subtracted from the life of the option and that the option must therefore be worth less money. However, that assumes that *all other factors stay the same*. We can use the Black-Scholes Model to see if time decay was the culprit. Figure 13 shows that if we use a volatility of 79.64% then the price of the call is $2.50, which was the market price at the time we considered buying the $33.375 call:

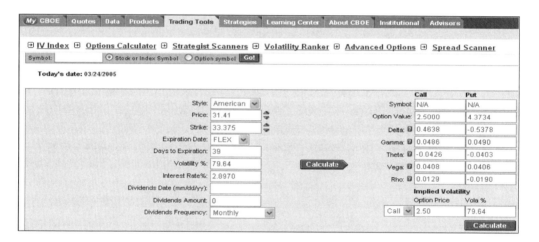

Fig. 13 *Is time decay the culprit?*

Thirteen days later, the stock rose to $34. Figure 14 shows the value of the $33.375 call thirteen days later (26 days to expiration instead of 39) would be $3.20 *assuming that volatility remained constant* at 79.64%:

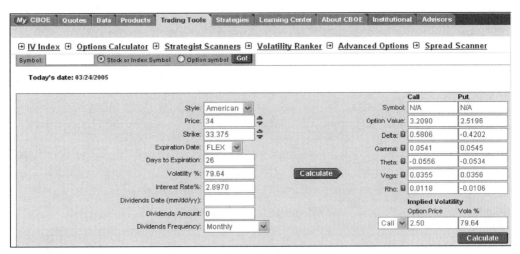

Fig. 14 *Value of $33.375 call thirteen days later assuming all else constant*

So the fact that time decayed by thirteen days was not the culprit of the loss on the VIP $33.375 call[3]. Had thirteen days passed and volatility remained constant, we would have been able to sell the call for $3.20 and gained a nice profit. Instead, we faced a loss with the call bidding only $1.80. Which volatility is necessary to create a $1.80 bid price?

Figure 15 shows that an implied volatility of about 40% (39.81%) equates to a $1.80 call price. This shows that the reason the $33.375 call lost money was not because of time decay but rather that the implied volatility was cut in half; it fell from 80% to 40% in thirteen days.

---

3. Technically speaking, to show the true effect of time decay we should have used the same starting stock price of $31.41 since time decay is a result of *all factors* remaining constant (with the exception of time). However, most traders believe that the reason this trade lost money is strictly due to time decay even though the stock price rose. To show that is not true, we need to account for the current stock price and use $34.

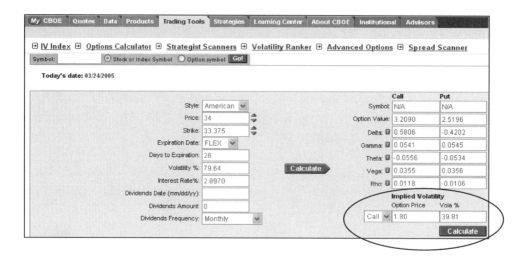

Fig. 15 *Falling volatility was the reason for the loss on the $33.375 call*

The Black-Scholes Model allowed us to see the volatilities that the market was using to price the $33.375 call. Had we not used the model, all we would see is the $2.50 call price and have to make our decision based on our belief of the *direction* of the stock. But as we've seen, knowing the direction is not enough to profit on options. We must also know something about the volatility that the market is using to price the options. Because the market's assessment of volatility was so high, we were faced with a very large premium ($2.50 market price versus our estimate of $1.30). In order to overcome this large premium, the call option had a high-speed component. Had VIP moved from $31.41 to $34 the next day, we would expect the call to be profitable. But it took thirteen days to get there and that's a different story.

Creating a Winning Trade

We've just demonstrated with a real-life example that option trading requires more than a directional belief about the underlying stock. In other words, just because you may be bullish does not mean that buying calls is the right strategy to capitalize on that outlook. The reason is that long positions have a "point spread" built into them in the form of a time premium. If that time premium is too high, we can lose on the option even though the stock may rise. By using the Black-Scholes model, we could guess that it's probably not wise to buy the

$33.375 call when it's priced at 80% volatility. Does this mean we should sell the call?

On the surface, many traders erroneously think that if the volatility appears to be too high then we should simply be the sellers of the calls but that is not necessarily true. There are two main reasons. First, in this example, VIP appears to be priced at high volatility levels but it's possible there is a good reason. If we sell the call and the stock price jumps much higher, we could end up with sizeable losses. So we do not necessarily want to sell calls "just because" volatility is high. Second, a high volatility does not equate to a bullish bias. It's certainly possible that the market is equally *negative* on the stock. Remember, high volatility just means that the market is expecting large price swings in the future; volatility measurements do not take direction into account but, instead, only the size of the price swings. So if the VIP $33.375 call appears to be priced high, it could be due to traders bidding up the price of the puts (as the price of puts rise so does the price of calls)[4]. Since we determined that volatility is exceptionally high, all we can really do at this point is decide to avoid the trade. We have tremendous insights into the price swings (volatility) that the market is expecting but nothing has been said about the direction. *And it is this point that makes candlestick charting so important for option traders.* If we can gain some insights into the direction of the stock, we can then determine whether we wish to buy or sell the bet. Let's see if we can use candlesticks to gain this critical additional information.

Candlestick Charts

At the beginning of this chapter, we said that Honma discovered that emotions play a significant part in the supply and demand for stock and therefore were important in determining price. In this example, all we know right now is that the market is bidding volatility to very high levels but that just means the market expects *large price moves* in the near future. We need to know if these large moves are due, for example, to an impending takeover (bullish) or corporate scandal (bearish) that is about to hit the news. Let's take a look at a candle-

---

4. There is a mathematical relationship called put-call parity, which states that the difference between the same-strike call and put prices must equal the difference between the stock price and the present value of the exercise price. The important point to understand is that call prices will rise if put prices rise (and vice versa).

stick chart on VIP and see if we can get a sense of how the supply and demand is stacking up. Figure 16 shows a two-month candlestick chart right up to the December 16th date of our decision:

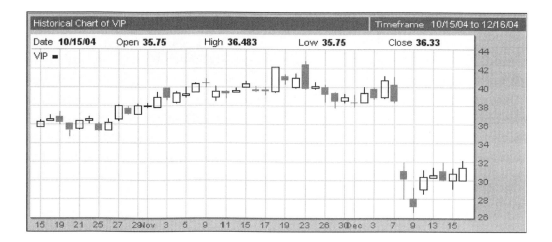

Fig. 16 *Bullish engulfing candle on our trade date*

At the right side of the chart, you'll see the last two candles forming a classic "Bullish Engulfing" pattern. In fact, the second "engulfing" candle never traded below the opening price, as there is no lower shadow. This shows us that the traders are stacking up as net buyers and we should expect the stock to continue higher. There is no way to get the information that quickly from a western style "open-high-low-close" chart. With one simple glance at a candlestick chart, we now know the two important pieces of information that are needed to trade options profitable – direction and speed. We know the market demand is stacking up to the bullish side *and* that volatility appears to be too high. So what type of strategy should we use? Because the market is bullish, we do not want to be caught holding short calls since that is a *bearish* bet. If the market is correct, we could end up with huge losses even though we were correct in selling theoretically high volatility. In order to create a winning trade, we need to take into account that we are bullish along with our belief that volatility is high. Because we're bullish, we obviously want a bullish bet. But because volatility is high, we do not want to *buy* a bullish bet. Instead, we need to *sell* the *bullish* bet. And that means we need to sell puts.

Figure 17 is a reprint of Figure 1 and Figure 2. You can see that selling the $33.375 put for $3.40 would yield a nice profit after buying it back thirteen days later for only $1.65.

VIP (NYSE)											31.41 +0.62
Dec 16,2004 @ 16:39 ET (Data 15 Minutes Delayed)							Bid 18.80 Ask 18.81 Size 14x6 Vol 29728				

Calls	Last Sale	Net	Bid	Ask	Vol	Open Int	Puts	Last Sale	Net	Bid	Ask	Vol	Open Int
05 Jan 31.625 (VIP AU-E)	3.00	+0.80	3.00	3.50	392	645	05 Jan 31.625 (VIP MU-E)	3.50	pc	2.40	3.60	0	249
05 Jan 33.375 (VIP AV-E)	2.10	+0.45	1.75	2.50	12	1348	05 Jan 33.375 (VIP MV-E)	3.30	pc	3.40	4.60	0	175
05 Jan 35 (VIP AG-E)	1.65	+0.45	1.15	1.75	48	977	05 Jan 35 (VIP MG-E)	5.20	+0.30	4.50	5.70	20	618

VIP (NYSE)											34.00 +2.50
Dec 29,2004 @ 12:56 ET (Data 15 Minutes Delayed)							Bid N/A Ask N/A Size NA/NA Vol 1845000				

Calls	Last Sale	Net	Bid	Ask	Vol	Open Int	Puts	Last Sale	Net	Bid	Ask	Vol	Open Int
04 Jan 31.625 (VIP AU-E)	3.20	+1.20	2.90	3.30	269	1515	05 Jan 31.625 (VIP MU-E)	0.90	-1.15	0.75	1.05	13	305
04 Jan 33.375 (VIP AV-E)	2.00	+0.95	1.80	2.25	217	1630	05 Jan 33.375 (VIP MV-E)	3.30	pc	1.20	1.65	0	186
04 Jan 35 (VIP AG-E)	1.25	+0.65	1.00	1.40	60	1396	05 Jan 35 (VIP MG-E)	2.30	-2.60	2.00	2.45	11	661

Fig. 17

How would the other puts have performed? The $31.625 puts could have been sold for $2.40 and repurchased for $1.05 and the $35 puts could have been sold for $4.50 and repurchased for $2.45. The sale of any put resulted in a significant gain for the simple fact that this simple strategy properly aligned both the directional and volatility aspects of options.

As we stated before, the purchase of any call resulted in a loss. And that's because the buyers were correct on direction (the stock did rise) but they were wrong about volatility (they bought the high volatility). Many traders believe that if calls are expensive to buy then they must be a great deal to sell. Let's see if that's true. Notice that if you had sold the $33.375 calls, you would have sold for $1.75 and repurchased for $2.25, which leaves you with a loss. By selling these calls, you were correct in selling volatility (you sold volatility when it was high) but you were wrong about the direction of the stock. In fact, the sale of any of the calls resulted in a loss. *It is only the short put trader that made money since that strategy properly aligned direction and volatility. Only when both components are properly aligned can you expect to make money with options.*

Once again, notice that the one-dimensional stock trader would have made money by purchasing at $31.41 and selling for $34. But in order to make money with options, you must be correct on direction and speed. And that means you must take volatility into account.

Your best source for understanding volatility comes from using the Black-Scholes Model and the best directional indicators come from candlestick charts. It is the trader who uses both tools that will be able to separate price and value of options.

Utilizing Option Information

The use of candlestick signals, in their proper positioning for identifying tread reversals and applying a few minutes of option analysis to a trade, can produce high profits that everybody always promises. Utilizing the same principles for evaluating high profit stock trades will make structuring successful option trades relatively easy.

Learning the candlestick signals enhances the ability to identify direction. Being able to identify price movement enhancements signals, such as gaps or bounces close off major technical levels, in conjunction with the candlestick signals, increases the probabilities of establishing a profitable option trade.

Applying that information to various option expirations provide profitable strategies. Able to recognize profitable trading patterns might allow an option investor to sell the near term calls while buying the calls of the next month strike price. Options strategies become measurably more fined tuned when having the ability to evaluate short-term direction based upon candlestick signals during a longer-term price pattern.

The Black-Scholes option pricing model adds an additional element for exploiting specific options that are over or under-priced based upon historic market conditions. As an example, if a bullish candlestick signal indicates a $53 stock as a strong buy, the Black-Scholes model creates an additional profit opportunity. In preparation of executing a call, the $50 strike price and the $55 strike price might be evaluated. If the model indicates the $55 strike price options are priced correctly and the $50 strike price options are undervalued, logic dictates purchasing the undervalued options. Or at least overweighting the $50 options if a combination of both options were being purchased.

The same rationale would be applied to selling calls or puts. When an option strategy was being implemented which involved selling calls are puts, selling the overvalued options becomes a better probability trade.

Putting Candlestick and Option Strategies Together

The serious option investor can make very strong profits utilizing correct trade analysis. The reduction of risk can be incorporated into the trade analysis. The same analytical tools for finding high profit stock trades can dramatically improve profitability with some simple option strategies.

A successful option trade utilizes a series of quick and easy trade entry steps. A successful option trader needs to prepare exit strategies the same as they would when trading the underlying stock. When the stock trade does not work, the option trade does not work. Unfortunately, this makes the effect of the bid/ask spread more pronounced.

The benefit of being in a successful option trade is the large percentage returns that can be made. Losses, as far as percent loss, on a particular trade will be much more exaggerated than a stock trade, of course. That makes the concept of the option trading "program" that much more important than each option trade.

Keeping in mind, the basis for successful investing is to put the probabilities in your favor. Probabilities imply that not all trades are going to be successful. The purpose of learning a trading strategy is to use the parameters and historic observations that have worked successfully a high percentage of the time. Utilizing the candlestick signals has that proven track record. Applying that information to option trading, leveraging the use of your funds, requires the same mental process as a successful stock trading program. When all the indicators/signals point to a successful trade, take advantage of what you have learned.

Chapter 8

Profitable Trading Insights

> *Ask the experienced rather than the learned.*
> *Arabian Proverb*

Candlestick analysis benefits all technical trading. Successful traders will incorporate candlestick signals into other technical methods. For the sake of providing the reader with other perspectives on how to use candlesticks, one of the leading traders, Tina Logan, has graciously contributed insights on her own successful trading methods. She is a well-respected investor and her reputation for utilizing excellent investment-discipline habits places her in the top ranks of investment trainers. Tina Logan is primarily a swing trader, but periodically day-trades or invests in longer-term positions, dependant upon market conditions. Over the years, Tina has had the good fortune to study with some very experienced traders, including an author, a seminar leader and a hedge fund manager.

The past decade has been devoted to studying and implementing successful technical analysis and trade implementation. Tina is an avid user of technical analysis and feels it is crucial to understanding when to enter, and exit stocks. She has spent thousands of hours trading, testing, designing strategies and developing very detailed and comprehensive training program for investors. For several years, Tina has been providing training to small groups and one-on-one private tutoring. Her insights illustrate the effectiveness of utilizing candlestick signals with Western techniques. Although some of the information will be redundant to what you have read so far in this book, it should illustrate that candlestick signals can be applied to simple but successful investment decisions.

Presented by Tina Logan

Rather than debate the superiority of Japanese candlestick analysis or western technical analysis, the smart trader utilizes them both. Savvy traders blend the two types of analysis in an effort to maximize their profits. Candlestick patterns can help strengthen other Western technical signals. The Japanese candlestick chart is visually more representative of investor sentiment than a western price bar. In addition, candlestick reversal patterns can help identify the likely turning points so traders can react quickly to changes in price direction. Western technical analysis is broader in scope. In addition to referencing the price bars, many books on western charting provide discussion of topics such as:

- **Volatility**
- **Retracement of previous price moves**
- **Drawing trendlines**
- **Divergence between price and indicators**
- **Support and resistance levels**
- **Identification of large chart patterns, such as triangles and channels**

Candlestick patterns provide a micro view of price action, while western signals provide a bigger picture look at the chart. Traders can combine these strengths to develop highly profitable strategies.

Combining Eastern and Western Analysis

Traders must survive before they can thrive. A major challenge for new traders is simply lasting long enough in the markets to learn the ropes. Those who do survive the early years eventually move from trading with emotion to trading with technique and discipline. As they gain experience, their focus shifts from that of mere survival to risk management and increasing profitability.

Cluster of Signals

Often more than one reversal signal occurs near the same price level. Multiple signals clustered together should give a trader more confidence that the set-up will follow through in the anticipated direction. An example would be when a Japanese candlestick pattern forms within a larger western chart pattern. For instance, often the second top of a bearish Double Top is a bearish candlestick reversal pattern. Figure 8-1 shows a Double Top that formed on the Waste Connections chart during the summer of 2005. An Evening Star formed at the second peak of the larger pattern. Stochastics confirmed by turning down from the oversold line.

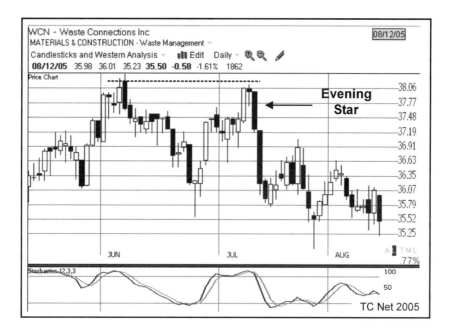

Fig. 8-1 *A bearish Evening Star formed the
second peak of a bearish Double Top.*

Another technical event that may make a set-up stronger is when price tests a long-term Moving Average, such as the 50- or 200-period. These Moving Averages are watched closely by experienced traders. They often provide support when price declines to those levels. Conversely, when a downtrend reverses, longer-term Moving Averages above may act as resistance.

Figure 8-2 shows a chart of Remington Oil & Gas. This is a good example of several signals coming together. A Double Bottom formed at the 200-period Moving Average. The additional support provided by the strong indicator should increase the likelihood of a reversal. In addition to the Western signals, a bullish candlestick reversal pattern formed the second bottom of the larger pattern. Usually the Stochastics will also curl up from the oversold level. However, if the second bottom is slightly higher than the first bottom, because of the loss of momentum on the second bottom, the Stochastics may not drop back below the 20 line. It should still curl up though.

Fig. 8-2 *A Hammer formed the second bottom of a Double Bottom pattern. The 200-period Moving Average also provided support and Stochastics turned up.*

Candlestick patterns are very common at reversal points. Figure 8-3 shows a bearish Head and Shoulders Top that formed on Take-Two Intera Software. A bearish candlestick pattern formed at each shoulder, and at the head, of the larger pattern. The larger chart pattern alone is bearish. The formation of a bearish candlestick at the right shoulder should increase the likelihood of follow through to the downside. Stochastics also confirmed the turns. By the time the right shoulder of the Head and Shoulders Top forms, price is already in a downtrend. Because of that downward momentum, Stochastics may not rise back up to the oversold level on the right shoulder.

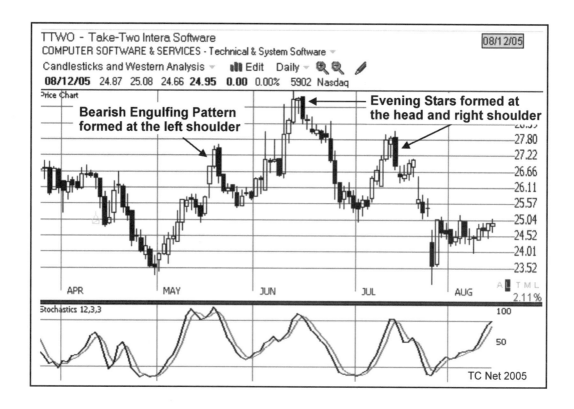

Fig. 8-3 *Bearish candlestick patterns are common at reversal points.*

To confirm a short position, price should close below the neckline of the Head and Shoulders pattern. The neckline touches the swing lows between the two shoulders. Traders may choose to take an early entry rather than waiting for confirmation, especially if there is bearish candlestick pattern that forms the right shoulder. By that time the neckline is breached, the move is well under way to the downside.

In the Take-Two example, there is potential support at the May low. If a short position is still open by the time price reaches a visible support level, it should be covered. Price generally bounces, at least temporarily, at a strong floor.

Consult the Sector

When a sector or industry group is in favor, the component stocks may run up for several weeks or even months. Eventually the overbought condition will cause a period of consolidation or a correction. A correction can be identified by a retracement of the previous trend.

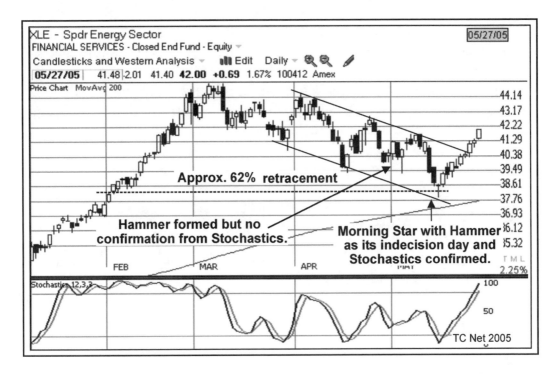

Fig. 8-4 *A Morning Star helped identify the end of a correction.*

A stock in a strong sector may resume the uptrend once price has corrected sufficiently. Traders who wish to participate in the resumption of the prior uptrend should watch closely for signals indicating that the correction may be ending.

Many stocks in the Energy sector made significant advances during 2005. Figure 8-4 shows XLE, the Spider Sector ETF for the Energy group. After the price advance from the January low to the March high, price retraced a significant amount of the previous uptrend. The retracement was approximately 62%, a well-known Fibonacci level.

A bullish Morning Star also formed near that level indicating a possible end of the correction. Several days later price closed above the top trend-line of a falling channel giving further evidence that price was rising again. The correction provided an excellent opportunity for traders to purchase shares at lower prices.

Oil stocks were a hot commodity during 2005. They were a major contributor to the run up in the XLE chart illustrated above. A challenge for traders was to know at what point the stocks in this industry had run up too far. Figure 8-5 shows a significant run up on Exxon Mobil. Traders who watched closely for reversal signals received timely warnings that Exxon was about to reverse direction.

Reversal candlestick patterns formed on both the daily and weekly time frames. Figure 8-5 shows a bearish Harami-Doji (also referred to as a Harami Cross) on the weekly chart. Figure 8-5a shows a Tower Top on the daily chart.

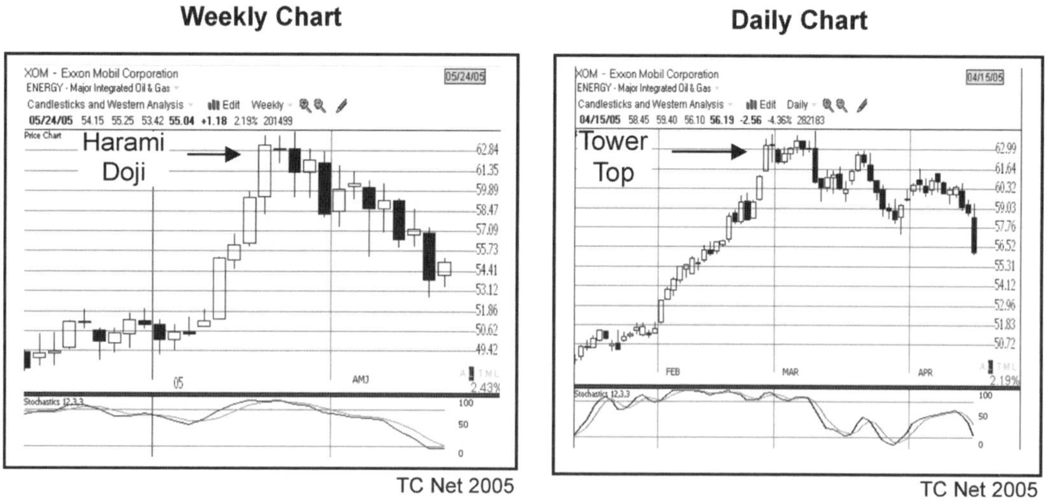

Weekly Chart   **Daily Chart**

Fig. 8-5 *Reversal patterns formed before a correction began.*

Traders who primarily view charts on the daily time-frame can gain an edge by also incorporating the weekly chart in their analysis. Support and resistance levels, that may not be seen within the time-period displayed on the daily chart, can easily be seen on the weekly chart.

Sometimes support and resistance levels formed months, or even years, in the past. However, they will be seen by chartists consulting the higher time-frames, such as weekly or monthly. Just because a support or resistance level is "old," does not mean it is not still strong.

Figure 8-6 shows a weekly chart of Hudson City Bancorp. On this view, it is easy to see that the stock has traded in a range for a couple of years. Looking at just a few months of data on a daily chart does not give as thorough a picture as can be seen on the weekly chart.

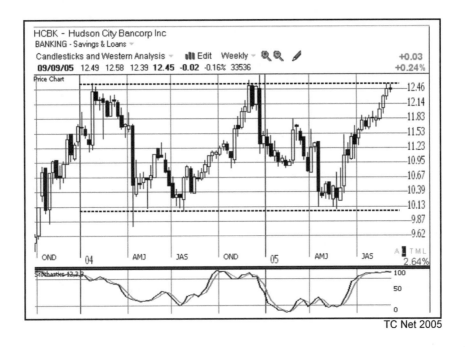

Fig. 8-6 *Support and resistance levels seen on a weekly chart.*

Candlestick patterns are visible on all timeframes. The higher the time frame the more meaningful the implication of the pattern. If a bearish reversal pattern forms at the end of an advance on the weekly or monthly chart, ignore it at your own peril!

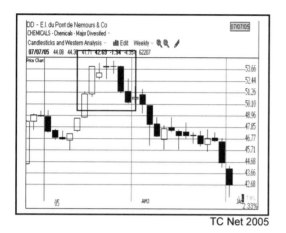

Fig. 8-7 *A bearish Tower Top formed on a weekly chart.*

Fig. 8-8 *A bullish Morning Star formed on a weekly chart.*

Trading with Multiple Time Frames

While browsing weekly charts, you may come across some interesting set-ups that offer great trading opportunities. For example, a Tweezer Bottom is a pattern where the lows of two or more bars are at, or very near, the same price. Often a Tweezer Bottom on a weekly chart will be a Double Bottom down on the daily chart. Vice versa for a Tweezer Top.

Figure 8-9 shows a weekly chart of SPLS with a Tweezer Bottom. The tweezer formed at a floor that had been established several months prior. On the daily chart, traders see a bullish Double Bottom. However, they may not notice that the pattern is testing a strong floor unless they compress the daily chart or shift to the weekly time frame. SPLS trended up for several weeks following the successful retest of the strong support.

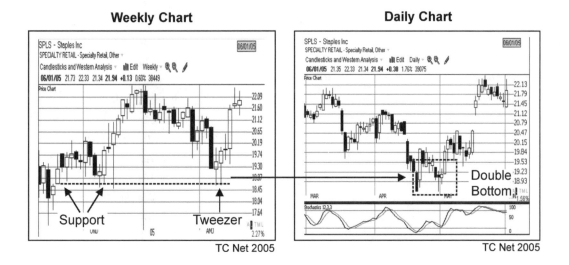

Fig. 8-9 *A Tweezer Bottom formed at a floor on the weekly chart. The daily chart showed a Double Bottom.*

Swing Trading Using Japanese Candlesticks

Swing trading can be a very profitable method of trading. It is a style that capitalizes on the concept that price does not usually move too far in one direction before pausing or pulling back. Swing traders can make substantial gains during those short-term moves. They then exit before price turns against them robbing them of their profits. This type of trade is generally held from two to six days. Some swing trades may be held longer, but usually not for more than a couple of weeks.

This method of trading has become increasingly popular over the past few years. It is not as demanding as day trading, and yet not as passive as a buy-and-hold strategy. The savvy swing trader has the ability to adapt quickly to changing market environments. Swing trading can be quite profitable in up or down trends.

Swings within a Trend

Intermediate-term trends generally last from several weeks to a few months. Within the trend, there may be several shorter-term price swings. A typical swing may consist of a distance the equivalent of about four to five average size bars for that particular stock. Every stock is different. The swings may vary dramatically from one stock to another.

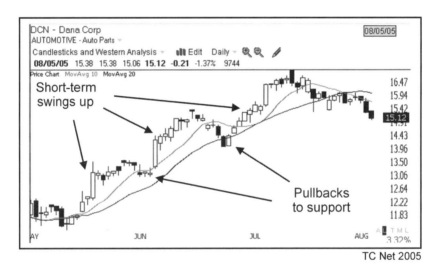

Fig. 8-10 *Shorter-term swings within a trend.*

You can enhance your swing trading skills by paying attention to overall market conditions. In a choppy or bearish market, the swings up may be shorter. In a bullish market, the moves up may be more significant as the broad market rallies. Additionally, if a stock is in a strong sector, price swings may last longer, and the dips to support may be shallower.

Sometimes stocks will trend upward making very recognizable price swings. Other times the swings are not as orderly. It takes practice to learn to trade the swings with precision. However, those who acquire the skill are usually rewarded with a steady stream of good trading opportunities.

Bearish reversal candlestick patterns often form at the end of an uptrend. But they also are quite common at the end of the shorter-term swings within the trend. These reversal patterns can be very helpful in assisting with exiting long positions on swing trades. Conversely, bullish reversal patterns can be used to fine-tune an exit on a short position.

Fig. 8-11 *Short term swings in an uptrend with bearish reversal candlesticks patterns at the swing highs.*

Trading the Swings

After a swing up, the decline that follows is often referred to as a pullback, or a dip, to support. Pullbacks are very common occurrences caused primarily by profit taking by swing traders. When price swings up, it moves away from the short-term Moving Averages. The 10-period and 20-period Moving Averages are popular short-term indicators. Price then turns down, often finding support at one of those short-term Moving Averages, but sometimes declining farther.

The pullbacks are often on low or declining volume. This is an indication of profit taking by short-term traders versus a more aggressive sell-off by a large number of traders and investors. These swings, followed by pullbacks, may give the appearance of a stair-step like motion in the trend.

The inverse can often be seen on swings to the downside when a stock is falling. However, it is not unusual to see downside declines of more magnitude than upside swings. Panic sets in and traders rush to eliminate pain. A wise trader once observed that, "The bull walks up the stairway, but the bear jumps out the window."

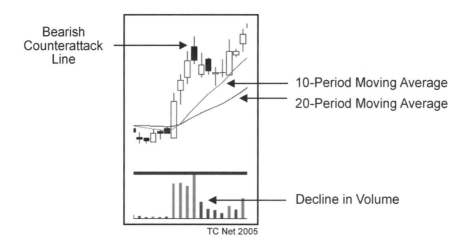

Fig. 8-12 *After ending the advance with a bearish reversal signal, price pulled back to support offering a new long entry.*

A challenge with holding through a pullback in a trend is that you cannot be certain how deep the decline will be. If price does not stop falling at the near-term support levels, a trader could watch much, or all, of the profits from the swing up disappear. Therefore, many swing traders attempt to sell the high of the swing and buy on the dips near a support level. Because of the short-term nature of this type of trade, traders can gain an edge by learning the warning signals that so often occur at the end of a price swing. Learning how to set price targets, and using protective sell stops, can also help traders avoid giving back profits.

Price Gaps

There are several types of price gaps. Their descriptions can be found in many books published on Technical Analysis. A price gap leaves a void on the chart where no trading took place. For a gap up to be present, the low of the current bar must be higher than the high of the previous bar. On a gap down, the high of the current bar must be lower than the low of the previous bar. All of the major price gaps—breakaway, continuation, exhaustion and island reversals— leave a price gap on the chart.

There is one type of gap that is not as often discussed in the mainstream publications, but is well known to experienced traders—the opening gap. An opening gap does not require an actual void on the chart. This type of gap is defined by the closing and opening prices of two candles. An opening gap up only requires that today's open be higher than yesterday's close. The shadows of the two bars can overlap. This leaves a gap between the two bodies. Vice versa for an opening gap down.

 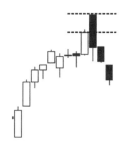

A price gap – A void was left on the chart
The gap was not filled in the same day.
This turned out to be an Exhaustion Gap.

An opening gap – No void was left on
the chart . Price reversed at the open
and filled the gap within the same day.

Fig. 8-13 *A price gap compared to an opening gap.*

The majority of opening gaps fill within the gap day. If price has already advanced for several days and then gaps open, the chances of it filling should increase. In most cases, exiting an opening gap will help maximize profits on a short-term trade. It is important to understand the difference between price gaps and opening gaps. Most gaps described in candlestick patterns refer to an opening gap, but may not require the gap leave a void on the chart. Traders should carefully read the description of the patterns.

Candlestick Warnings to Exit a Swing Trade

One way traders can gain an edge is to recognize a timely sell signal that warns that the swing up is probably over. That's where Candlestick charting can be very helpful. One type of warning traders may see, at or near a swing high, is one of the many bearish candlestick reversal patterns. These patterns can inform traders that price may be about to pull back. With some reversal patterns, by the time the pattern can be identified, it is too late. Once the pattern becomes apparent, the pullback is already beginning and the gains from the swing trade are slipping away. The Dark Cloud Cover and Bearish Counterattack (Meeting) Line patterns both start out as an opening gap. Some, but not all, Bearish Engulfing Patterns also start as an opening gap.

Figure 8-14 illustrates these three bearish patterns. The difference between the patterns is the depth of which the bearish candlestick intrudes into the previous day's bullish candle. The deeper the bearish candle, the further price is into a pullback by the close of the bar.

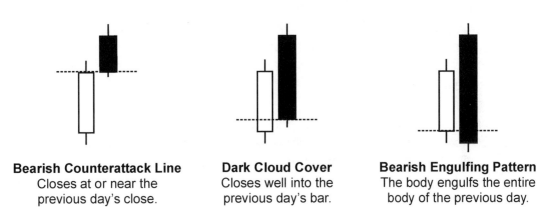

Bearish Counterattack Line
Closes at or near the
previous day's close.

Dark Cloud Cover
Closes well into the
previous day's bar.

Bearish Engulfing Pattern
The body engulfs the entire
body of the previous day.

Fig. 8-14 *Bearish reversal patterns.*

The Bearish Counterattack Line stops at, or near, the previous day's close. The additional gains that could have been locked in at the open are erased. The Dark Cloud Cover is more ominous. It closes more than midway down the body of the previous day's bullish candle. The additional gains at the open, plus most of the previous day's gains, are erased. The Bearish Engulfing Pattern engulfs the entire body of the bullish candle. It erases even more of the gains than the other two patterns.

For a swing down, the inverse of the patterns mentioned above are the Piercing Pattern, the Bullish Counterattack Line and the Bullish Engulfing Pattern. In most instances, when price gaps up after an advance, or gaps down after a decline, exiting at the open is the best strategy for a short-term trade. Waiting until the end of the day to exit would result in a less profitable trade. It is true that traders cannot know for sure until the close of trading how the end of day bar will look. However, because of the likelihood of an opening gap filling within the same day, they can anticipate that the bar will probably end the day bearish.

Many Hanging Man patterns also start as an opening gap and can be exited at the open. By the close, a trader can look back on this pattern and realize that having sold at the open would meant not having held through the decline that formed the long black candle. With this pattern, price does rise back up and closes near the high by the end of day. However, the trader has to watch a considerable amount of their profits disappear intraday before price turns back up. Many traders may end up closing out the trade before price turns back up. They could just sell the opening gap and avoid the roller coaster ride.

There are other bearish reversal candlestick patterns that may not gap up at the open, but by the close of the bar, it becomes apparent that the opportunity to sell near the swing high was missed. For example, on those reversal patterns that have long upper shadows, such as the Shooting Star or a Gravestone Doji. Wherever an upper shadow remains, the candle was one a bullish body that traded up to the high of the shadow. Vice versa for a lower shadow.

A **Shooting Star** was a long bullish candle at some point during the trading day.

A **Hanging Man** was a long bearish candle at some point during the trading day.

A **Gravestone Doji** was a long bullish candle at some point during the trading day.

Fig. 8-15 *Bearish reversal patterns.*

It is always easy to look back on a chart and wish you had sold at a higher price. These patterns aren't as easy to anticipate as those that gap up at the end of a swing. However, sometimes they can be exited with more profit if a target has been calculated in advance. For instance, if there is overhead resistance on the chart, a target can be set for a bit below that resistance level.

Figure 8-16 is an example where a sell limit order could have been placed in anticipation of the resistance being tested. The sell order, set for just below the ceiling, would have triggered while the candle was still bullish. By the close, the candle had formed a Spinning Top and pulled back more the following day.

Fig. 8-16 *A Spinning Top formed at resistance.*

Maximizing Profits on Swing Trades

For traders to increase their profitability, they must learn how to maximize the profits on their trades—not through greed or fear, but through technique.

Sell the Opening Gap

A gap up at the end of a swing is a warning. It is usually a last blast of buying just before a pullback begins. Once price turns down after a several day advance, there are no more buyers willing to pay the higher prices. Suddenly sellers have to turn their sites downward to find buyers at lower prices. The stock begins to collapse on the intraday time-frame. This is an unfortunate scenario for inexperienced traders who bought at the swing high. They find themselves immediately in a losing trade that continues to decline. The higher the volatility of the stock, the more, and the faster, the pain will set in. They may end up exiting during the decline, often just before price turns back up.

Skilled swing traders know that the gap is a bonus at the end of a price move. It can be looked at as a stern warning to take profits before a pullback begins.

A high percentage of gaps that occur at the market open are filled within the same trading day. This is true of gaps up or down. Often a trader can lock in additional profits by immediately exiting an opening gap that forms at the end of a price advance or decline. In some cases the additional profits can be substantial, for example, on a Dark Cloud Cover formation.

If the stock is trading actively in pre-market and the spread is narrow enough, which is likely if price is set to gap at the open, the stock can be exited before the open. A limit order can be used to exit a trade in pre-market. Market orders are held until the open—they will not be executed in pre-market or after-hours trading.

If waiting until the open to exit, traders can begin monitoring the price action on a low intraday time-frame, such as a 5-minute chart. If price holds up in the first few minutes, it may run in the opening direction for a short time after the open. There is a good chance price will still reverse by approximately 30 minutes into the trading day. The first few minutes after the open, and again near 10:00 a.m. Eastern Time, are strong reversal times.

Some traders like a "stop and reverse" strategy. They may exit the long position and go short, or vice versa on a gap down. They may sell short on the high likelihood of the gap filling. Traders should be cautious shorting against a strong uptrend. The pullback may be short-lived if the stock is in favor with traders or belongs to a strong sector. The stop and reverse method may be more profitable if the swing up was quite significant, or if the swing up encountered resistance.

Set Price Targets

Often a swing target can be determined in advance. Traders can place a limit order to trigger automatically as price approaches the target. Alternatively, an alert can be set to warn that price is approaching the target. When the alert is triggered, price can be observed on an intraday time-frame for an optimal exit point. Rather than setting an alert or limit order for the exact target price, it is usually best to exit a bit before the actual target price. Too often price turns just before the target is reached resulting in a missed opportunity to exit at a desirable price. It is penny wise but pound foolish to hold out for every cent.

If a stop order is in place for protection (recommended), then a limit order to exit can be placed as a one-cancels-other order. Most brokers offer this type of order. If this order is not familiar, contact your broker for instruction.

> **Tina Logan is located in San Diego, California. She is an experienced trader and provides private tutoring for individuals and small groups. For more information, visit her company website, Trader's Roadmap, at www.tradersroadmap.com.**

Each individual investor will have their strong points and their weak points. Their likes and dislikes. Trading styles that fit their schedule and trading styles that they would like to do but do not have the time to execute them properly. Applying candlestick signals to a multiple of technical methods and timeframes allows an investor to cultivate investment programs that is successful for them. Utilize whatever methods work. Cultivate trading techniques to your comfort level. Successful investing is easily achieved when an investor can put all the parameters in the right places.

Chapter 9

Profitable Candlestick Entry and Exit Strategies

> *It is a great folly to struggle against such things as thou canst not over-come.*
>
> *Desiderius Erasmus*

Candlestick signals are in existence today because of their statistical probabilities. As can be imagined, the signals would not be in existence today if they did not produce noticeable profits throughout history. Profits showing significantly more than random luck or normal market returns. The purpose for utilizing the Candlestick signals is to put as many probabilities in your favor as possible. The fact that a signal is still around is due to its observed results over centuries. Assuming that the probabilities of making a profit from that signal is above 50%, maybe 60%, 70% or even 80%, and those percentages can be enhanced by an additional factor. The signals indicate when to get out of failed trades immediately, thus cutting losses. *(To date, statistical performance has been difficult to obtain. The combination of severe misunderstandings of when a signal is truly a signal by most investors has been a deterrent. That lack of knowledge and the multitude of parameters required to do a statistical analysis makes programming for statistical results an overwhelming task. What can be visually accessed in the matter of milliseconds involves a multitude of numeric calculations and parameters. The Candlestick Forum is currently directing projects to accumulate these statistics and will make them available to Candlestick Forum members as results are obtained. Because of the magnitude of this project, information will most likely be released in bits and pieces as completed.)* How a position is performing, once the signal has appeared, is an immediate filtering element. We are all eternal optimists and want every position to go up as soon as we buy it. However, keep in mind, even with the possible phenomenal results of 80% positive trades, that still leaves 20% that will not work. The more steps taken to reduce bad trades, the better your results will be in your investment funds.

The information revealed in this book and on the Candlestick Forum website is not the revealing of ancient "secrets" or the development of sophisticated computer generated formulas. It is the assembling of commonsense observations from centuries of actual profitable experience.

Candlestick information has been around in the U.S. investment arena for several decades. Everybody knows about them. They use the candlestick graphics for better viewing of charts. However, most investors do not know how to apply the signals for effective results. You, taking the time and effort to research the Candlestick method, are still in an extremely small minority of the investment community. The Japanese rice traders made huge profits from the Candlestick method. They used rice paper to draw charts and backlit the charts in candle boxes. The concepts applied to Candlestick analysis eventually became the backdrop of the Japanese investment culture.

Common Sense

As you learn about the Candlestick method, keep in mind that the commonsense approach is what distinguishes this investment technique from most investors trading practices. The information you are receiving is knowledge that is available to everyone. However, you have the benefit of learning the correct interpretation, which means you get the desired results. Take advantage of this knowledge. It will create a confidence in investing that most people never experience.

Just as the signals produce valuable information as to when to buy a position, they are just as valuable for demonstrating when to sell. This, sometimes, is much sooner than expected. Simple logic tells us that if a Candlestick "buy" signal appears in the right place with the right confirming indicators, the trade should have a high probability of being a profitable trade. Unfortunately, reality may show a different outcome. How a price 'opens' the next day is a very important indicator as to how aggressive the buyers are. (The same parameters apply to sell transactions, but for illustration, the buy side will represent all trades.) Utilizing that information can be instrumental in weeding out less favorable trades.

The logic behind the results of an opening price the next day after a signal is simple. Is there evidence that the buyers are still around? That information is readily available through inexpensive live-feed services. Being able to view how a stock is going to open, before the market opens, improves an investors positioning dramatically. Returns expand dramatically by eliminating bad trades.

The shorter the trading period, the more critical the 'open' pricing. Options are trading vehicles that require as exact timing as possible. Longer-term investors have more leeway when putting on a position. A six-month trade or a one-year trade is usually being bought when the monthly, weekly and daily candlestick charts all coordinate, each chart shows that it is time to buy. (The monthly and daily charts are the pivotal charts for long-term investors. The weekly chart is sometimes out-of-sync. It is better to do your own testing with a four-day, six-day, seven-day, or eight-day chart. They may have more relevance than the one-week chart.)

> *Buy stocks that are going up; if they don't go up, don't buy them.*
> *Will Rogers*

Each formation is not a signal. A Candlestick "buy" signal in the overbought area does not mean the same as a Candlestick "buy" signal in the oversold area. Conversely, a Candlestick "Sell" signal does not mean the same in the oversold area as it does in the overbought area. Many investors confuse the formations as signals. They do not take into consideration where the overbought or oversold indicators (Stochastics, settings of 12,3,3) might be.

When do most investors want to buy into a stock? They usually want to buy after the price has gone consistently up for days or weeks! Finally, they become convinced that the stock is going to go up forever. That is the reason an inordinate amount of volume appears at the tops. Finally, everybody has gained enough confidence and wants in. After a sustained uptrend, the broadcasts begin on the financial news stations. The "experts" discuss how great the company or the industry is doing. The average investor perceives they will be left behind if they do not get into the stock. Of course, that is usually the first sign that the top is near. Prices start to pull back because of profit taking. The new investors hang on anticipating the uptrend will continue after some profit taking. However, the pullback lasts a few weeks longer than everybody expects. Then it moves slowly up to the area that those investors bought, bumps into resistance, then pulls back again. Soon they are sitting in a stock they have owned for three months where the price still is not back where it was bought. This is not a good return on the invested dollars.

Alternatively, the inexperienced investors are going to try another approach. They are going to buy a stock that they have followed because it has pulled back a hefty percentage. This is at least more logical than buying a stock because it has gone up a great deal. However, this also has its flaws, if done without using any buying parameters or signals. Enron Corporation is a prime example of not buying a stock just because it has backed off a good percentage from its high. The person, buying a stock without any buying signals because it has gone down, is just grabbing for the fallen knife. One of three things can happen from that point and two of them do not make you money. The price could easily continue its downward trek. Buying because you think that the sellers have sold enough may not be a viable approach. The stock price could level out and trade flat for the next six months, not a profitable endeavor. Finally, because you have a wonderful sixth sense, you happened to buy the stock at the bottom and it turned up reasonably quick. If that is the case, you do not want to read this book or any book that would screw up that talent.

The best investment strategy is to buy a stock that has bottomed and the buying is becoming more prevalent. Tall order? Not really, when you can visually see the buy signs. The probabilities are much greater to find the stocks that are just starting to make an 'up' move. It is better to buy a stock where fresh buying is recently coming into the stock and getting in on strength. Participating with other buyers at least indicates that there are other buyers, logical! As in the famous investment strategy of Will Rogers, "Buy stocks that are going up, if they don't go up, don't buy them". As backward as that philosophy appears in the real world, the Candlestick signals get investors close to that concept.

How Prices 'Open' Reveals Valuable Information

After the above wordy dissertation, the meat of this subject is being aware of how to get into trades properly. What is the message of a "buy" signal? As expressed in the *Profitable Candlestick Trading* book, *a signal is the cumulative knowledge of all investors participating in that stock that day*. If this is the only statement that you remember about Candlestick analysis, you will easily comprehend the ramifications behind the signals. A "buy" signal forms by the reversal of investor psychology in downward trend. That formation becomes visually evident to the Candlestick investor.

Simply stated, the signal is showing the evidence of buyers coming into a stock, reversing the previous downtrend. The Candlestick trader can identify those signals, 12 major signals and approximately 50 secondary signals and continuation patterns. As discussed earlier, the signals each provide a positive percentage of profitable trades. Upon recognizing a candlestick reversal signal, the best test to determine when to establish your position is based upon one simple question. "On the open of the next day, are the buyers still showing their presence?" This may appear to be elementary, but that is the basis for getting into the position in the first place. The Candlestick signal represents a change of direction. The magnitude of buyers present is an important factor on how strong the reversal will perform.

Fig. 9-1, the Pinnacle Entertainment chart opens near the previous close. This clearly indicates that the buyers have not backed away. Witnessing the price advance at the 'open' reveals that buyers are stepping in without hesitation. Buy immediately. You have all the parameters evaluated. The probabilities are in your favor. There should be no reason not to get into the position.

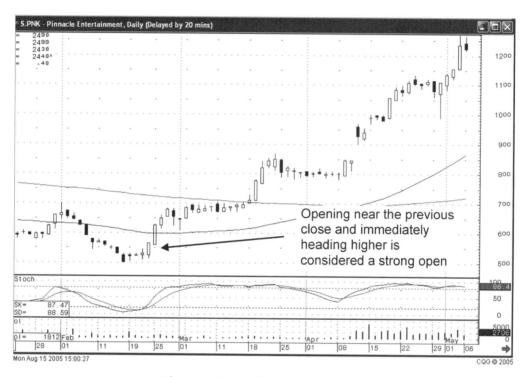

Fig. 9-1 *Pinnacle Entertainment*

An open very near the previous close is a strong open

Fig. 9-2 *Province Healthcare Co.*

Note in Fig. 9-2 Province Healthcare Co. that the buyers were still present. The open, by remaining in the area of where the buyers closed the price the night before, indicates that there was not a change of heart during the evening. "In the area" can mean a slightly lower opening price. Consider the action of the price the previous day. It had a big up day. As the end of the trading day is getting near, the shorts may have realized that buying was the overriding influence. The shorts may have covered, pushing the price up further on the close. Profit taking or sellers still wanting to get out of the stock could lower the price on the open. The next morning, prices opening slightly lower and immediately moving higher indicate that the buyers have not disappeared. As soon as the first few minutes of trading transpire after the open, an investor should be able to ascertain how the stock and markets are performing.

If the market in general is not falling out of bed and the stock price does not appear to want to move lower, it is time to start establishing the position. A prudent method would be to buy half the position at the slightly lower level and put a buy stop at the previous days close for the other half. The rationale being that if the price comes up through yesterday's price, the buyers are still present.

The most promising form of evidence, indicating the price is getting strong buyers' attention, is the gap up. Note in Figure 9-3, Meritage Corp,. a gap up formed. As defined by the gap, the strength of the buyers is very strong. A gap-up, at the bottom of a downtrend, and after a candlestick reversal signal, is one of the best signs of buying strength. One should be committing funds immediately.

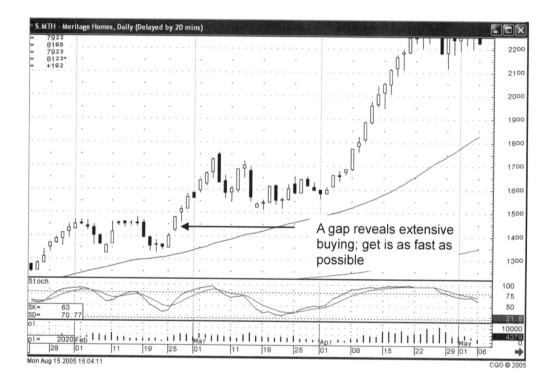

Fig. 9-3 *Meritage Corp.*

The gap up at a beginning of a trend bodes very well for an extended rally. Whether the indexes are opening up weak or strong, a gap up in a stock deserves immediate attention. The buying coming into this stock is not concerned about the status of the markets. Try to get into the stock as fast as possible. The advantage of being able to view the bid and ask prior to the open is that it prepares an investor for an entry strategy. Seeing a stock price biding up before the open and knowing what a gap up indicates after a Candlestick signal allows for placing a market order on the open.

Use that buying force to your advantage. Get in early as possible. Again, the probabilities are in your favor and this time the gap is adding to the force of the move.

Sometimes you are going to see a gap up; you get in and then watch the price head back the other way. Don't worry. The buy signal was the reason to buy. The buyers were still around if prices gap up. If profit taking occurs after that, no big deal, the buyers are still around. Wait for a day or two and the signal should confirm itself.

A substantial gap up may require watching to see if there is any immediate profit taking. This might be better accumulated by buying one-half the position on the open, the second half after observing the price move. In some substantial gaps up, the opening price might be the high for that day, creating a black candle. The fact that it had many buyers on the open, followed by some immediate profit taking, still reveals that there was a strong change in sentiment.

> *I hear and I forget. I see and I remember. I do and I understand.*
> **Chinese proverb**

Note in Fig. 9-4, the Meridian Gold Inc. chart, how the large bullish engulfing pattern clearly illustrated that the bulls had stepped in. This shows a great buying influence. The next day gaps up. This could be the beginning of a very strong rally. This has all the makings of a strong run up. There would be no reason not to get into the position. However, once the position is filled, the profit taking sets in. Is this time to worry? Remember what the bullish engulfing pattern told you. The buyers were coming into this stock with great force for some reason. It would seem very unusual that the next day they would all of a sudden disappear.

Fig. 9-4 *Meridian Gold Inc.*

It is not unusual to see some profit taking after a 10% to 15% run up in two days. The underlying factor remains that the buyers have come into this position with vigor. Sit comfortably for a day or two to see what happens after the profit taking disappears. In this case, the strong 'buy' signal was the prelude to more buying.

The appearance of a gap up is a clear indication that the "buy" signal is having the follow through that is required to sustain a strong rally.

Fig. 9-5, The Exploration Co. has every sign of strong buying. A Bullish Engulfing pattern is the first signal. The gap up and the strong buying afterwards is more evidence. There would be no reason for not getting into the position on the next show of strength.

Once you have gotten into the position, the price rolls back. Profit taking, or the market in general starts getting weak. Your peace of mind is still in the strong buy signals. As in this illustration, it took a few days for the trend to start back up. During those few days, note that the sellers could not knock the prices down.

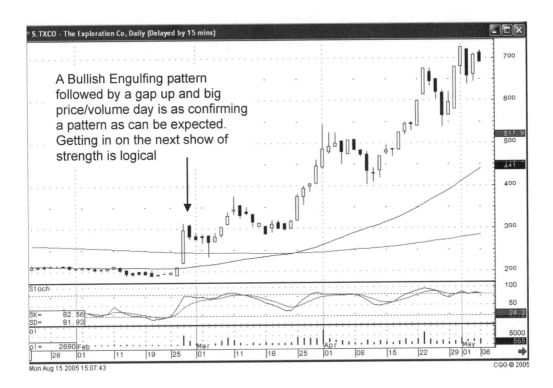

Fig. 9-5 *The Exploration Co.*

It may have tested some nerves, but after 3 or 4 days, the bulls starting gaining confidence that the sellers did not have enough strength to push the price back down. This leads to the continuation of the upward trend. It took a few extra days but that is reality. Some positions look great when you get in but will be a laggard for a few days. Nevertheless, if the message of the signals is correct, the trend will be continuing. Sometimes that will take patience but the probabilities will be in your favor.

BUY on a Strong Open

"Buy on a strong open." What does that mean? Once a Candlestick "Buy" signal has made itself present, investors want to see one obvious element in the next day's opening price; that the buyers are still committing. The signal in itself reveals that buyers have moved into the stock. Will that buying continue? That is easily identified the next morning.

Establishing an initial position requires a small amount of research. What is the direction of the indexes? What is the direction of the sector index most related to that particular stock? How are the other stocks doing in that sector, the ones closely associated to the stock you are ready to buy?

The first hour has always been considered the amateur hour. However, that reputation was created years ago when stockbrokers were directing everybody's funds. They were buying with the orders they received before the market opened. Buying early in the first hour, having the advantage of the Candlestick signals allows an investor to exploit the buying of the first hour. Use that to your advantage.

The entry instructions "Buy on a strong open" has two definable variables. What is considered strong, and what is considered the open? First, let us discuss the definition of the open. Some investment gurus recommend not trading in the first thirty minutes of trading. The volatility is too great during that time. Most traders know the best trading opportunities present themselves in the first and last hour of each trading day. Probably 60% plus of the total daily volume occurs in the first hour and the final hour of the trading day. The pent up research since the close of the previous day, is implemented during the opening hour of the next day. This is the time to take advantage of the Candlestick signal.

A new dynamic is in force during the first hour of trading. Investment decision-making processes are put into action with buy and sell orders in the opening hour. The inordinate volume is crossed and matched in market conditions. Once this volume is consumed by the joining of buy volume and sell volume, the price will begin moving in the direction of the remaining order balances. This inordinate volume makes the first hour more volatile than the other trading hours during the day. It also influences the direction and the magnitude of the move. Take advantage of the first hour.

Use Pre-open Indicators to Improve Profits

Knowing that the open consists of a period of inordinate volume, the Candle-stick investors can watch the movement of the stock price. If it is consistent with the other factors of a strong or weak open, the trade can either be executed or withheld until the proper factors are evident.

The 'other' factors are simple indicators of what the market direction should be once the market opens. Each morning the futures can be observed in many places. CNBC has the DOW, NASDAQ, and S&P 500 futures posted in the lower right hand corner of the T.V. screen. If a position were ready to be implemented, it would not be prudent to place the trade on the long side if the futures were illustrating heavy selling on the open. The signals need continuing confirmation that the buyers are still around. Dramatic selling pressure on the futures before the markets open is an indication that the buyers may not want to fight the selling pressure that morning. The direction of the index may be projected by what formations appeared prior to the next open. If it is expected to be in an upward direction that day, then the futures should be confirming that sentiment in their activity before the open.

If the direction of the market is projected to go higher, a small pullback of the futures should be tolerable. If the futures leave the "open" as questionable, check the pre-open price of the stock itself. Having software that shows pre-market bids and asks provides a clear indication of what is happening in the demand for that stock as it gets near the opening time. That will be the most important illustration of how the buyers and sellers are lining up on the open. That does not mean that is the final indication. Sometimes a buyer or seller will commit their buy or sell order immediately after the market opens, not wanting to show their hand too early.

If the level of the bid and ask does not produce any concrete decisions, investigate how some of the companies in the same industry are acting on the pre-open. If they are opening above or below the previous nights close, that information should add some insight as to how the stock in question is going to act. (Take notice of the volume, if possible, pre-market. Sometimes very little volume will move prices more than what the regular market conditions warrant.)

The first thirty minutes after the market opens it will swing around a bit. The general analysis should have reduced some of the potential possibilities of what might happen the next day. Buying 'long' when there is overwhelming evidence that the indexes are going lower should not be done aggressively. Part of the previous nights evaluation involved seeing continued buying strength in the markets in general the next day.

Buy on a strong open. Your analysis leans toward an "up" day. The stock you are trying to buy had a bullish signal the prior day. Four combinations can occur on the open.

1. The Indexes/Futures appear to be opening positive. The pre-market indication on the stock price is opening higher than the close of the night before. The buyers have not disappeared. This scenario best fits with your analysis. In this case, there is no reason why the position should not be bought as quickly as possible. Buy at the market on the open.

2. The Indexes/Futures are showing strength but the stock position is opening lower than the close of the previous day. Analyze the situation. If the "buy" signal was created by extensive buying, which created the signal, some of that buying may have been 'fearful' short covering near the close. That buying may have caused an extra boost in the price on the close. It would not be unusual to see some traders taking quick profits, moving the price slightly down on the open. If this scenario happens, watch how the price acts for the early minutes of trading. If there does not seem to be any sustained selling and the rest of the market seems to be staying strong, pick up a partial position. The "buy" signal showed a reversal the day before, the market is staying up, and there is not any major selling going on in the stock price. Anticipate that the lower open was just some quick profit taking. As soon as you notice buying coming in, fill the rest of the position. On the other hand, if you want to be more conservative, try this strategy. When the price opens lower, put a 'buy stop' at the previous days close. The rationale being if it opened lower but came back up through the previous days close, then the buyers were still around.

3. The Indexes/Futures appear to be opening weaker and the stock price is opening higher. The signal from the previous day is the overriding factor. The buyers are still around, but the indexes are not acting well. The buyers are witnessing the weaker market indexes also. In this case, watch what the stock price is doing. If it appears that the buyers are coming into the

stock despite the lower market in general, the buying force is not considering the market conditions, they want the stock. Buy it. Conversely, if the
stock opens higher and the market indexes are heading lower, watch to see
if the price does not fizzle and start backing off. If so, wait for a while. See
what the markets are going to do for the day. A safe approach under these
conditions would be to put a buy stop at the open price. The rationale being
if the price comes up through the opening price later in the day, the buyers
are back in control.

4. The worst scenario in the grid is a weak open on the indexes and the stock
opening lower. There is not much of a decision here. The trade should not
be considered. However, a buy stop at the previous day close acts as the
same beneficial strategy as before. In this situation, if the markets and the
stock price start coming back up before the end of the day, the buyers
should be back.

The Basic Entry Assumption

The primary element that should go into every entry decision is simple. Is there
the evidence of buying, continuing the trend as indicated by the reversal signal? Being able to recognize which trends are going to get stronger 'buy' par-
ticipation will increase your portfolio returns impressively.

For example, a signal has indicated that the trend has reversed. It may be
a slow reversal; it may be a power move. The signal revealed that a new trend
was probable. Reviewing past charts to see what signals occurred at the reversal points is a well-advised practice. Identifying the historical trading patterns
of a particular stock adds to the arsenal of information. Learning to recognize
how a strong up trend performs in the previous trading environments puts the
probabilities in your favor. The signals are going to reveal plenty of buying
opportunities. Evaluating the follow-through of the signals will allow you to
filter the best of those opportunities. Visual analysis of previous reversals will
take mere seconds of time.

Invest with the Probabilities

Not every trade is going to shoot straight up after the buy signal appears. There will be many entry points that fit the perfect buying conditions, yet fade just after you fill your position. Mistake? Depends on how the rest of the day finishes. Will every trade work the way the signals indicate? Definitely not! Nevertheless, back to the basics. You are looking for the best possible place for your money to make the best returns while minimizing risk. Hopefully, the signal itself is representing well above a 50/50 probability of making money. This ratio may be 60%, 68%, or 74%. Fine-tuning the entry process may increase the probabilities another 3%, 4%, or 5%. A good evaluation of the entry also has the element for limiting the losses. If a trade is placed, and the basis for entering the trade disappears immediately, and the buyers have disappeared, then liquidate the trade immediately. The loss may only be 1%, 3%, or maybe as much as 5% if it is liquidated that day or on the open the next day. The gains get an opportunity to run when the buy signal is not negated. The losses are trimmed immediately if the signal fizzles. All from a simple premise! Are the buyers still in control?

There is a good rule of thumb for protecting a newly established position. If after a buy signal, a position is established, and the prices back off by the end of the day, closing more than halfway down the bullish candle that identified the buy signal, close out the position. Statistically this represents that the sellers still have the upper hand. However, keep in mind that a buy signal did form at the bottom of the trend. Despite having to exit the trade at a small loss, be prepared to see new buying evidence soon. If so, re-establish the position. The initial buy signal occurred for some reason.

The most important decision-making area is at the reversal points. Is it a reversal or is it a pullback in the trend? That is where the analysis and monitoring is most important. A buy signal requires follow through. The weight of a sustained downtrend needs strong change of sentiment to reverse its course. If the reversal has only two or three days of an up move, do not be hesitant to take quick profits once a weak signal appears. There may be a more opportune time to get into a position if a pullback occurs. Will the current low hold, acting as a support level? You should be watching for a new buy signal. This is your opportunity to get into the position again.

If the previous low does not hold and prices go lower, watch for the next buy signal to occur at lower levels. This is true whether a short-term trader or the long-term holder.

Fig. 9-6, Hovnanian Enterprises Inc. illustrates the Candlestick investors' minor dilemma. All the parameters say to buy this stock. A Hammer is followed by a Bullish Engulfing pattern. The stochastics have turned up, volume is picking up. But the next day the price opens much lower than what would indicate that buyers were still active. What is the best way to enter this position? Are the sellers taking back control for some reason? Maybe the indexes opened much lower. In keeping with the practice of buying a stock that is going up, the best entry strategy would be to put a buy stop at the close of the previous day. If the buyers are still participating, it will be evident when the price moves from the lower 'open', and then back up through the close of the previous day. Buying the stock at a slightly higher price is a small premium to pay for knowing that you are getting in a position when the buyers are around.

If the buy stop never gets executed, the lower open and a close below the previous days close would form a Harami. This formation would indicate that the buying had stopped. You are not in a position where the sellers may be taking control again. If the buy stop is executed, a buy signal is being confirmed.

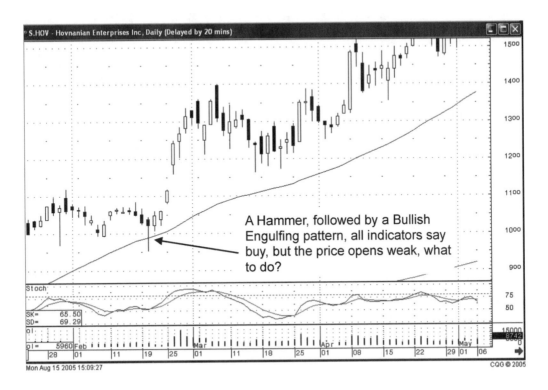

Fig. 9-6 *Hovnanian Enterprises Inc.*

As described in "Profitable Candlestick Trading" a Hammer signal can show the investor great amounts of information. In the example of Hovnanian Enterprises Inc, the buyers did come into the stock, executed the stop, and continued to show strength. This made for a good trade.

If market conditions were weaker or profit taking comes into a stock, it can create a different evaluation after the close. Fig. 9-7, Movie Gallery Inc., for example, creates an evening of less positive possibilities for the next day. In this case, the price opened lower, came up during the day and executed the buy stop. Now the position closed lower than where it was bought, forming a Doji/ Harami. That could lead to a few days of consolidation. However, it is still early in the up-trend. Stochastics are heading up. Fortunately, the buying continues the next day and moves prices positive. Again, the overriding factor boils down to the appearance of a Morning Star "buy" formation. As seen in the chart, the Morning star formation was the bottom reversal point for a strong uptrend.

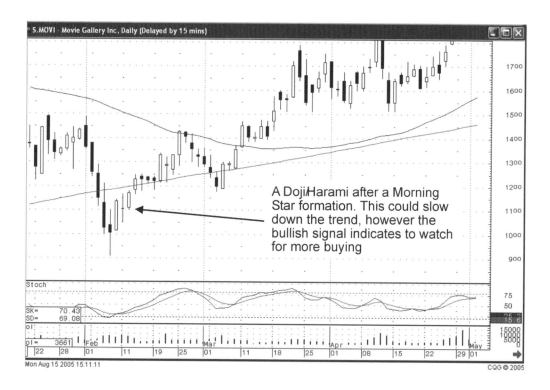

Fig. 9-7 *Movie Gallery Inc.*

One of the most common chart patterns is the Doji after a big up day. Consider the dynamics that are occurring in the investors' minds. In an example such as

Fig, 9-8 (following page), Scansoft Inc., there has been a recent distinct downtrend. All of a sudden, a Bullish Engulfing pattern emerges. The buyers are stepping in. They have overwhelmed the sellers to the point of reversing the trend. The following day, after the big up surge, there will still be sellers that will take advantage of being able to get out at a higher price than just a couple of days prior. This continued selling is met with buyers coming into the position. It is not unusual to see a Doji day after a big up day. However, when the sellers see that the buying is now soaking up all the selling, they get concerned and step out of the way. The following day should see higher prices.

Don't let the Doji Day concern you. It is the transfer of stock from selling hands into buying hands. If the price opens higher the next day, you can be assured that the buyers have now gained control. The rally should continue.

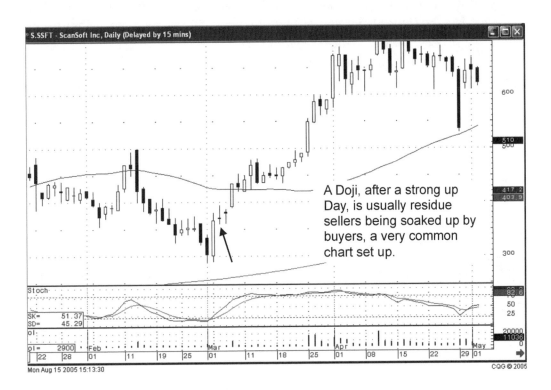

Fig. 9-8 *Scansoft Inc.*

Entering a trade involves a combination of evaluations. Just as you would make a decision about what you are going to wear today involves a number of observations. You may have heard the weather report saying that it is going to be cold and rainy today. You peer out the window to see what conditions are. You look at the thermometer to see what the temperature is doing. You may open a door to see if it is windy or calm. You do the same process when getting ready to enter a trade.

You investigate. You have already done your research and decided on what position you want to buy in the morning, if the conditions are right. You check the futures in the morning to see what the general market sentiment appears to be. You can check to see if the bid and ask have moved one way or the other during the non-market hours. You can check on other stocks in the industry to see how they will open. You may look for any news reports since the close yesterday that would influence the stock price.

If nothing seems out of kilter, based upon what the "buy" signal was indicating to make your "buy" decision, then the final input will be how prices are actually opening. If nothing appears to be out of line, purchase the position. That is what the Candlestick signal had indicated should be done.. Fine-tuning the entry process will minimize getting into a bad trade. For each bad trade that can be avoided, the more opportunities are available to put investment funds into a good trade. Eliminating a very small percentage of losing trades will increase your returns in geometrical proportions. Avoiding a loss negates having to make back those losses with a positive trade, while using up that next trade and time to get back to even.

If skills could be acquired just by watching, every dog would be a butcher.
                                                    Turkish proverb

When is it Time to Get Out?

O.K., you have the position on. You are in it to maximize your profits with minimal risk. We all want to see a huge rally once we put the position in place. But, reality tells us that hitting the right stock at the right time in the right market conditions is a very long shot. Multitudes of events are going to happen that will make us question whether to stay in or get out of a position. Fortunately, the candlestick formations provide a simplistic visual depiction of what is going on in the minds of participating investors.

The probabilities of being in an up trend, after a bullish Candlestick signal, are extremely good. The up trend may last for a day or two; it may last for three weeks. The signal itself cannot convey this information. As illustrated from some of the examples, there are signals that will show more potential than others. The Gap and Kicker signals are likely to foretell a strong rally.

The up trend is assumed, but many factors can terminate a rally. Market conditions, news events, rumors, many outside influences can affect a stocks upward move. Profit taking is another common pullback factor. Having knowledge of the common "sell" signal formations improve the exit strategy. Combining the knowledge of "sell" signal recognition with stochastics helps the Candlestick investor distinguish between sellers stopping an up trend, or whether profit taking is occurring. There are a number of continuation patterns that reveal profit taking versus reversal patterns.

The same logic should be incorporated in the exit strategies as in entry strategies. The bottom-line thinking should be, "have the sellers taken over?" This can be easily analyzed by evaluating the buying that got the price to the current level and the condition of the stochastics. Numeric formulas do not work for Candlestick formations. The buys and sells are based upon a change in investor sentiment. If the last candle represents buying, the trend should continue until the sellers demonstrate that they have overpowered the buying. A sell signal or a weak price move will demonstrate the buyers are exiting the trade.

Note in Fig. 9-9, Meridian Gold Inc. had strong buy signals a few days before the actual major run up. A gap up (Kicker Signal) formed followed by another day of buying. Nothing in this chart would have indicated the next three down days. How do you protect from this event? Each evening, analyze each position. What would the price action have to do the next day to reveal that the sellers had taken over, more than just some profit taking? In the Meridian Gold price movement, it would have been logical that if the price closed below the halfway point of the previous days trading range, the sellers may have taken over control.

How does one protect from this action. When a buy signal is negated by a "sell" signal, there should be some immediate evaluation as to what the trend is doing. In this day of inexpensive commissions, if the situation is causing some doubt as to the direction of a trade, get out. With Candlestick signals providing more excellent picks every day than what any investor could utilize, why stay in a position that is casting doubts. Liquidate the trade and go on to a high probability trade.

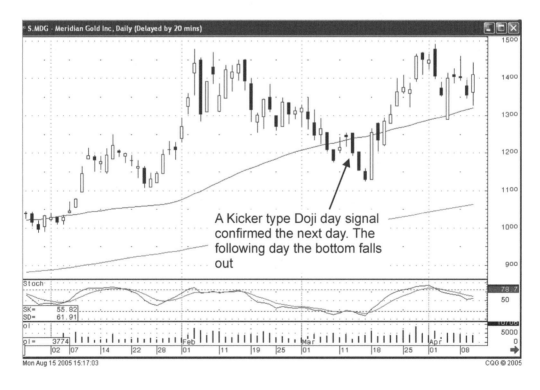

A Kicker type Doji day signal confirmed the next day. The following day the bottom falls out

Fig. 9-9 *Meridian Gold Inc.*

As mentioned in "Profitable Candlestick Trading" there will be a common price action described as a "scary" day. A scary day usually occurs about two, three, or four days into a new trend. After moving up for a few days, the sellers or profit takers knock the price of the stock down hard early in the day. However, by the end of the day, some of the sell-off is recovered. It creates an evening of great investment decision turmoil. Was this day just a last gasp sell-off or was there some new dynamic that was changing the trend direction. If the stochastics, as well as the other indicators, appear to be acting strong, let the price play out the next day. Stocks do not go straight up; expect a trend to have some pullback days.

The ultimate up trend is a majority of white-bodied candles with an occasional dark body candle created by profit taking. Note in fig. 9-10, the up-trend of Horizon Offshore Inc. the appearance of dark candles. Though scattered through the up trend, they never formed a "sell" signal, just periodic profit-taking days.

Fig. 9-10 *Horizon Offshore Inc.*

Exiting a trade uses the same simple premise that the buying side of the trade uses. Are the buyers still present? It is not uncommon to witness a double bottom at the bottom of an extended downtrend. It represents the buyers coming into a stock, moving it up, and then the last of the sellers come back. This moves the price back down to, or close to, the recent lows. This formation is observed after a few days of up move; the trend experiences some small sell signals and moves back down to the recent lows. Recognizing the small sell signals may take some time to get accustomed to, but it is easy to review the price action at the beginning of trends by looking through past charts. Find up trends. Examine what price actions occurred. This will accomplish two functions.

If you are still learning the signals, it will reinforce the recognition of signals at the turns. The next thing investors want to become familiar with is what formations appear in strong up moves versus what formations appear in rallies that fizzle out quickly. The visual advantage of the Candlesticks is the definite contrast created by the dark and light candle bodies. As can be imagined, the more dark bodies seen in a trend, the tougher that trend is having moving to the upside. The earlier you witness dark bodies, the greater the probability the trend is experiencing new selling.

Studying the previous trading in this chart provides the insight that a trend will continue because no definable Candlestick "sell" signal appeared. There were some potentially doubtful moments, but the up trend was completed because the selling candles showed consolidation versus an outright reversal, no major change of investor sentiment.

Simple Rules

Being that the Candlestick signals are formed by price moves, and not by any numeric quotas, percentage stop points cannot be applied. The basis for stop losses in Candlestick analysis is simple. If a signal is created by the evidence of buying, then a complete retracement of that signal reveals that the sellers have undone what the buying did. Simply stated, if the confirmation of one of the Candlestick formations was a price move from $10.50 to $11.25, then it would be assumed if the sellers push that price back down through $10.50 they were back in control. In other words, price coming back down through the beginning of a buy signal negates the signal.

Once an uptrend starts, if an opening price appears more than one-half way down the previous white body, be ready to liquidate immediately. This implies that something changed during the non-market hours. Be prepared to sell if prices appear to want to trade lower, especially if there is bad news reported overnight. When a stock price gaps down dramatically, profitable strategies can be implemented based upon the trend, prior to the announcement.

Some charts will reveal a day that shows strong buying followed the next day with some selling. Expect this as a new trend is developing. However, if the Day 3 shows buying, then Day 4 shows selling, there is reason to be concerned. The sellers are not stepping out of the way. The strong buying is not evident. Take a tiny profit and find another trade with more upside potential.

When in doubt, get out. There is no economic reason to not get out of a trade if it shows weak indications after you have just bought it on a strong buy signal. First, there are many more trades to be found. Second, there is no rule to say that if a position looks doubtful, get out and watch for the next buy signal. Not all stocks go up on a "buy" signal. The majority do! It is sometimes prudent to get out of a position, and then come back in later when the signals demonstrate a more bullish situation. The point is not to make the most money from each trade; the purpose of successful investing is to make the most with the dollars available.

The Trend has Started

Once the trend has gotten out of the initial up turn, it becomes much easier to set stop losses. Buying because of a 'buy' signal now becomes selling because of a 'sell' signal. The beginning of a trend reversal has the additional weight of clearing out all the previous trend sentiment. That is why double bottoms are so prevalent. The initial reversal moves prices up. The sellers, feeling that they are able to get out at a better price, start selling again. Be prepared for the typical bottoming patterns. The advantage of the candlestick signals is that it prepares investors for instantly acting upon a pattern setup.

As a trend begins to move, create your own mental image of what would have to happen to indicate that the forces of the trend have been altered. The review of charts showing turning of trends will give you an idea of what price movements occur, as the reversals get underway. It is visual. Occasionally a sell signal will appear after a few days into the uptrend. The stochastics may be the indicator that reveals that profit taking is occurring and not a trend reversal.

The most important investment defense should be, "When in doubt, get out." If your original game plan was to trade the position, or hold it for a two-week move, two-month move, six-month move, it makes little difference if you liquidate a trade because it does not appear to be maintaining a direction. There is absolutely nothing wrong with closing out a trade when it doesn't look good and buying it back when it does, even if it is at a higher price. The hang-up about buying a position, closing it when things look sloppy, then buying it back when all indicators look good again is our own egos. "What if after I sell it, it turns right around and goes back up?" That is what most investors fear. How foolish we would look after selling out of a position, and then it made a major move up without being in it. But that would have been true ten years ago. Back when it took thirty minutes to hear back from your broker and the cost was $250 or more in commissions.

Today, if you decide to get out of a position, or you get stopped out, and then the position turns back up, buy it! Today's commissions, getting in and out, can be as low as $10.00, maybe as high as $54.00 roundtrip. If you have a $12,000 position on, $54.00 to get out when things looked bad and back in when everything in that price movement looked good again, is very small insurance to protect your downside.

Our egos get really bent out of shape if there is the possibility of having to get back into a position at a higher price than we got out. How stupid we look! We could have just left our position alone and made out much better. Except for two things: 1. The position was closed when all indications were that the price could head lower and 2. Look stupid to whom? Over ninety-nine percent of the time, no one else sees any of the trades you put on. A punch of a button and a bad situation is closed. A touch of a button and the position opens again. If you had to get back in at a little higher price than what you just sold for, so what! The point of maximizing profits is not to make the most on each stock move. Maximizing profits involves making the most with the invested dollar. Nobody cares that a stock you were in went up ten dollars and you only netted seven dollars. If the probabilities were not always good to stay in the position, the prudent strategy was to be out. The important function of investing is to make the most from your invested dollar, not the most from every trade.

Get in when the probabilities say to get in. Utilize the signal, the stochastics, market direction, sector activity and any other parameter that indicates it is time to buy. Get out when the signals tell you to get out. Sometimes that will be tomorrow, sometimes that will be two weeks, two months, or two years. The signals reveal when the buyers have taken over. The signals reveal when the sellers have taken over. Nothing in the structure of today's investment world requires you to stay in a position any longer than needed. If a trade does not appear to be doing what it is suppose to after being in it twenty minutes or two days, get out. Go find a trade that has all the probabilities in your favor. There are dozens of profitable trades every day. Once your knowledge encompasses the general thought processes behind the signals and high profit patterns, your investment acumen will expand immensely.

There is a vast difference in investment philosophy between buying stocks with fundamental potential of going up and identifying stocks that *are* going up. Most investors live and die by the theory that a good company, held long-term will reap the best returns. This is not the best investment strategy available today. Look at Enron, Lucent, Worldcom Inc., or dozens of other stocks that were the leaders of their industries just a few years ago.

Today's market requires today's investment strategies. Those strategies require the ability to identify when a trade is not working. Use the insights developed by the Japanese rice traders to decide when a trend has been stifled. There is nothing wrong with taking two or three 3% losses, and not taking a 20% loss, to finally get into the 30% gain. Profits should be you ultimate motive.

Chapter 10

Candlestick Stop Loss Strategies

> *Progress always involves risk; you cannot steal second base and keep your foot on first.*
>
> *Frederick B. Wilcox*

Protecting your assets is the main function of putting on stop losses. It is to provide a point where the reason for "buying" becomes null and void. Many trading strategies incorporate them into their trading formulas for closing a trade that has gone sour. Usually this is done by establishing a percentage loss as the parameter. The Candlestick method completely disregards a preset formula for stopping out.

There is a major flaw in using a prescribed percentage loss as the stop loss. Your purchase price becomes an important function of where you are to stop out. Some investment advisors recommend three percent as the stop out level. Others suggest eight percent. But where you buy a trade position now becomes the quantitative element of where you should place your stop. A couple of extreme disadvantages become apparent.

A buy recommendation is placed on a stock. You are advised to place a stop at a preset number, for example, three percent below your entry price. The buy is placed on a stock at $50.00. However, by the time you get executed, you have paid $50.80. Buying the stock at $50.00 would have meant your stop out level was $48.50. Your entry at $50.80 now means that the stop loss is to be placed at $49.27. As often mentioned in candlestick analysis, where you bought a stock or sell a stock does not mean a hill a beans to the market. Your arbitrary level of where to come out of a trade has absolutely nothing to do with what the price trend should be doing. What if $48.50 is a level that negates the uptrend move, but $49.27 does not change the trend direction.

Your entry level, although may not have been the ultimate point to get in, does noy have anything to do with what the trend is doing. Prices coming back down through $49.27 may not be a level that affected the uptrend. The "percentage stop" may have stopped you out while the trend direction was still valid.

> *Everything comes to he who hustles while he waits.*
>
> *Thomas A. Edison*

Additionally, the volatility of a particular stock has a great bearing on whether a trend has been affected. A three percent pullback on some stocks might be more than big enough to reverse a trend, while a ten percent move in others stocks is common and isn't a factor on the trend direction.

The most important factor for establishing a stop loss is very basic. What price point would indicate that the established trend has been negated? This now becomes a stop loss level that is established based upon the trend being stalled and/or negated. As with all of Candlestick analysis, this becomes a "common- sense" evaluation. If you have put on a long position, based upon a bullish buy signal, where would the price have to pull back in order to confirm that the sellers were still in control?

The simple visual evaluation establishes the proper stop loss point as it pertains to that specific stock position, taking into consideration the volatility of the stock and the signal that created the buy signal. A stop loss on one stock may be relevant at a close level where as the next stock position requires greater latitude. Candlestick analysis allows the investor to establish a stop loss that would logically indicate when the sellers were still in control, and the buyers have been overcome.

What Does the Signal Tell You?

Keep in mind, not all trades work. "Probabilities" of a successful trade, after witnessing all the parameters that make for a successful trade, is the key word. Although the probabilities are greatly in your favor, there is also the small probability that a trade will not work.

The signal itself is still the result of centuries of observations. Observations that were reinforced by profitable trades! The signals have meaning. They represent the change in sentiment of the buyers and sellers. The signal comprises that new change. The candle formation is the basic element of the reversal signal. However, when that reversal signal illustrates that a new force has entered the market but it is immediately negated by the original trend force, that makes it clear that the new trend is now nullified. Get out of the trade immediately.

Does that mean the analysis was not correct after identifying the signal? No. If a buy signal was formed in an oversold condition, Candlestick analysis establishes that there is a high "probability" for that trade to make money. Again the word "probability" is what needs to be addressed. The trade should make money. However, if the trend does not establish itself, it becomes obvious when knowing the candlestick signals. Your stop loss strategy now becomes customized to that particular trade setup. This is an easy visual process. Take each signal setup, knowing what makes it work, and set your stop loss price based upon where that signal would be negated.

Negating the Signal

What created the signal? The Bullish Engulfing pattern, the Doji followed buy a bullish confirmation day, a Hammer signal confirmed, a Kicker signal? When a signal is created, we will see the candle formations that established the new trend. Trading back down through the signal formation indicates the sellers are still in control. That becomes the stop loss criteria. The same rules for what makes a successful signal can be used for showing what makes the signal unsuccessful.

A candlestick investor is able to establish the level where the signals demonstrate the trade is not working, gaining more control in the investment psyche. Establish where to get in and out of the trade instead of arbitrarily setting stops that have nothing to do with how a trend should be performing. That control can be directed to making pro-active decisions versus reactive decisions. It also allows the candlestick investor to prepare strategies to re-establish a trade in the same position, selling when the trade was not working and getting back in when the trade was working again.

Initiating a Trade

A signal has significant meaning. Knowing that, the thought process for when to stop out of a trade becomes easy. A buy signal indicates a new trend. What would counter that "indication"? Being in that trade has favorable odds for profitability, not any guarantees. Even though a majority of the trades should work from using the signals, it also means that some trades will not work. Keeping that mindset in focus, stop loss analysis creates a format for identifying when a trade is not working and getting out of the trade as soon as possible.

Establishing the stop loss point is using the same commonsense approach that is incorporated throughout the candlestick method. Examine the chart of Wynn Resorts Ltd. Fig. 10-1. Note the three spinning tops on July 23, 24, and 25.

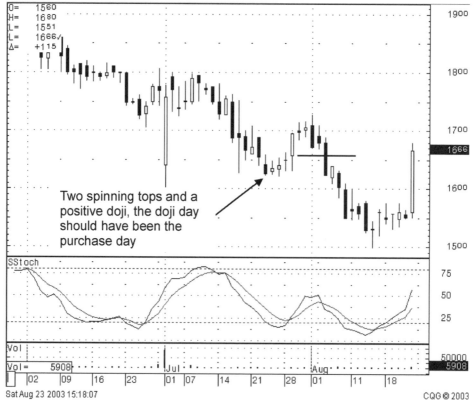

Fig. 10-1 *Wynn Resorts Ltd.*

The gap up on July 28 should have been the buy signal, the entry being at $16.50. A big bullish candle forms the next day followed by a couple of Doji. The Bearish Engulfing signal the following day, with stochastics still heading up, may not have convinced anybody that this uptrend is over. What becomes an obvious level that would indicate that they were not taking the trend up anymore? That is where a stop should be placed. The bottom of the large white body on the 29th becomes a logical level. If the sellers take it back down through that level, the trend is obviously not 'up' anymore.

What does that do for profits? Break even. But if you can break even on the bad trades, that is not bad at all. Built into the candlestick trading concept is a factor not evident in most other trading systems. The signals provide an extra day or so, getting in earlier than the other technical methods; other technical methods needing more confirmation than what the candlestick signals provide. Getting in at a more optimal level makes the sellstop more effective. The negation of a 'buy' signal is less extensive. For example, getting into a position at $10.00, when the $9.50 level indicates a failure of that trade, is much better than getting in the trade, using other techniques at $10.70. The failure level, after entering the trade using a candlestick signal, makes the loss much smaller and less time consuming.

What are you expecting to witness after a buy signal? More buying, of course! That sounds trite but that is exactly what the buy signals should reveal. Note in Fig. 10-2, the Millennium Pharmaceutical chart, the Bullish Engulfing pattern on January 23, 2002.

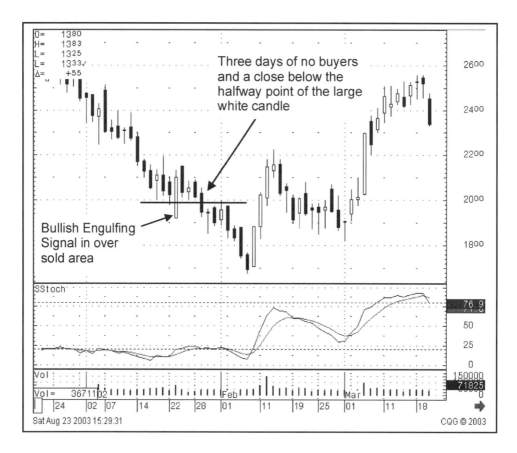

Fig. 10-2 *Millennium Pharmaceutical*

Stochastics oversold and turning up, and the Bullish Engulfing signal followed by a gap up open the next day, represssents is the perfect buy scenario. However, as we see, it closes lower that day. Not disconcerting, it is not unusual to see residue selling from the previous trend still around. The important point is that a Bullish Engulfing signal, in an oversold area, has appeared. The following day a Spinning Top signal, a good sign, the selling of the previous day may have stopped. The following day begins with a higher open, but then closes lower. What should now be gleaned from the chart? The obvious, there is no extensive buying now for three days after the buy signal. Common sense tells us that if a buy signal occurs, then we should see the buyers continuing the trend.

The fourth day after the bullish engulfing signal results in a close more than half way down the Bullish Engulfing candle body. The half-way point of that body represents an important factor. The sellers are now more evident than the buyers that formed the white Bullish Engulfing signal. The sellers are stronger, get out of the trade. Plus it is now four days after the buy signal and no additional buying has been evident. The trend is not up. Move to a better trade.

The half-way point of a body, that created a signal, is the pivotal point. At that level, the existing trend has negated the new trend indicator. This works for both directions, bullish and bearish trend reversals. Does that mean the trade should be ignored? Definitely not! The reason for buying in the first place was due to a buy signal appearing in oversold conditions. The conditions have not changed. It is still oversold, and there were buyers that stepped in once at these levels. If the first entry does not work, keep an eye open for the next buy signal. That will be stronger because the sellers will see that even though the sellers overcame the first buying signal, another buy signal illustrates that new buying is starting again. The sellers usually give up and get out of the way.

The half way point is crucial. As seen in Fig. 10-3, the Kana Communications chart, the bullish breakout signal indicated new investor sentiment. Trading at the $3.00 range for six weeks suddenly experiences a new dynamic coming into the price of the stock. This is a good time to buy. But the next day it backs off. Should that be a worry? Not really. Remember, it is not unusual to see some residue selling after a big percentage move. A Harami is formed. At this point in the new trend, the Harami indicates a day or two of consolidation before the next leg up.

The next day continues to back off. However, note the candle formation, a Hammer. That alone reveals that the buying has started back in. Secondly, notice where it closes, above the half-way point of the body of the white candle that initially indicated the new sentiment in the stock. More importantly, that day reveals the buying has presented itself again. It illustrated that the buyers were still slightly in control.

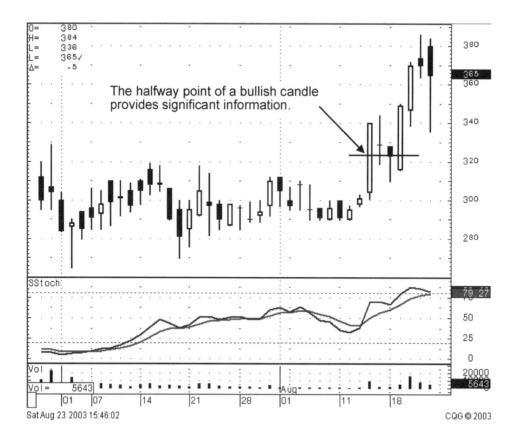

Fig. 10-3 *Kana Software Inc.*

Now the stop loss decision making process becomes simplified. If the price closes below the halfway point of the large white candle on the third day after the bullish candle, it should be obvious that the buyers are not around anymore. The sellers are a stronger force. Close the trade. On the other hand, the overriding facet to this trade was that strong bullish candle day. That should have been evidence that a new attitude was being applied to this stock price. The direction will persist until there are signals to indicate the direction has been negated. Expect the 'probabilities' to continue the uptrend. As seen in the chart, the third day showed the buyers continuing what the first big bullish candle indicated.

To reiterate, use the half-way point of the bullish candle as the level that would demonstrate that the buyers were not in control anymore. Also, a buy signal should represent that the buyers were taking control. After the third day, if no new buying becomes apparent, that should imply that the buyers are not around. Take those funds and move to a better "probability" trade.

The Inverted Hammer is an excellent buy signal. Remember the basic rule when witnessing an Inverted Hammer signal. Seeing the price open positive the following day, with stochastics in the oversold area, the probabilities are extremely high this will be a profitable trade. As expected, the trend should continue upward. With that knowledge, placing a stop becomes very logical. A positive open indicates that the trend should be up. It will usually continue up immediately, but if it does close below the open of the previous day, the bottom of the Inverted Hammers small body, that would indicate that the signal did not work. Put the 'sell stop' at the previous days open price and be ready to close out immediately.

Review Fig. 10-4, the Kana chart again. June 16, 2003 created the perfect set up for an Inverted hammer trade. It opened higher that day with stochastics curling up. This is the exact proper set up for starting an up move from the Inverted Hammer signal. But there was no follow through in the buying.

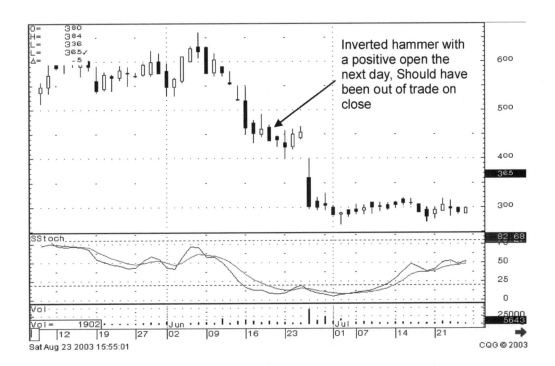

Fig. 10-4 *Kana Software*

The price, moving back down through the previous days open, the bottom of the white body of the Inverted hammer, would be the telling story. The buyers are not present, as hundreds of years of candlestick charting analysis revealed that they should be. Breaching that point should be the stop loss level.

The same analysis can be seen in Fig. 10-5, the Neoware Systems Inc. chart. The Spinning Top signal, followed by the bullish candle creates a perfect Morning Star signal in the oversold stochastics area. Two days after the Morning Star signal, a black candle closes more than halfway down the white body of the Morning Star "buy" formation. The sellers are still dominant. Take those funds and move to a higher probability trade.

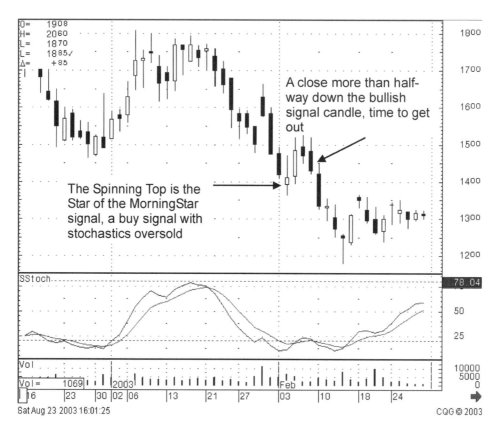

Fig. 10-5 *Neoware Systems Inc.*

The same rationale can be applied to the Hammer buy signal. To review, upon seeing a Hammer signal in the oversold stochastics area, with a positive open the next day, indicates that the buyers are back in the trading. There is a high probability that the trend has reversed. That given, the trend should be moving up from that point. Rarely will you see a Hammer in the oversold area, with a positive open the next day, fizzle and move back down. That is the reason that we utilize the signal after hundreds of years. The signal discloses that a new investment sentiment has entered the stock price. However, the operative word is "rarely".

This same scenario should not see a positive open and a close below the body of the Hammer signal. A close below the body, whether a white or black body, negates the concept of the bullish implications of the signal. Close the position. As seen in Fig. 10-6, the Kindred Healthcare stock price, the buy signals are followed by sell signals. Even what should be considered a strong Doji/Hammer signal, confirmed the next day with a positive open, immediately shows weakness. This now becomes a trade that has no follow through buying, not a trade you want to be in.

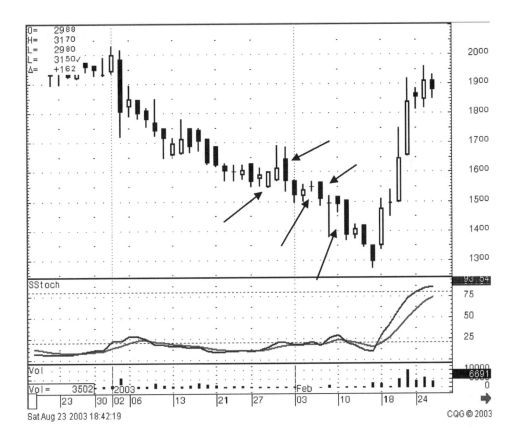

Fig.10-6 *Kindred Healthcare*

Fig. 10-7 Advanced Micro Devices illustrates a chart pattern that set up with a Doji at the bottom. Followed the next day with a positive open, a strong buy indicator. Even the next day it gapped open to the upside. But it traded lower from that point, creating a black candle. The black candle, three days after that Doji, becomes a significant indicator. The close, being lower than the Doji that first indicated the reversal to the upside, now reveals that the sellers have overpowered the buyers. Not a position that represents buying anymore. A bad trade? Close it and move those funds to a strong chart.

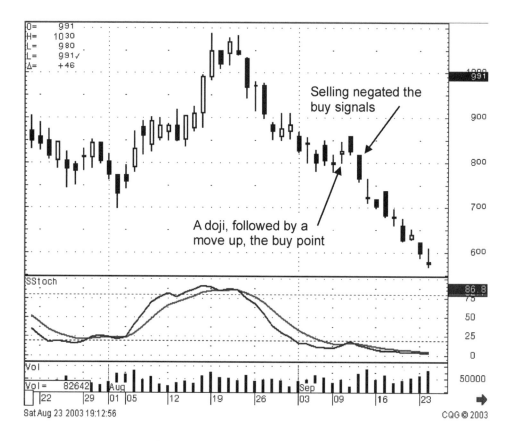

Fig. 10-7 *Advanced Micro Devices*

Illustrated in Fig. 10-8, the Sports Authority Inc. chart is another Inverted Hammer that is set up exactly as it should for producing a profitable trade. The stochastics nearing the oversold area and a strong Inverted hammer should have prepared the candlestick investor for an opportunity the next day. That opportunity would have presented itself by revealing a positive open after the Inverted hammer signal. Buying on the open that next day was the right execution. The little selling day after that did not change the direction of the trend. However, the fact that the sellers could push the price back down through the body of the Inverted Hammer gave a clear indication that the sellers had overpowered the buyers.

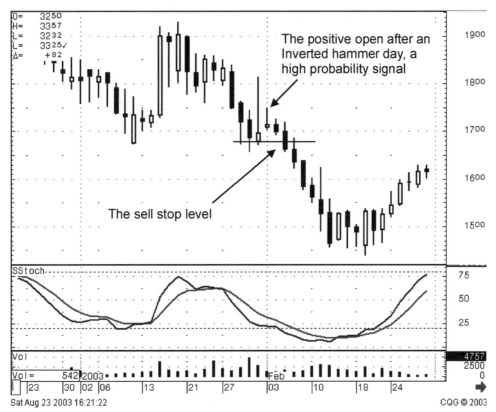

Fig. 10-8 *Sports Authority Inc.*

As illustrated in the chart examples, the basis for proper stop loss levels, using candlestick analysis, boils down to one simple observation, **what level demonstrates more sellers than buyers.** That revelation can occur the next day or after three days or more. If no new buying has come into the stock price, the buy signal is not being confirmed. Take those funds and move to a chart that shows buyers.

Does that mean that trade is dead? No. Watch it. It has already been evaluated as being oversold. The buyers may still be ready to buy in at that price level. Again, the next buy signal will reveal that the buyers are back again. This same message will be noticed by the sellers. They may start backing away from their selling or start covering their shorts.

Stop Losses During the Uptrend

The previous examples were illustrating stop loss reasoning in the initiation of a trade. The next strategy to consider is, "what should be done when the uptrend has started." This again incorporates commonsense planning. Back to the basics, what does the candlestick buy signal represent? It is the change of investor sentiment, the "trend" should be up. Does a trend go straight up? As much as we would like it to, there will be zigs and zags in the price movement. The only reason for putting a stop loss on, during a good trending situation, is to protect yourself from that rare catastrophic announcement. Otherwise a stop loss, too close to the price oscillations, could stop you out at a low point of an up-trending trade.

Once the trend starts, candlestick analysis can be applied. The same thinking process can be used for evaluating whether a trade is still working or not. A price level can be predetermined as to where it would be indicating that the sellers have taken control. During an uptrend, more latitude can be given. The longer the uptrend continues, the more definite a 'sell' signal needs to be to reveal that the trend has terminated.

Note in Fig. 10-9, the NASDAQ chart the trend was apparent until the gap down in price broke the trend lines.

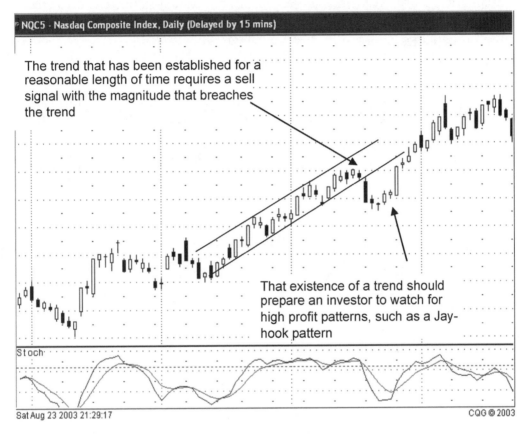

Fig. 10-9 *NASDAQ*

Since March 10, 2003, the NASDAQ chart has shown a steady uptrend. These trends would continue for a month and a half at a time. Upon closer observation, it will be seen that there were definite sell signals in those periods. Does that diminish the validity of the signals? No, the signals need to be heeded. However, they need to be evaluated based upon the environment that they are being viewed.

As seen in Fig. 10-10, the DOW chart, the signals divulge selling at the top of the trend channel. That provides valuable information. For the short-term trader, it becomes evident that the upside channel is not going to be breached. Individual stock charts may have already produced a strong run up. The charts showing toppy signals can be liquidated. Why own a stock that appears to have great probabilities of going back down? Take profits! Positions can always be bought back when sell signals are negated.

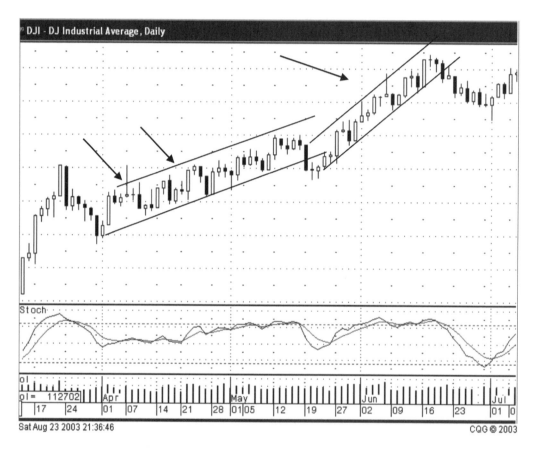

Fig. 10-10 *Dow Jones Averages*

Will the stocks with toppy chart patterns be finished as far as further upside? That can be determined by seeing what the next down move will do. Observation reveals that for the past few weeks, the pullbacks have been supported by the bottom channel trendline.

If not as aggressive a trade, the longer-term position holder can sit through a pullback, using the bottom of the trend channel as a guide, alleviating the need for bopping in and out of a trade.

Note the third week in May; the bottom of the trend channel is breached, occurring about three months after the start of the uptrend. Not a bullish sign. Take some profits. But keep in the back of your mind that a strong reversal signal is required to change the trend. The longer the trend, the more powerful the reversal has to be demonstrated. That is a function of the investment psychology in the markets. The longer a trend continues the more compelling a sell signal needs to be to show investors that the trend is finally over. The optimistic (or pessimistic) attitudes that are being ingrained during the trend are hard to dispel as the direction of the trend changes.

Further analysis of the NASDAQ chart shows that the selling that broke through the bottom of the trend immediately stopped with the appearance of a couple small hammers, and then continued buying. Other technical analysis would have evaluated this as consolidation in the beginning of a downtrend. The Candlestick analyst has the benefit of visually seeing that buying is occurring, stochastics at the bottom, curling up. Instead of a full fledged selling program, the candlestick investor would be watching to see if continued strength was coming back into the market.

Would a sell stop have been prudent when the trading breached the lower trend channel? The "probabilities" indicated that the sellers were taking control. However, the individual stock positions should have been evaluated as to what their chart signals indicated. This would have eliminated a mass selling spree. Seeing the hammers, after the bottom of the trend channel was breached, gave a forbodence of the downtrend not being a powerful move. If stopped out, it was probably done in positions that had good profits from the preceding uptrend. That does not preclude an investor from getting right back in to the same positions after they have consolidated and started moving back up. Better yet, those funds could be moved to new sectors/positions that were coming out of oversold conditions, with much greater upside potential and lower downside risk.

Stop Losses/ Exit Strategies at the Top

The other major concern for most investors is where does one start trying to protect profits. The easy answer is, "when you start witnessing sell signals." That should be the ultimate method. But that does not work for all investors. If the trades cannot be watched at the beginning of trading or the end of each day's trading, a problem that most working investors face, then a stop-loss strategy can be implemented that protects most of the profits. The phrase "most of the profits" has a significance.

Our ego's have a severe deterrent for allowing us to make money. The majority of investors feel that a trend needs to be bought at the very bottom and sold at the very top. To take profits before a trend peaks out or after the high has been seen is a blow to the ego. "Why didn't I get out when it was a point and a half higher?" the question always asked with a tinge of anguish in the voice. A defeat to the ego if that trade was not maximized to the hilt. The point to maximizing profits is not to maximize the profits from each trade. It is to maximize the profits in the account. Two completely different objectives!

The aspects of the 'built in' psychology behind the signals produce immense advantages. Knowing what the normal investor flaws occur in investment actions provides an effective trading strategy. Placing stop-losses, based on where a price should *not* move back to in an uptrend, becomes an easy function. The depiction of human emotions is charted in the price action of the trend. To reiterate, the average investor panic sells at the bottom and is an exuberant buyer at the top. Knowing this (and probably having experience with those flaws in our own previous investing habits) the candlestick investor can be prepped for when a sell signal should be occurring.

What do we see at the top of the trend? Exuberant buying! Buying that is usually shown as larger white bodied candles after an extensive uptrend. Or, a gap up at the top. Being armed with that knowledge permits the candlestick investor to extract a high amount of profit from a trade.

As seen in Fig. 10-11, the Tivo chart, the gap up when the stochastics were peaking out indicated that the exuberance had culminated. The gap up was the signal. What is the best way to exit from this trade? First, the gap at the top is the sign to be ready to sell. A couple of simple stop-loss applications make getting out of a trade an easy mechanical procedure. When the price gaps open in the overbought area, a few things can occur. The price can continue to go up from that point. The price can stay the same, or it can go down. Undoubtedly, these are not earth moving revelations. Fortunately, dissecting what each will do, as far as a candlestick signal indicates produces an easy-to-execute exit strategy. This is where placing stops becomes an excellent mechanical process.

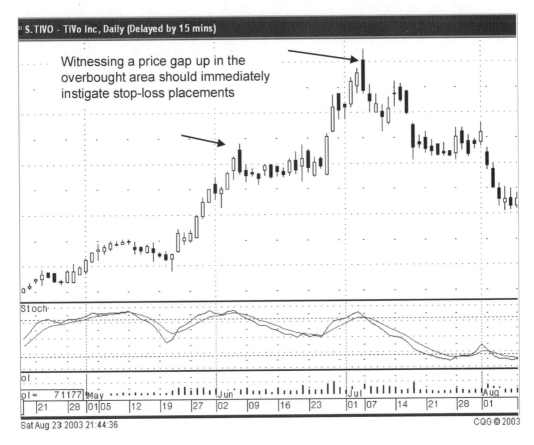

Fig. 10-11 *TIVO Inc.*

If the price gaps up, the first action should be to place a sell stop at the previous day's close. If the price gaps up and immediately shows strength, moving higher, place a sell stop at the opening price. What is the rationale behind these moves?

Consider what signals will be created after a gap up move. Closing at or below the open now produces a Shooting Star signal or a Doji/Shooting Star, both sell signals. Even a close slightly above that day's open will produce a Shooting Star. A close back at the previous day's close will form a Meeting Line signal. A close half-way down the previous white body produces a Dark Cloud signal. A close below the previous day's 'open' produces a Bearish Engulfing pattern. All sell signals.

If the price gaps up, the first procedure is to put a sell stop at the previous day's close. If prices immediately back off from the open price and the 'stop' is executed, the probabilities indicate that the majority of the profits have been extracted from a trend.

If the price opens higher and continues to move higher, moving the stop up to opening price becomes more advantageous. If the price moves up, then back down through the open price, the probabilities lean toward a candlestick sell signal forming.

The only bullish scenario that can occur after the price was up and came back down through the open would be to turn around and have the price move back up substantially. Substantially, being far enough up not to create a Hanging Man signal. A gap up at the top, whether it opens and continues higher or it opens and immediately retraces, has many more sell signal opportunities versus the continuation of the uptrend. Back to a basic premise, maximize profits for the account. A gap up at the top is now a high probability profit-taking situation. Be ready to move the funds elsewhere.

Fig. 10-12, Siebel Software is another example of the gap up at the top. A sell stop at the open would have provided a very profitable execution. Not all trades will give you time to place the order at the open price, if upon opening, it immediately moves up and quickly falls back. The next safe stop is at the last white candle close, which in this case did not get executed until the following day.

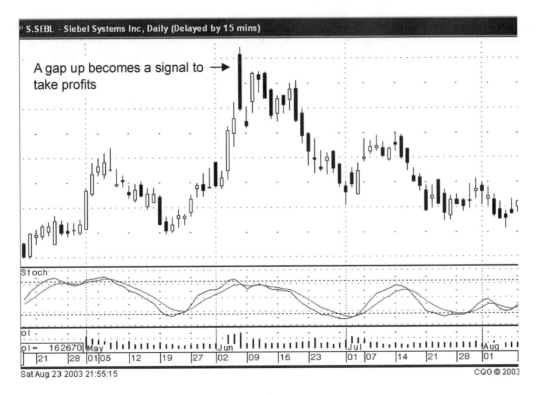

Fig. 10-12 *Siebel Systems Inc.*

Fig. 10-13, Cree Inc's chart illustrates another example of the open or the previous closing price becoming the best strategy point for placing a sell stop. This chart reveals the warning signal four days earlier, a Shooting Star. It would have taken a huge up move, after pulling back through those levels, to eliminate the possibilities of a sell signal forming. Upon seeing the stochastics in the overbought range and a gap up at the top of the trend, get out. Why try to buck the odds. Take the profits and go to a low risk, high probability trade.

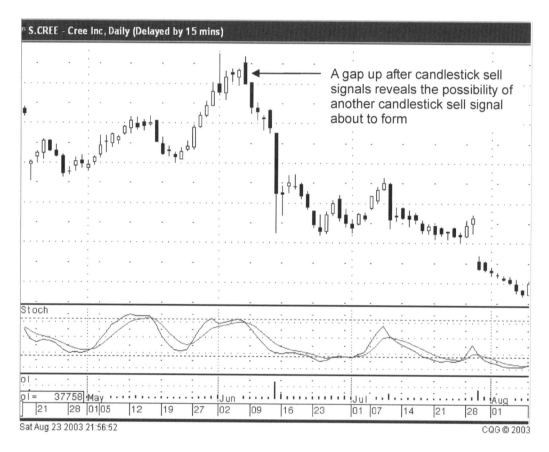

Fig. 10-13 *Cree Inc.*

Candlestick Stop Loss Reasoning

Limiting your losses, using visual analysis, with the candlestick method has immense advantages. Understanding the signals, knowing why it is time to enter a trade, makes it easy understand when to be out of a trade. Applying arbitrary percent movements do not pertain to what the price movement is expected to do.

The basic premise being that the majority of trades will be profitable utilizing candlestick analysis. That still means some trades are not going to work. Having a prepared mind set for addressing the losing trades keeps funds moving to the best probabilities. Most investment programs teach very little about getting out of losing trades. Cutting losses short is prudent advice. Yet very little is taught on how to recognize the losing trade. Even less is taught on how to effectively close out the losing trades.

Learning when a trade is not working has two benefits. Limiting the loss is the obvious benefit. Additionally, getting those funds out of a nonproductive trade and placing them immediately back into a potentially positive trade greatly enhances the ability for those funds to create gains for the portfolio. Doing so immediately creates more opportunities to make profits. Plus it keeps the mind clear, not having to use mental energy worrying about a position that should be closed out.

How often do we hear investors say when their stock position is going down, "that's alright, I'm in this position for the long term, and it will come back?" Poppycock!!! That is the answer of somebody that does not have a strategy for coming out of a position.

Know why you are going into a position. Know why you want to be back out. That gives you control of your portfolio management. The price moves are not throwing you around; you are maintaining control of your portfolio. The constant cultivation of placing investment funds where they should be or closing positions that are not doing what the signals indicated will greatly enhance the profit potential of a portfolio. Remember, this is not rocket science, this is simple commonsense evaluation of what the buyers and sellers are doing.

Chapter 11

Trading Rules

> *If you step in a puddle, do not blame the puddle.*
>
> *Japanese proverb*

Having the ability to identify reversal signals creates an extremely beneficial dynamic for investors. Once an investor becomes comfortable that the signals represent a high-probability situation, investment trading rules can be better followed. The elimination of emotions, especially fear and greed, should be the prime goal for investors.

The biggest failure factor for most investors is the emotion element. Investment trades become skewed with investors "hopes" versus what indicators are telling. Every time an investor puts on a position or takes off a position, a mental decision process has been made. Our mental decision process! Our egos come into play. Of course, we are all smarter than the rest of the world. That is what we all like to believe. To confirm that, our mental prowess becomes quantified every time an investment decision is made.

To buy a stock and watch it go down not only hurts the pocketbook but also hurts the ego. We cannot be smart in somebody else's eyes if our investment decision was wrong. When we are right, and get into a position of big profits, our sell parameters become fluid. What was our original selling strategy now gets modified by the euphoric rhetoric that may be surrounding the circumstances. The "sell" decision now becomes based upon other people's opinion or a few more points higher will allow us to buy a better car, new set of golf clubs, pay for next quarter's tuition, or anything else that has absolutely nothing to do with what the price should do.

The candlestick signals produce a high-probability format for when it is time to buy and when it is time to sell. Utilizing that format creates a self-imposed discipline. Why trade against the probabilities? As we are often told by the professionals, you cannot time the markets. However, as can be clearly seen, the Japanese Rice traders have successfully timed the markets for centuries. The ability to see high-probability potential reversals in market trends allows an investor to apply simple trading rules.

The following list of rules has been derived from many years of investing experience from numerous sources. It will also incorporate rules specifically applied to the use of candlestick signals. Since investing has become a more active part of people's lives, general investing rules are also included in this chapter. The mental state of an investor, as well as mechanically imposed disciplines, is important to successful investing.

Incorporate Good Investment Procedures

Just like any profitable endeavor, investing requires a structured business plan. Successful money managers establish a set of business disciplines. Money allocation, trading environment, consistent evaluation processes, and clear and concise planning are all required to maintain a good mental analytical process. The analysis of candlestick signals and patterns, although a primary element of a successful investment program, still requires a business atmosphere for successful implementation. The trading area should be organized, whether at a business office, a home office, or a laptop on the back deck overlooking the lake. Having one's mind clear of distractions allows for better evaluation of the investment signals and patterns.

Document Winning and Losing Trades

A well-maintained accounting of transactions and writing the results of good and bad trades in a journal is a good investment habit. Having a journal of what the thought processes were during a good or bad trade situation frees an investor's mental energy for analysis versus trying to remember previous trade occurrences. The mind is a very nebulous entity. Important factors that should be remembered can often slip away through time or be lost when trying to analyze massive amounts of information. Having a documented journal of past trades allows an investor to refresh their memory on what worked or did not work in the past. Keep a journal at your workstation.

Do Not Trade When Not Feeling Well

Investing requires clear mental thinking. Most people experience different mental outlooks when feeling under the weather. Having a bad cold, the flu, a toothache, headache or a multitude of other ailments can dramatically affect an individual's outlook.

Investing is just like any other activity. There will be times an investor may not "feel like" investing. Take a break. Getting mentally refreshed is often a crucial aspect for thinking clearly. Investing does not require participating in the markets every single day. Investing should be taking advantage of market conditions when the investor wants to participate in the markets.

There are times when the market is not moving well enough to produce profits that would warrant spending mental time and energy. Often, during the summer, market activity/volume decreases dramatically when everybody is vacationing. Do not try to squeeze blood from a turnip. Go relax, rest up.

There will be times when trades do not seem to work. Positions put on, despite how strong a signal indicates a high probability trade, do not seem to work. Take a break. Go clear out the cobwebs. When you come back after a few days of rest, the analysis process should be clearer.

When in Doubt – Get Out!

The most important aspect about investing is the ability to put the probabilities in your favor. The primary function of candlestick signals is to identify high-probability investments. The purpose of the step-by-step analysis of the markets, sectors, related stocks, and other trading entities, that would support the reasons for a candlestick signal to be acted upon, is to develop a high-probability correct trade scenario.

The primary reason for establishing a trade is the identification of favorable indicators. Taking advantage of centuries of observations of investor reactions has created signals that make a profitable trade very plausible. That was the reason for putting on the trade. The investor has made an evaluation of a trade set up that has worked correctly in the past.

The candlestick signals are indicators of what price movements should occur in the future, with a reasonably high predictability. If the trend/price movement, after the candlestick signal, does not produce the results expected, or the price action starts creating some concern, close out the position. The reason for establishing the trade was to benefit from the probabilities established from historic previous results.

Why remain in a position where the favorable probabilities appear to have diminished? Remaining in the position puts your investment funds exposed to market moves that do not enhance your profit potential. A high probability profitable trade signal still has the potential for creating losses. Hopefully the potential of a loss is diminished. Keeping funds exposed to a position, where the favorable probabilities have disappeared, makes the potential of losses that much greater.

If the premise of your investment strategy is to keep placing funds in high-probability trade situations and a trade does not appear to be working, close it!!! Preserve your capital when ever in doubt. The capabilities of the candlestick signals and patterns are always going to be available. The purpose of investing is to maximize your profits. The benefit of candlestick signals is to identify high profit situations. When a candlestick investor does not have a strong feel for what the trend is indicating, close the position. There are more strong trade signals occurring every single day/week/month, one minute/five minutes/ fifteen minutes on a candlestick chart somewhere. Preserve the capital to take advantage of the next trade.

Preserve Capital

The concept of preserving capital is as important as the function of maximizing profits. That is the mainstay of most investment advice. How does maximizing profits and preserving capital intermix? Utilizing the candlestick signals and high-profit patterns establishes expected price movements. Once a trade has been established, historic results demonstrate price movements that should be anticipated. Results should be somewhat predictable. If the projected trend does not confirm those expected results, then another analysis should be made immediately.

The analysis should be made on a very simplistic basis. Are my funds being allocated into a position that will benefit the portfolio? Are those funds utilizing the benefits provided by the signals in the patterns? If an evaluation does not confirm both of those questions, then investors needs to ask themselves, "Why am I in this trade?"

There will always be a supply of excellent buy signals or sell signals provided by candlestick signals. Each day or whatever time period you are trading, there will be more trade opportunities than most investors will ever be able to take advantage. Why stay in a trade where you do not have analytical control? There is always somewhere to invest your funds where the signals indicate a high probability trade direction.

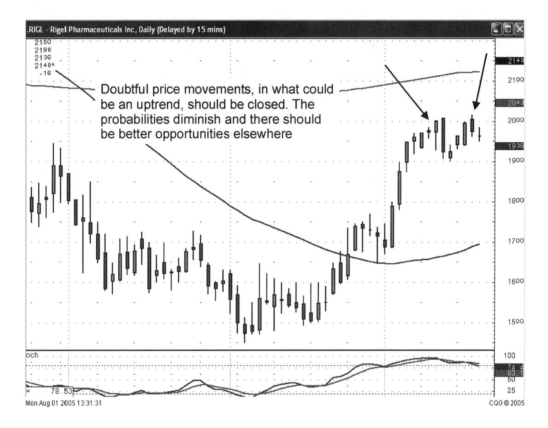

Fig. 11-1 *Rigel Pharmaceuticals Inc.*

The decision process is made easier with a doubtful chart, as seen in fig.11-1, the Rigel Pharmaceutical Inc. chart. When there does not appear to be a strong probability of upside potential, moving funds to another trade such as the Daystar Technologies Inc. chart, fig, 11-2, makes sense. The probabilities for upside potential are much greater when all the indicators line up. Moving funds from the low probability positions to high probability positions will produce consistent profits over the long run.

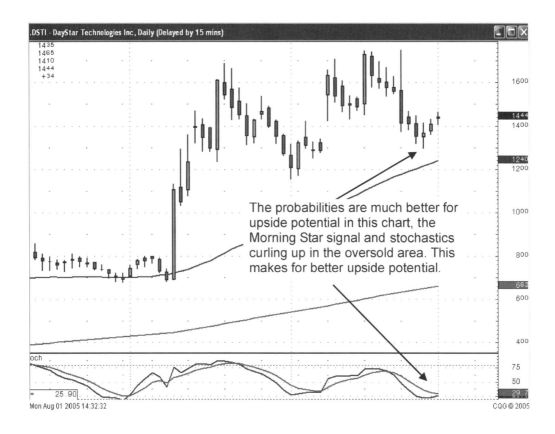

Fig. 11-2 *Daystar Technologies, Inc.*

Don't Look Back!

The two emotional factors that affect investing the most are fear and greed. These emotions are found in many situations. Fear can be found when everything in the investment world looks terrible; there is no viable reason to be putting money into the markets. Greed is jumping in to the markets/stocks as they have continued moving up over an extended period of time and the world looks rosy. Everybody wants to jump on board because nothing can go wrong.

Those are the normal circumstances for identifying fear and greed. However, fear can be experienced when it's time to sell a profitable position. For example, a stock is bought for $10 a share. Over the next two weeks it moves up to $14 a share. Candlestick sell signals start appearing. What happens when a stock price gets strong? Everybody finds great things to say about the company.

What is the fear factor for selling the stock? What if!!! What If the stock is sold at $14 and after a few days it goes straight to $18? Boy, would we look stupid! So what do most investors do? They hang on to the stock even though the candlestick "sell" signals said it was time to get out. Finally they get out of their position at a much lower price. All for the sake of not looking stupid had the stock gone to $18.

The candlestick signals produce an important message. They visually demonstrate when the "probabilities" indicate it is time to sell. The effectiveness of candlestick signals is the ability to show high probability buy and sell situations. *When the signals say it's time to sell, close out the position.*

There is nothing wrong with buying when it is time to buy and selling when it is time to sell. If, for some unforeseen reason, the price immediately spikes up after you sell it, don't look back. The trade was closed based upon high probability factors. To hope for additional price increases is exactly that, "hope." If a trade was closed based upon the signals indicating that it was time to sell, that was the trade.

The purpose of using candlestick signals is to get investors into a position when the probabilities say it's time to buy and get them out when it is time to sell. Under that investment philosophy, those funds coming out of a sold position should have been put into another trade where the probabilities were in the investor's favor.

Worrying about a stock price moving up after the position is sold becomes detrimental to rational investment thinking. Stocks prices **will** move up after the signals shows "sell". Not nearly as often as prices will continue down. Even if the price of the stock moved up after the sale, it was now in a higher risk area. Those funds should have been moved to another chart signal where the probabilities were great and the risk factor was much lower.

Take profits when it is time to take profits. There is absolutely nothing wrong with coming out of a position when the probabilities say it is time to come out. There is absolutely nothing wrong with buying that position back if the sell signals are negated. The J-hook pattern is a prime example of getting out when the signals said to sell and getting back in when the J-hook pattern shows buying. The purpose of investing is not to maximize your profits on every trade. The purpose of investing is to maximize your profits for your account.

Cut Your Losses Short, Let Your Profits Run

Cut your losses short and let your profits run is the advice provided by practically every investment adviser in the world. The only problem with their advice is they do not tell you how to do it. Candlestick analysis provides a framework for keeping losses small. The visual analysis that identifies a buy signal or a sell signal incorporates the change of investor sentiment. The result of the investor sentiment change should lead to confirmation of a new direction.

If a candlestick buy signal, which should indicate a new upward trend, is immediately negated by more selling, the message provided by the buy signal loses its relevance. Simply stated, if the sellers are still present, after a candlestick buy signal is formed, to the magnitude that prices move back down to a point where they override the buy signal, close the position immediately. The buy signal did not work.

Trades are established based upon a signal providing a high-probability situation. If that signal is negated, the high-probability situation does not remain. Close the position. Move on to an identified high-probability situation. Does that mean this trade will not work? No, it just means that is not working right now. If that trade was implemented because of a candlestick buy signal in an oversold condition, and it does not work, the oversold condition has not disappeared. Continue to watch for the next buy signal. However, the next buy signal may occur two days later or two months later. If a trade is not working, get back out immediately and use those funds to take advantage of another high- probability trade.

Set Your Stops

A major human flaw, setting a stop, and then changing our mind when prices get near the stop price. That process defeats the purpose of setting the stops in the first place. Why do investors change their minds? When making irrational evaluations, investors will make irrational decisions. However in the heat of trading, emotions come into play. As demonstrated in our Entry and Exit Strategy chapter, candlestick analysis places stop losses based upon logical selling indications. If you find yourself in a situation where you are questioning your own stop-loss decision, remind yourself that you made that stop- loss point based upon clear, non-pressured analysis.

Setting a stop at a pre-derived percentage movement means nothing. The markets do not care where you bought. The price is going to move up and down in a trend. Trends can have short-term pullbacks. *The basic reason for establishing a stop loss is to be out of a position if it is not confirming the reason for being in the position.* Candlestick signals make stop-loss procedures relatively easy. If you are buying based on what a candlestick signal implies the buyers should now be in the trend. Price moving back down through the level that suggested the buyers were taking control, reveals that the sellers were still in control.

Entering a position is based upon a signal. Visually, a trading level should be recognized as an area that would indicate that the buyers did not follow through; the sellers were still in control. Use that as your stop. Prices breaching that area negates the reason for being long. Close out the position. That is how you cut your losses short.

When you visually analyze where the stop loss point should be, it will not change the scenario once you have put your position on. If you anticipate that a percentage of the established trades may not work, then utilize the candlestick stop-loss process.

There will be more high-probability trades to move your investment funds into. Get out of the bad ones immediately and move to the good ones.

The Fear of Selling Too Soon

Fear works against most investors when it is time to take profits. Fear and greed! The fear after taking profits on a trade, greed in that the price may continue higher! How stupid we would look after buying a stock at $10, took profits at $16 and two weeks later it was trading at $24! The first question should be, "looking stupid to whom?" 99.9% of the time nobody other than yourself, knows what trade you have made. The other .01% doesn't give a hoot. They have their own problems. What it boils down to is not looking stupid to you. Unfortunately this ego problem induces the majority of investors to continue to hold a position well past the optimal "sell" time.

The inherent attributes candlestick signals provide is a format that indicates when the "probabilities" say it is time to sell. Most investors lose sight of the premise of their investment program. A good investment program indicates when it is time to buy and when is time to sell. These are the outstanding features found in candlestick signals.

Profitable investing requires discipline. That discipline involves following the signals/indicators that are the basis for one's investment program. There is nothing wrong with buying a position when the indicators say to buy. There is nothing wrong with selling a position when the indicators say it's time to sell.

Will there be occasions when a price continues higher after you close out a position? Definitely! There are two ways to resolve the emotions of that issue. First, when an investor comes to the realization that if they execute their trades based upon a trading program that provides a high percentage of profitable results, they can always look back at a trade that continued higher with solid investor logic. They bought when it was time to buy and they sold when it was time to sell. That trading discipline will work in favor of the investor over the long run.

There is nothing wrong with taking profits when the probabilities indicate that it is time to take profits. Are there times when the signals are indicating a profit-taking pullback in an uptrend versus a full-scale reversal? Certainly, but being able to identify candlestick signals in the formation of high-profit patterns allows an investor to take advantage of anticipated price movements.

The perfect example is the J-hook pattern. After a strong positive move, candlestick signals usually indicate the probability of a sell off.

Will that sell off be 5% or 55%? That is a question that cannot be answered when the reversal signals first appear. Why take the chance of holding a position that may give back most of the profits?

The worst case scenario is a candlestick sell signal indicating it is time to take profits. Four days later the price starts moving back up. If it appears as if a trading pattern is forming, buy the position back. There is nothing wrong with buying it back at a higher price. The point of investing is to put funds in positions that show a high probability of producing profits. That will mean there will be trends that provide opportunities to make "most" of the profits available from that price move. *The point of investing is to maximize your profits for your account, not to try to maximize profits on every trade.*

Averaging Down

The concept of averaging down should not be in the realm of candlestick analysis. Averaging down is performed by investors that do not incorporate a trading strategy. Averaging down is the rationale for holding a position too long in the first place. The swing trader clearly has analytical benefits using candlesticks signals. Once a trade is executed, the negation of the candlestick buy signal should create cause to close the position quickly. Cut your losses short, let your profits run. Utilizing the simple stop loss analysis that candlestick signals offer eliminates the need to consider averaging down.

The long-term investor may have a different perspective. Averaging down might occasionally be applied if the long-term chart has experienced a pullback but not a sell signal. Even then, the analysis needs to involve one important factor, "Is this the best place to be committing funds at this time?" Money should not be allocated to a position for the sake of averaging down just because an existing position is already in place.

Do Not Preset Profit Targets

Analyzing profit targets and setting profit targets are two dramatically different functions. To arrange taking profits at a specific percentage gain is like cutting off your nose to spite your face. Unless an extensive statistical study has been made upon a specific trading entity, discovering what the average/median price move has been historically, then a lot of effort may be wasted. For most investors, it is difficult to find positions that will move in a profitable direction. If a trading program has been devised to identify high probabilities of a trend direction, then it should be utilized to its fullest potential.

When analyzing a reversal from a chart pattern, profit targets should be utilized for anticipating what the potential gains might be. That will be taking into consideration where the next resistance level might be. This analysis would involve trend lines, moving averages, Fibonacci numbers, or any other technical indicator that might reveal the potential end of the next trend. Logic dictates that a bullish signal or pattern that has a potential of a 15% return is much better than a chart analysis that reveals only a 5% return. Use that analysis to decide which trade to enter.

Once entering the trade, do not let the target be the sole 'sell' factor. The candlestick signals remain the main factor for when to sell. A signal to sell the position may occur well before the target is reached.

The candlestick signals identify when a price reversal has occurred. Indicators can project the potential strength of the price move. Other technical factors can project potential targets. However, the majority of the time the signals simply indicate that a new trend is in the making. To interject a self-imposed profit target greatly reduces the benefits that candlestick signals provide. Once a price trend moves, which was bought based upon a candlestick buy signal, it becomes a relatively simple procedure to analyze when to sell. Identifying the candlestick sell signal should be the determining factor.

The time and effort of finding positions that are going to move in a profitable direction should not be compromised by a preset function that has absolutely nothing to do with how far the price will move.

Take Windfall Profits

The major benefit of interpreting candlestick signals is that it tells you when buying or selling is coming into a position. You may not necessarily know why buying or selling is coming into the position but apparently somebody does. The smart money, or the money that has knowledge of a company or a trading entity, will be making buy and sell decisions based upon their knowledge. The graphics of the candlestick signals is the representation of that knowledge.

The results of that knowledge will create candlestick signals. Information from candlestick signals becomes a source of recognizing where buying and selling is occurring. They visually portray what is occurring. This often leads to being able to participate in situations where the signals indicated something major is about to happen. Essentially the signals position an investor to be in the right situations at the right time.

When a big price move does occur, do not be hesitant to take some profits immediately. Most investors are happy when their portfolio or a position provides a 10% return annually. Getting a large price move, in a one or two-day period, warrants taking some profits. If stock price moves up 10%, 20%, 40%, or 100% in one day, sell half the position. Moving profits into your account was the purpose of being in the position in the first place. Could the price move higher? Certainly, and you will still make profits with the remaining half of the position. Will there be profit-taking after the first big move? Certainly, if so, you can formulate your strategy for exiting now with half a position. If you get a big move fast, take profits. Remember, greed has killed more men than lightning.

Do Not Formulate New Opinions/ Strategies as a Trade Progresses

If you are buying based upon a daily signal, sell based upon a daily signal. If a daily candlestick "buy" signal is the reason for entering a trade, then let a candlestick "sell" signal indicate when to come out of a trade. A common mistake technical investors make is exiting a trade because of price movement occurring contrary to expectation on a shorter timeframe.

An example would be buying a stock or commodity position based upon the criteria of a good bullish trade; a candlestick buy signal with stochastics in the oversold condition, starting to curl up. After two or three positive trading days the price sells off hard early in the day. It would form a candlestick sell signal if it closed at that level. However, the stochastics or other trend parameters may still be in an upward trajectory. What should be the course of action? Nothing! Wait until the end of the time frame that your investment program involves. If you are buying based upon a daily buy signal, then sell based upon the *completion* of a daily candlestick sell signal. Whatever price movement occurs in between the open and the close is noise. The signal is created at the end of the timeframe.

Will there be selling during an uptrend? Of course. If the price goes into the close at the same levels it did during the early part of the day, it would create a candlestick sell signal. Although stochastics are heading up, a new investment strategy can be analyzed with that information. More than likely, prices may end up near the top of the trading range at the end of the day. Keep in mind, the candlestick buy signal provided a high probability indicator that a trend reversal had occurred. Allow the signals to dictate what prices should do. The signals are formed at the END of the timeframe.

Other Opinions

One major human flaw is listening to what other people verbalize. Hearing somebody else's opinion can start causing doubt when maintaining a position. The exposure to financial news stations and a multitude of investment chat rooms creates the opportunity to hear many 'opinions'. If you buy based upon a set of parameters, do not change your investment decision parameters midstream. Everybody will have an opinion on what should be done with specific investments. Your decisions should be based upon your analysis for entering and exiting trades.

There are two major reasons for not letting others influence your decisions. First, the establishment of a trade was based upon evaluations of the indicators that you know, or are learning, for making profitable trades. To circumvent the exiting of a trade, because of another source's influence, does not allow the investor to correctly analyze the success or failure of that trade. If the trade does not work, an investor wants to be able to analyze the result based upon the failure of the indicators they are using. Exiting a trade based upon other criteria does not add information to your program knowledge.

Secondly, the opinions of others may be formulated by completely different or unknown factors. Their viewpoint could be influenced by a multitude of factors that have nothing to do with the reason you have put on a trade. Their timeframe, their risk tolerance, the information that they based their opinion on may not have anything in common with your investment technique. Does this necessarily mean that all other opinions need to be ignored? Not necessarily, but that information should be assimilated into your total analysis, not as a prime decision factor.

Watch the Charts – Not the News

The major benefit of candlestick signals is that it tells you exactly what investors are doing. The strongest element of the signals is that it provides a graphic account of what investor sentiment is doing *right now*.

Consider the definition of smart money. Smart money usually knows what is going on in a stock/industry well before it becomes public knowledge. When the average investor gets the news, it is usually old news. That is plainly illustrated when a chart has been declining for two months, then gaps down at the bottom on bad news.

It has to be assumed that the smart money knew what was going on months ahead of time. They were selling anticipating the news coming out sometime in the future. A gap down or a big candle day to the downside on a news announcement should invoke one important question. When everybody else was selling, who was buying?

There are usually very few surprises in the investment world. Somebody usually knows things well in advance of a news announcement. When news stories are being reported on the major financial news stations, the news has probably been built into the stock for a long while. Watch the candlestick signals. When the news appears so bleak that there can't be any possible way that anybody would want to buy and the charts start showing candlestick buy signals, it provides some very important information. Somebody is buying. Conversely, how often do you hear investors complain when a company comes out with a great announcement and the price of the stock goes down? The announcement/news is already built into the price.

The candlestick signals produce a visual confirmation of what is actually happening. Buy when candlestick signals indicate a buy, even though the news is terrible surrounding that company/sector. You will have a high likelihood of making profits. Sell when the candlestick signals indicate a sell. Although the future appears tremendous, the question always remains, why is somebody selling if the news and the outlook is so wonderful?

Trade the Chart Pattern, Not the Name

Often an investor will not put money into a trading entity when they have lost money in it before. "I lost money in that stock in the past; I don't want to touch it again." Remember, the markets and stocks do not give a hoot what you think, what you're going to do, or what you've done in the past. Prices are going to move in the manner that will be predictable based upon patterns.

If you run across a chart pattern that shows a very strong signal but then you see that it is a position that lost you money before, do one simple procedure. Put your hand over the name and look at the chart. If the chart reveals a strong reason to buy, do not let the name influence your decision.

Stay With Your Indicators

The candlestick signals are statistically proven reversal patterns. The candle formations are the illustration of investor sentiment, more specifically of **actual** investor sentiment. The financial news programs or financial newspapers are full of so-called professional opinions. Do not let others affect the analysis of a chart pattern. *If you are buying based upon technical reasons, then base your selling upon technical reasons.*

The advantage candlestick investors have is being able to see a graphic depiction of what the true investor sentiment of a price is doing despite all the verbal rhetoric. Quite often negative commentary will persist about an industry/sector/stock. At the same time, the candlestick signals indicate buying. The signals illustrate what is actually happening.

Once an investor learns to successfully interpret the signals and the confirming indicators, all other opinioned information will become incidental. If your indicators work successfully a high percentage of the time, follow what they express. This allows an investor to cut through all informational rhetoric.

Stay With Your Trading Program

Trading programs should be defined. If an investor does not understand what their trading program should be, they will not make money. A large percentage of investors do not have a trading program. They get money to invest, and then look for something to buy immediately.

Once you have developed your trading program, stay with it. First of all, it will help identify which trading techniques are working. To move from one investment program to another whenever something is not working never allows an investor to figure out how to correct what is not working.

Using the candlestick signals as a basis for a trading program allows an investor to trade and analyze the results of a signal formation. It permits an investor to stay with a trade that may not currently be producing big profits, knowing through past experience that the signals have not been negated.

Set your parameters based upon the candlestick signals. Other indicators can be applied in specific market conditions. Whether using candlestick signals or not, moving from one trading strategy to another will never allow an investor to analyze changes that can be profitable as market conditions change.

Learn a trading strategy extremely well. Constantly tweak it as conditions change. If somebody recommends another trading strategy or system, research it before jumping into it. Once it's researched, experiment by taking its good points and applying it to your existing trading program.

Too often investors will buy stocks based upon the availability of information when they have funds to invest with no strategy for getting in. This means there is probably no strategy for when to get out. Learn your investment trading strategy well. Then start improving upon it, by integrating what you learn as you go, into YOUR own program.

Why Use Rules

> *Not to have control over the senses is like sailing in a rudderless ship,*
> *bound to break to pieces on coming in contact with the very first rock.*
> *Mahatma Gandhi*

Trading rules are established to provide guidelines. Are there exceptions to the rules? Definitely! But rules for your investment program should be for the development of proper trading habits. Correct investment perceptions are developed through a minefield of emotional hurdles.

Utilizing a set of rules keeps the investor from backsliding into old habits. The statistical value of candlestick signals provides a format for an investor to have the probabilities constantly in their favor. Establishing a set of rules for your investment procedures is also putting favorable guidelines into an investment program. Utilize the experience conveyed by successful investors. The rules that were expressed in this chapter were provided by the investment knowledge of successful investors throughout the years.

Trying to formulate a successful investment program without guidelines is like running in quicksand. The basis for the successful consistent extraction of profits from the trading markets is not only learning a high-probability trading technique, but also establishing investment procedures to keep those profits.

Chapter 12

Candlesticks Applied

> *A man, although wise, should never be ashamed of learning more and must unbend his mind.*
>
> *Sophocles*

What was the term most often used in the explanation of candlestick signal benefits? *"Probabilities!"* The primary factor for placing investment funds at risk. Having the probabilities in one's favor for making good investment returns! Investments are made because they have a good probability to make money. Many investment methods promote favorable investing results. Many investment methods have elements incorporated into their system that improve investor probabilities. Some have been tested for a reasonable length of time, 10 years, 20 years, and 50 years. The trust in what candlestick signals provide is based upon hundreds of years of proven results. They do not work 100% of the time, BUT to ignore what candlestick signals are conveying is to go against the odds.

The information gleaned from the appearance of candlestick signals provides immediate knowledge. Because results can be analyzed, with a high degree of accuracy, candlestick analysis contains important trading components. It provides a signal for when to enter trades. It also provides the graphic information for when a high-probability trade situation is not performing. Simple inferences can be made for what a price or trend should do, when candlestick signals appear in the correct conditions. Evaluation can be acted upon with some certainty. The ensuing price move has expected results. The price move, not performing as expected, should provide additional information. The high "probability" expectations were not occurring. Move the money elsewhere.

Patterns can be employed to further increase the probabilities of being in a correct trade. Patterns occur for the same reason candlestick signals form.

Human emotions involving investment decisions have recurring characteristics. The fear factor! The greed factor! Both become assimilated in the price as trends move. Visually recognizing a pattern increases investment probabilities. The reason a pattern can be recognized is because of the results it has produced many times in past trend situations.

The basis of technical analysis is the recognition of chart formations that perform consistently. The results of a chart pattern become greatly enhanced when applying candlestick signals into the patterns evaluation. This is nothing more than taking two "probability" oriented graphics and combining their positive results.

This book was written for the purpose of training the eye to instantly recall profit 'potentials.' The ability to identify the graphic set-ups of having had high profit trade situations in the past, becomes very advantageous. 'Fundamental' reasons for a price to be moving may not be known to all investors. However, the educated eye can detect when price behavior resembles previously witnessed price behaviors that have produced profits. Utilizing consistent investor behavior patterns provides a format that can increase investment returns dramatically.

Human emotion becomes the fatal flaw for most investors. Candlestick signals and trading patterns are a graphical depiction of those flaws. Being able to eliminate the presence of emotions in investment decisions is the discipline most investors should strive for.

Discipline

Candlestick signals and high-profit patterns create the groundwork for eliminating the emotional input involved in financial decision-making processes. As a result, understanding what a signal or pattern should cause as a result, calms the jitters. The simple process of watching a pattern develop and knowing what that pattern should be doing, allows an investor to exhibit composed patience until the pattern completes itself. At the same time, an investor can establish stop loss areas. These levels can be established by projecting what and where would constitute a failure of the pattern.

Fundamental-based investing incorporates a much longer timeframe for an anticipated price move. The fundamental factors that should cause a price to move may not be recognized for months or years down the road. Holding a position long-term, with the anticipation of particular results, becomes a risky endeavor when not analyzing price movement. The application of candlestick signals and high profit patterns as a guideline for a long-term hold has beneficial aspects. If fundamental results 'should' produce a positive move in a trading entity, the analysis of its chart pattern can be valuable. A price movement contrary to what should be expected from fundamental improvements of a company, would indicate that something might have altered the future potential of that company. Whether an investment decision is made or not, based on price patterns, at least it would forewarn the "fundamental investor" that further research was required. Something may have changed the outlook for that company.

A "technical investor" executes trades based upon expected results from chart patterns. The discipline that should be followed becomes a function of adhering to simple rules. Letting your profits run and cutting your losses short does not need to be a nebulous investment procedure. As discussed previously in this book, the candlestick signals are as effective for illustrating when a trade is not working as well as when a trade is working. The maintenance of good discipline involves making decisions based upon rational analysis. The candlestick signals and high-profit patterns incorporate price levels that would indicate an investment situation NOT working. When they do, closing a trade immediately is the proper investment process. The purpose for establishing a trade is that the 'probabilities' are all in alignment. When the signals or patterns reveal that the probabilities are no longer favorable, an investor can close a trade without emotions hampering the decision.

Money Management

If emotions are the downfall of most investors, then everything possible needs to be put in place to eliminate emotional aspects. That process should be carried through to the money management of a portfolio. Unfortunately, as debilitating as fear and greed are to most investment decision-making processes, the human ego is also a major hurdle. Of course, we are all smarter than the average investor. Unfortunately, that thought process usually skews good money management.

As important as it is to take the emotions out of when to buy and when to sell, it is also important not to have egotistical reasons to stay in a trade. The easiest way to eliminate that factor is to pre-establish and maintain uniform position sizes. Why should each position be the same size as the next position? To keep from putting our emotions into the decision-making process!

For example, after going through a scanning process, an investor finds the perfect trade. It has every confirming indicator in the exact correct conditions. The chart suggests this could be a killer trade. What is the first inclination?

Because we are a little bit smarter than everybody else is, we put 1 1/2 times the normal investment funds into this perfect trade. What has just been created? A position that has a little bit of our ego involved. Reality check! What has occurred when all the indicators have aligned perfectly? A trade where the "probabilities" are extremely high that it will be profitable. Unfortunately, the qualifier to this statement is the word "probabilities." The best trade setups still have the possibility of not performing.

After putting a more than normal allocation of funds into this trade, a new mental dynamic occurs. "This trade should go up" because our mental processes said it should go up. What happens when the trade does not perform as expected? We give it another day or two longer than we should because our 'smarter than average' investor prowess expects the price to eventually do what we evaluated it will do. Instead of making a decision on a 'unit' of our portfolio, we are trying to prove ourselves right and hold a position too long. Money management involves simple and mechanical processes for correctly executing the positioning of a portfolio.

Establish a Money Management Plan

Just as an investment strategy needs to be learned and maintained with discipline, money management in an investment account needs to be planned. The establishment of a successful investment strategy involves identifying signals and patterns that are going to be successful. Once that strategy is put in place, an investor becomes more comfortable because entry and exit strategies have been thought out. That same comfort should also be extended to how funds are allocated. The function of a successful investment strategy is one that produces profits and does not overburden an individuals time constraints. Additionally, the allocation of funds should not be such that it causes tossing and turning at night.

Having too many positions will involve extensive analytical time. Fortunately, not very extensive when utilizing candlestick scans. Not having enough positions could involve too much possibility of one position greatly hurting the portfolio. An optimal number of positions for a portfolio should range between 6 positions and 14 positions, depending upon the size of a portfolio. Commodity accounts and futures accounts will have different position numbers. The main purpose of establishing a comfortable position number is important. The exposure of each individual position should be small enough as to not severely hurt returns if something drastically bad occurred in a particular position. On the other hand, the number of positions should not be so great as to require extensive analysis for when to get out of positions. Additionally, the size of the position should be significant enough to warrant attention every day or every time an analysis is made.

Once the number of positions has been established as a comfortable number for the investor, the size of those positions should be an equal dollar amount. That produces the element of a 'unit.' Each time an analysis is done, it is to evaluate whether that 'unit' is going to be a positive factor or a negative factor to the overall performance of the portfolio. The component of being an emotionally derived decision is dramatically reduced.

Develop Your Own Investment Style

The major advantage of candlestick signals and high-profit patterns is that they can be incorporated into any trading strategy. Whether trading stocks, bonds, currencies, commodities or day trading, swing trading, or long-term investing, the signals and patterns can be used profitably wherever fear and greed are involved.

Unless you are an investor with super analytical capabilities or have access to research staffs that can follow an immense number of stocks/sectors/industries, your investment program should be suited to your schedule. The candlestick signals dramatically reduce the time required to analyze what is affecting price movements. The signals and patterns are the accumulative results of everybody's research. The billions of dollars spent annually, for projecting and anticipating the future price movements of all trading entities, can be seen in the signals themselves. Once an investor becomes comfortable with the information that can be extracted from candlestick signals, investment strategies can be put in place that fit each investor's schedule and capabilities.

The graphics portrayed in this book are the result of centuries of profitable observations. High-profit patterns are going to occur constantly. The human psyche will not change. Experienced investors become wiser. Newbie investors will make the same investment faux pas. The supply of "newbie's" into the investment markets is constant. The trading results of trends will remain constant for centuries to come. Use the candlestick signals and high-profit patterns as the framework for your investment strategies. As new investment techniques are introduced, they can be applied to your existing chart knowledge. Some investment techniques will improve your trading strategies. Others will not. Some will work during certain market conditions and then fizzle out in other conditions.

Using candlestick analysis as your basis for your investment strategies provides a format that can continuously improve your investment results.

As seen more than once in this book, *this is not rocket science*. This is common sense investment philosophies put into a graphic depiction. Use it and make money.

www.candlestickforum.com

Investing requires practice. The experienced investor became that way because of 'experience.' There is a vast difference between knowing what to do and doing it. A ground ball hit to a professional baseball first baseman requires an action from the pitcher. The pitcher needs to move in a path to first base, giving the first baseman a target to throw to. A very simple maneuver. However, this defensive maneuver is practiced over and over. The fact that it is practiced over and over has important implications. Although professional baseball players fully understand what is needed to execute the play, as simple as it is, it is practiced so that the thought process is automatic when a real-life situation occurs. The same input is required for successful investing. The study of the major candlestick signals and the reviewing of high-profit patterns should be a constant practice. This is so that when an actual trade set up is forming; an investor is not only considering whether to do the trade, but how to properly execute the trade. It is strongly suggested that the investment process be shared with an investment partner or friend. This provides mental reinforcement for learning and remembering the signals.

The Candlestick Forum website was established in 2002. Its' sole purpose is for providing a forum where investors continuously hone their investment abilities, utilizing candlestick signals. The website offers daily stock and commodity picks. This service is not to provide a 'pick' service. It is to constantly illustrate the investment rationale made for a chart pattern to be recommended. The opportunity to master a powerful investment technique is constantly available.

There are evening live audio/video chat training sessions, twice a week, describing and teaching the ramifications of signals and patterns occurring in the current market conditions. These sessions provide continuous education as well as interaction from the participants wanting to learn candlestick patterns. The website provides an open forum where investors can ask questions about specific topics and get feedback from other candlestick investors.

The Candlestick Forum provides a library of training CDs that delve into specific topics of candlestick analysis in great detail. These learning CDs are highly informational and provide valuable insights into the profitable use of candlestick signals.

This is not rocket science! Learn the important candlestick signals. They will transform investor thought processes. Preparing one's mind with graphic information that has proven itself for centuries will become the basis for a successful investment outlook for the rest of your life.

> *Learn as though you would never be able to master it; hold it as though you would be in fear of losing it.*
>
> *Confucius*

Glossary

The following is a list of terms used in association with Japanese Candlestick Analysis. Some terms are purely of Western origin; others are purely of Japanese origin. Many are used for description in both Western and Japanese techniques, becoming intermingled through the years.

Bar Charts: The conventional graphic depiction of price activity. The trading range is illustrated with a vertical line representing the high to low prices during a time period. Open price is shown by a short horizontal line attached to the left side of a vertical line, the close is a horizontal line to the right side. Price is represented on the vertical scale of the chart. Time is represented on the horizontal scale

Blow-offs: A topping or bottoming action. Occurring at the end of an extended move. Prices move sharply and rapidly in the direction of the current trend on high volume. If the price reverses direction after this movement, a blow-off has occurred.

Breakaway gap: When prices gap away from a technically defined area, such as a congestion area or a trendline.

Breakout: The movement that pushes through a resistance level or a support level.

Confirmation: When a move or an indicator substantiates the anticipated action resulting from another indicator.

Congestion area: Trading activity where the price movement stays within an observable trading range for an extended period of time.

Consolidation: Trading in a range of the congestion area with the implication that the trend is resting and will resume the direction of the current trend.

Continuation patterns: A pattern that has been observed to indicate that the current trend will continue.

Cradle pattern: formed with the appearance of a large dark candle at the bottom of a down trend. A flat trading period consisting of Doji, Spinning Tops, and small indecisive trading days is then followed by a large bullish candle.

Dead cross: When short-term moving averages cross under the longer-term moving averages and a bearish signal is given.

Deliberation pattern: Also known as a stalling pattern, prices are coming to a point of a reversal.

Divergence: The disparity between indicators when a price action has made a move. One indicator confirms that the move was correct, the other shows the opposite. For example, if prices hit high and the relative strength index does not, a divergence has occurred.

Double bottoms: An easily recognized technical pattern illustrated by a W-shaped bottom where prices reverse at approximately the same lows.

Double tops: Price movement that resembles an M where the highs are approximately the same.

Downgap: Prices gap down in the next time period to levels below the total trading range of the previous time period.

Downtrend: Prices trading lower usually represented by lower lows and/or lower highs.

Elliot wave: Ralph Nelson Elliot developed a system for forecasting price movements based upon oscillations in investor sentiment. The basis of the theory revolves around five waves in a general direction (five-wave upmove) followed by three corrective waves in the opposite direction (three-wave downmove).

Exponential moving average: A moving average calculated by exponentially weighted input.

Fibonacci numbers: The series of numbers that are derived by adding the two previous numbers to obtain the next number. That number added to the previous number results in the next number. The series of numbers produces ratios used extensively by Elliot wave advocates, 38 percent, 50 percent, and 62 percent.

Filling the Gap: A gap becomes filled when prices move back into the black area of trading. Candlestick terminology describes this as "closing the window".

Fry Pan Bottom pattern: A slow downward trajectory of a trend consisting of indecisive trading days is then followed by a slow upward trajectory of a trend. When prices come back up to the beginning of the pattern, strong buying occurs as investor confidence has built back up.

Gap: A price void where the trading range between one time period does not overlap with a price trading of the next time period.

Golden cross: A bullish signal created by the short-term moving averages crossing above the long-term moving averages.

High-wave: A group of candlesticks with long upper and/or lower shadows. This grouping of formations foretells a market turn.

Implied volatility: A measure for the market to forecast future volatility.

Inside session: This is a trading session where the high and the low of a trading period remains within the high and the low of the previous trading session.

Intra-day: Trading periods that begin and end within a one-day time frame.

Islands: A formation created at the end of a trend where prices gap away from the current trend, trade for two or more days at those levels, and then gap back in the opposite direction. This leaves an island of trading at the end of the trend. Commonly known as island reversals. Strong reversal indicator.

Jay-hook (J-hook) pattern: A formation identified with candlestick sell signals at the top of a strong uptrend, followed by a pullback that wanes when small candlestick buy signals stop the downtrend. New buying creates a hook back up to the recent highs with a good possibility that the new uptrend will breach the recent highs and continue.

Locals: Floor traders that make their living by trading a particular entity.

Lower shadows: The trading range below the body of a candle.

Meeting lines: At the end of a trend, the open of the final day opens away from the previous days close, gapping up at the top of a trend or gapping down from the bottom , and by the end of the day the price has come back to close at the previous days close. This is a secondary reversal signal

Momentum: Related to the velocity of a price move. The most recent close is compared to a specific number of closes in a specific time frame.

Morning attack: A Japanese definition for a large buy or sell order on the opening that is designed to significantly move the market.

Moving Average Convergence-Divergence oscillator (MACD): A combination of three exponentially smoothed moving averages.

Neckline: The level that indicates the lows of the head in the head and shoulders formation or the high points in an inverse head and shoulders formation.

Night attack: A large order placed at the close to move the market.

Offset: The term for closing trades. Longs are said to liquidate. Shorts are said to cover.

On-Balance Volume (OBV): A cumulative volume figure. If prices close higher than the prior trading session, the volume for the higher day is added to the OBV. Conversely, volume is subtracted from the OBV on days when prices close lower than the previous day.

Open interest: Pertains to future contracts. It is the number of contracts that are still outstanding. It will be equal to the total number of long and short positions, not the combination of the two.

Oscillator: An indicator based upon a momentum formula that moves above or below a zero line or on a chart grid between 0 and 100 percent. They depict overbought and oversold conditions and positive or negative divergences; r measures the velocity in a price movement.

Overbought: A term associated with specific oscillators to denote when a price has moved too far, too fast in an upward direction.

Oversold: The same as the overbought definition except for it being in the downward direction.

Paper trading: A popular method using real-life trade circumstances and trading with imaginary trading funds.

Petrifying pattern: Another name for the Harami cross.

Protective stop: An order placed to limit losses on an existing position. If prices move to that level, a trade is initiated to liquidate the position avoiding further loss potential.

Raindrop: Another name for the star formation.

Rally: Usually a strong upward price movement.

Reaction: A price movement that moves opposite the current trend.

Real body (or body): The boxed area from the open to the close is what forms the body of the candle. When the close is lower than the open, a black body is produced. A close above the open causes a white body to be formed.

Relative Strength Index (RSI): An oscillator developed by Welles Wilder. It compares the ratio of positive closes to negative closes over a specific time period.

Resistance level: A trading level where obvious selling keeps the prices from advancing any further.

Retracement: The price movement in the opposite direction of the recent trend.

Reversal session: After a move experiences a new high (or low), the next close is below (or above) the previous day's close.

Rickshaw Man: A long-legged Doji where the body, although small, is in the center of the formation.

Selling climax: After a move downwards, prices push sharply lower on heavy volume. If prices move higher from these levels, a selling climax has occurred.

Selloff: The downward movement of prices.

Shadows: The extreme price movement outside the body of a candle creates the shadows. The lower shadow extends from the bottom of the body to the low price of the day. The upper shadow extends from the top of the body to the high price of the day.

Shaven bottom: A candlestick with no lower shadow.

Shaven head: A candlestick with no upper shadow.

Simple moving averages: The smoothing of price data where prices are added together, and then averaged. The term *moving* is included due to the fact that as each new day's information is added to the numbers, the oldest data is dropped.

Spring: When prices break below a congestion area, and then spring right back above the broken support area, it has produced a bullish signals.

Star: A small body that gaps away from the previous long body. A star indicates the reduction of force illustrated by the previous long candle. A star following a long black body is called a raindrop.

Stochastics: An oscillator that measures the relative position of closing prices compared to the trading range over a specified period of time. %K indicates the fast stochastic, %D indicates the slow stochastic.

Support level: An obvious level where buyers are shown to step in and hold prices above that level.

Tick volume: The number of trades occurring during a specific time interval.

Time filter: A price level that prices have to stay above or below for a specific period of time to confirm that a technical level has been broken.

Toppy – Toppiness: Term for indicating that prices can not move higher, signals start forming that would show selling coming in at the top of a trend.

Trend : A price's prevalent directional movement.

Trend-line: A line that can be drawn along a series of highs or lows. This requires at least two points for a line to be drawn. The more points that are associated with the line, the more strength the trend-line carries.

Trend reversals (or reversal indicators): Price action that indicates the high probability of a trend reversing its direction.

Tweezer tops or bottoms: Highs or lows of a trend that are duplicated in back to back trading days or within the next few sessions. The name is derived from the price movement to those levels forming a tweezer-like visual. It is a minor reversal signal, however, its significance becomes greater if the highs or lows are touched with long shadows or if the identical bottoms are part of another reversal signal.

Upgap: A gap in prices to the upside.

Upthrust: The price movement that carries prices through and above observed resistance areas. If these new price levels do not hold and prices pull back under the breached resistance level, it is called an upthrust. It now becomes a bearish signal.

Uptrend: Prices that are trading higher.

V bottom or top: A sharp reversal forming a V pattern at the bottom of a trend or an inverted V at the top of a trend.

Volume: The total number of shares or contracts trading in a given day on that trading entity.

Weighted moving average: A moving average where the most recent data is given greater value than the oldest data.

Window: The same as a Western *gap*. Windows can indicate the beginning of a strong trend as well as the end of a trend, exhaustion window. As Western technicians say that prices will always fill the gap, the Japanese expect to close the window.

Yin and Yang: The Chinese name for the black (Yin) and the white (Yang). Good and bad, positive and negative.

Index

Preferred Investment Information

Books

Profitable Candlestick Trading, Stephen W. Bigalow
A Complete Guide to Technical Trading Tactics, John L. Person
The Discipline Trader; Developing Winning Attitudes, Mark Douglas
Trading in the Zone: Master the Market with Confidence, Discipline and a Winning
Attitude, Mark Douglas
An Investor's Guide to Understanding and Mastering Options Trading, Bill Johnson
The Single-Stock Futures Revolution, Bill Johnson
10 Biggest Mistakes in Option Trading, Bill Johnson
McMillan on Options, Lawrence G. McMillan
Japanese Candlestick Charting Techniques, Steve Nison
Candlestick Charting Explained: Timeless Techniques for Trading Stocks and Futures, Greg Morris

Websites

WallStreetTeachers.com A web site that develops and utilizes high probability patterns and waves using cutting edge computer technology. Candlestick signals are an integral part of accurate short-term trading programs. Operated by David Elliott.

Nationalfutures.com A website utilizing Pivot Points and candlestick signals, operated by John L. Person.

21stCenturyoptions.com A website specializing in option trading strategies. It provides a comprehensive educational package for a multitude of successful option trading techniques. Operated by James DiGiorgia.

www.worden.com An excellent software program for scanning for stock selections. This software has numerous valuable technical indicators. Worden Brothers Inc. Five Oaks office park, 4905 Pine Cone Dr. Durham, NC 27707 Ph. 800-776-4940 or 919-408-0542

Candlestick Forum Educational Products

available at www. candlestickforum.com

Profitable Candlestick Trading $47.95

A book that will forever improve your investment perceptions. Hundreds of years of proven, tested and profitably successful Japanese Candlestick signals incorporate powerful ramifications. You will learn how to identify the profitable signals quickly and easily.

The Major Signals Poster $23.95

View the major candlestick signals every day in your home or office trading area. A 2 foot by 3 foot poster provides a quick glance to identify candlestick signals.

Candlestick Trading Forum Flash Cards $29.95

These unique Flash Cards will allow you to be "trading like the Pros" in no time. Now a faster and easier way to become an expert Japanese Candlestick Trader! Ideal for: Self-study drills. Practice with your "Trading Buddies." Their use is only limited by your imagination!

Candlestick Training Seminar Video $795.95

Eight hour training video (2 DVD set) filmed during a live seminar

Candlestick Analysis Training CD's

Do you want to master your investment future? Do you want to create wealth with the probabilities in your favor? You will find these training CD's to be an invaluable educational investment. Each CD video contains approximately one hour of specific training to accelerate your portfolio profits.

The Major Signals Educational Package

Buy all 12 CD's - valued over $500 for packaged price of $397.00

Candlestick Scans for TC2000ITCNet $34.97

See how to set up the simple scans for finding the best Candlestick trades each day. This is a simple step-by-step process that is easy to follow. Very simple! Be able to set up your own search scans. (get immediate results. You'll want to have this instructive lesson to refer to when establishing your search program. Find the best Candlestick trades each day in less than 20 minutes. Let this program work for you. You're in control. Use it over and over, whenever you need to refresh your memory.